1947

1947

Making the World Over

Richard A. Leiby

McFarland & Company, Inc., Publishers
Jefferson, North Carolina

This book has undergone peer review.

LIBRARY OF CONGRESS CATALOGING-IN-PUBLICATION DATA

Names: Leiby, Richard A., 1954– author.
Title: 1947 : making the world over / Richard A. Leiby.
Other titles: Nineteen forty-seven, making the world over
Description: Jefferson, North Carolina : McFarland & Company, Inc., Publishers, 2025. | Includes bibliographical references and index.
Identifiers: LCCN 2024062177 | ISBN 9781476695341 (paperback : acid free paper) ∞ ISBN 9781476654867 (ebook)
Subjects: LCSH: Nineteen forty-seven, A.D. | Civilization, Modern—20th century. | History, Modern—20th century | World War, 1939-1945—Influence.
Classification: LCC CB425 .L37 2025 | DDC 909.82/4—dc23/eng/20250111
LC record available at https://lccn.loc.gov/2024062177

ISBN (print) 978-1-4766-9534-1
ISBN (ebook) 978-1-4766-5486-7

© 2025 Richard A. Leiby. All rights reserved

No part of this book may be reproduced or transmitted in any form or by any means, electronic or mechanical, including photocopying or recording, or by any information storage and retrieval system, without permission in writing from the publisher.

Front cover: (top, left to right) Dennis FitzGerald, Lt. General Lucius D. Clay, Herbert Hoover, and Brigadier General William H. Draper, Jr. (National Archives); (bottom, left to right) Muhammad Ali Jinnah (Columbia University), Wendell Smith (National Baseball Hall of Fame and Museum, Cooperstown, New York)

Printed in the United States of America

McFarland & Company, Inc., Publishers
  Box 611, Jefferson, North Carolina 28640
    www.mcfarlandpub.com

Table of Contents

Acknowledgments   vii
Preface   1
Introduction   5

Chapter 1. The "Reluctant Spring": How the Winter of 1947 Affected Europe's Historical Trajectory   11

Chapter 2. "Sustaining Virtues": Herbert Hoover and the Rehabilitation of Germany   28

Chapter 3. "A Stitch in Time": Arthur Vandenberg and the Truman Doctrine   54

Chapter 4. "Up from the Dust": Mohammad Ali Jinnah, Masood Ghaznavi, and the Creation of Pakistan   75

Chapter 5. "One-in-a-million": Sgt. Paul Shimer and the Rise of the Anglo-American Partnership   100

Chapter 6. "Making Democracy Practical": Wendell Smith's Crusade for Racial Equality in Sports   117

Chapter 7. "Nervous Frustration": Stan Kenton and the Decline of the Swing Band Era   140

Chapter 8. "See Yourself!" Irene Murphy and American Television's *Coming of Age*   166

Epilogue   193
Chapter Notes   197
Bibliography   217
Index   225

Acknowledgments

There are many people, both in the United States and abroad, whom I need to thank for their assistance. My gratitude goes out to the staffs at the National Archives and Records Administration in Washington, D.C., and College Park, Maryland; the Harry S. Truman Presidential Library and Museum in Independence, Missouri, and the Herbert Hoover Presidential Library and Museum in West Branch, Iowa; the Bentley Historical Library of the University of Michigan; the George C. Marshall Foundation in Lexington, Virginia, and the archives of the National Baseball Hall of Fame in Cooperstown, New York. I am also indebted to the Archives of the City of Southampton, the Gloucestershire Archives, and the Chipping Campden Historical Society in the United Kingdom; the Chambersburg Historical Society in Franklin County, Pennsylvania; and to the countless other local repositories and libraries I relied upon for the information that makes up this book. Most importantly, I'm deeply indebted to all the individuals who agreed to share their life experiences with me, especially Irene Murphy McInerney and the late Masood Ghaznavi, and to the family members of many of the key actors including Theresa Rosa, Jill Tunkavage, and Diane Conklin. Several others who were instrumental in providing me with information for this book have since passed away, including Walter Boeck, Kathryn Ruggiero, and John R. Shimer. I hope my efforts do their memory justice.

A number of friends and scholars read parts of the manuscript and weighed in with their own expertise, including Professors Sharon Hirsh, Richard G. Wells, and Rekha Datta. A special thank you goes to Professor Kenneth Campbell for poring over the chapters and providing me with invaluable suggestions for improvement. I also benefited from the research conducted by graduate students Cathy Colborn and Joseph Magee. Donna McKeever provided me with expert editorial assistance. My eternal gratitude goes to my wife, Cathy Jo, not only because she is a fine research assistant and travel partner, but also for enduring my frequent bouts of sour disposition while I was writing and revising the text.

Finally, I wish to acknowledge the assistance of the Connelly Foundation, whose grants have underwritten my travel to archives and libraries for research. Any factual errors in the text are my sole responsibility.

Preface

Those who have experienced the trials of advanced graduate studies know that a researcher's worst enemy is boredom. While working in some dim and dusty archive, sifting through and reading mountains of documents, the mind wanders easily from the task at hand to something—anything—more exciting. In truth, such mental diversions are not always unwelcome; they can keep you from going bonkers. Sometimes, they can even stoke the imagination. Such was my experience doing research for my dissertation on postwar German history in furtherance of my Ph.D. studies at the University of Delaware. As I immersed myself in the documents, I noticed how pivotal the year 1947 was to the success of the Allied occupation and to the subsequent history of the two Germanies. In one of my many daydreams, I wondered whether that year was equally important in other countries and in other areas of human endeavor beyond geopolitics. The more I read and researched, the more I became convinced that 1947 was a special year, not just for Germany but also for the world. And thus was born the idea for a book.

I contend that the events of 1947 were more decisive than those of 1945 in transforming the wartime era into the contemporary age. That thesis will require some argument, since the notion that 1945 was both an end and a beginning is entrenched in public consciousness. Many historians have also advanced the *Stunde Null* concept, which holds that the cessation of hostilities in 1945 marked the "zero hour" when a new age emerged. Although that interpretation has its attractions, it rests upon a premise that war and armed conflict constitute the most decisive "moments" in the course of human history. If we reject that premise, or at least give it no more weight than any other, we can see that the "wartime era" lasted well beyond the cessation of hostilities. Europeans and indeed much of the world still had to contend with the disruptions brought on by war many months beyond its conclusion. Industrialized nations that once produced enough coal to fuel their factories found themselves facing energy shortages. Disruptions in trade patterns and transportation systems meant that food still had to be rationed. Millions of refugees, evacuees, and displaced persons set out to return home or find a new one, creating one of the largest mass migrations in all of human history. And there was also the ubiquitous destruction to homes, public facilities, and physical infrastructure brought on by years of bombings and ground combat. Those realities did not suddenly vanish in 1945; they would take years to overcome.

This book examines the year 1947 in an attempt to describe a world in transition. The chapters come from multiple perspectives including, but not limited to, politics, international affairs, the arts, music, and intellectual thought. I make no pretense of being an expert in any of these areas but, as a devotee of the liberal arts, I wanted to illustrate my point by sampling as broadly across the spectrum of human accomplishment as I could and tell those stories in narrative form. Fortunately, I had many good examples of scholarship using a similar approach to guide my efforts.

The works of Robert Darnton, particularly his essays in *The Great Cat Massacre* and *The Kiss of Lamourette*, come to mind as evidence of this sort of history at its best. Another such influential book is David Clay Large's *Between Two Fires*, which highlights key events in Europe's interwar period. More recently, Erik Larson (*The Devil and the White City, Dead Wake*, et al.) has captured the imagination of countless readers with his evocative storytelling.

These authors and their works convinced me of the value in writing narrative history for the public and not just for academic specialists—and their works ignited a fire in me to write similar books. I certainly make no claims to be in the same league as Darnton, Large, and Larson, but I do hope that this book will inspire some of my readers in the same way that their works inspired me.

Several caveats are in order. First, I make no claim that there is some mystical dynamic that unites all of the events discussed here, other than the fact that they all are responses to the dislocations and deprivations of the Second World War. Hence, each chapter stands alone as a story of specific experiences in specific places. Second, the rationale behind my selection of topics was to tell the stories of the people, places, and events of 1947 that often do not get sufficient attention in history textbooks or even make it into history textbooks at all. That is why I paid more attention to Muhammad Ali Jinnah and Arthur Vandenberg than to Mahatma Gandhi and Harry S. Truman.

The reader should therefore be aware that my choices were highly personal, conforming as much to my personal tastes as to my academic research interests. Simply put, I took the advice of many authors and wrote a book to please myself. Consequently, some readers may be disappointed when they do not see their favorite topics (like, for example, the Marshall Plan or Flying Saucer mania) discussed in detail.

Finally, I make no claim that my work is in any way groundbreaking.

Preface

The key events of 1947 have already been described in great detail by other authors and historians, and my narratives owe a great deal to their work. It was not my intention to rewrite these histories, but rather to summarize and elaborate on them within the context of epochal change. I encourage those readers who desire to know more about any given topic to consult the bibliography for a list of more authoritative sources.

Introduction

New Year's Eve is traditionally the time to reflect on the past and envision a brighter, more promising future. Never was this more true than at the close of 1946, the first full year of peace following the Second World War. Sixteen months since the surrender of Imperial Japan ended hostilities, everyday life was still anything but "normal." Reminders of war still lingered across the globe but particularly in Europe, the epicenter of the conflict. Wartime rationing was still in place, and citizens had to contend with shortages of everything from sugar to gasoline. Even food, which had always been available during the war, was now a scarce commodity owing to the deficient 1946 harvests across most of the continent.[1]

But even if agricultural production had kept up with demand, the bombing of railways, roads, and ports hindered the distribution of commodities. Coal shortages made generating electricity and heating homes extremely difficult. Chapter 1 details how the terrible winter weather of 1947 in Europe exacerbated all of these lingering reminders of wartime privation and created several new problems of its own. In terms of day-to-day survival, there was little to suggest that the war had ended other than the end of fighting.

No one could have known it, of course, but 1947 would prove to be a memorable year filled with events symbolizing an end to the wartime era and a transition to modern postwar society. As if to usher in this new age, President Harry S. Truman held a surprise press conference on the morning of December 31, 1946, to declare an official end to the period of hostilities. Proclamation 2714, as it is known, gave expression to everyone's hopes and aspirations for the future.

> With God's help this nation and our allies, through sacrifice and devotion, courage and perseverance, wrung final and unconditional surrender from our enemies. Thereafter, we, together with the other United Nations, set about building a world in which justice shall replace force. With spirit, through faith, with a determination that there shall be no more wars of aggression calculated to enslave the peoples of the world and destroy their civilization, and with

the guidance of Almighty Providence great gains have been made in translating military victory into permanent peace. Although a state of war still exists, it is at this time possible to declare, and I find it to be in the public interest to declare, that hostilities have terminated.[2]

On the surface, Truman's proclamation seems little more than a symbolic act. However, the declaration did have important repercussions for domestic politics in the United States because it meant that many of the wartime powers granted to the President would now lapse. In truth, Truman had not invoked those powers recently anyway, but there were several emergency laws of some consequence that would be set aside (most notably the Smith-Connally Act, which gave the government the right to take over mines and industrial plants and limited the rights of labor unions to strike). It also meant the reduction of certain taxes as the financial burdens of war eased.

Although he had not intended to answer questions, Truman fielded several queries from the assembled press reporters, most of whom seemed more interested in the timing of the announcement and the politics behind it than in its substance. The Republican Party leadership had clamored for the removal of executive wartime powers for some time. And now, in late 1946, after a victory at the polls gave the Republicans a majority in both houses of Congress, there was a very real threat that the division might cripple the government.

The Truman administration's willingness to relinquish wartime powers seemed to portend at least the possibility of bipartisan cooperation, and the Republican leadership welcomed the announcement as a step in the right direction.[3]

The next 12 months witnessed dramatic changes in the United States' approach to foreign policy. Chapter 2 addresses how the United States reevaluated its attitudes toward defeated Germany. In order to share the occupation and administration of the defeated Reich, the Allies had divided Germany into zones of occupation at the war's end. Those zones allowed the Allies to govern their areas of responsibility more effectively, but it did nothing to further any revival of Germany as a single economic and political unit. On January 1, 1947, the United States and Great Britain took a critical step toward German recovery when they united the administration of their two zones. The new unit, appropriately enough called "Bizonia," allowed the occupation authorities to share raw materials, industrial production, and export capacity across zonal boundaries. Some postulated that a successful Bizonia might serve as the nucleus of a new Germany, but such a result was not in the immediate future as the French and Soviet occupation authorities showed little interest in any grand strategy to create a unified Germany.

Their reticence was of little consequence anyway since the Allies had much more immediate and severe humanitarian and economic problems on their hands. Germany's industrial production limped along at inadequate levels, and policy makers in both Washington, D.C., and London realized that if Germany were ever to become a self-sufficient economic unit again, punitive wartime controls had to be rethought. More importantly, insufficient agricultural production threatened a return of widespread hunger and malnutrition, exacerbating the general famine that much of the world experienced the year before. Chapter 2 chronicles the steps the United States took to end the industrial and nutrition problems in 1947 and focuses specifically on how former president Herbert Hoover became an unlikely but critical agent in solving these crises.

As efforts to rehabilitate Germany proceeded apace, Communism soon replaced Nazism as the greatest threat to democracy. The Soviet Union's victory and its occupation of Eastern Europe gave Stalin the opportunity to woo suffering populations and fragile governments with Marxist promises of mutual prosperity for all. Greece and Turkey proved two prime targets. Chapter 3 relates how and why the United Kingdom surrendered its oversight of those two countries to the United States. That chapter focuses on Senator Arthur Vandenberg and how a Michigan Republican became instrumental in what was otherwise President Truman's and the Democratic party's initiatives to stop the rising "red menace." The result was the Truman Doctrine, which cast the United States into the role as protector of democracy and committed the country to millions of dollars in spending to support fledgling democracies worldwide.

The era of British hegemony had ended; the new age would be one of American dominance within a network of defensive and social alliances anchored by a strong Anglo-American partnership in world affairs.

Chapter 5 discusses how wartime cooperation became the roots of a trans–Atlantic friendship that lasts to this day. It also chronicles how a chance meeting between two men, one an American soldier and the other a British politician, symbolizes that mutual friendship.

The Truman Doctrine relieved Great Britain of a massive financial burden; however, a return to economic and social normality was still a long way off. Nevertheless, 1947 began with glimmers of hope that the quality of life might soon improve. On January 1, the United Kingdom took control of the ailing coal industry pursuant to the Coal Industry Nationalization Act of 1946, a move which Prime Minister Clement Attlee said "offers great possibility of social advance for the workers and indeed for the whole nation."[4] For a country experiencing coal shortages and intermittent electricity outages, nationalization held the promise that all of society could share the benefits and burdens of energy consumption. Many hoped that government intervention would mitigate the vicissitudes of capitalistic free enterprise, rationalize production, and end the shortages. It was part of the United Kingdom's grand postwar experiment in Socialism, but could the experiment succeed?

The answer depended on how well the British government would manage its financial crisis in the postwar period. Chapter 1 describes how the terrible weather drained the Treasury's resources, and Chapter 2 details how the ensuing need for relief at home figured into the Labour Government's decision to quit Greece and Turkey. The rationale for quitting Britain's overseas commitments was equally valid for the country's colonial possessions. Decolonization had already begun before the war, but the bankruptcy of the treasury forced Clement Atlee's government to concede what had previously been unthinkable, a withdrawal from India. That decision unlocked a host of new problems as the Indian subcontinent prepared to terminate British control in August of 1947.

Chapter 4 discusses the history behind the British dominion over the subcontinent and the events the led to the creation of Pakistan and India as independent nations. It focuses primarily on Pakistan and Muhammad Ali Jinnah, the leader of the Pakistani independence movement, and the experiences of a young Muslim college student named Masood Ghaznavi. The bifurcation of India turned out to be one of the most catastrophic events of the immediate postwar period, as atrocities and massacres fueled by religious and ethnic hatreds spilled blood all over the subcontinent. The antagonism and distrust spawned by that horrific experience still plague the region to this day.

Politics and foreign relations were not the only areas to change course in 1947. In the United States, the return of peacetime gave Americans an opportunity to confront the country's dark history of racism and bigotry. It was a cruel irony that African American soldiers who had served valiantly in Europe fighting Hitler returned home to a society that discriminated against them in ways reminiscent of Nazi policies toward Jews, Sinti-Roma, and other minorities. Would their service bring about an end to Jim Crow? Chapter 6 concerns one victory in the civil rights struggle. As most fans of American baseball know, 1947 saw the breaking of color barrier in the Major Leagues by Jackie Robinson. But instead of focusing on Robinson, this chapter tells the story of Wendell Smith, the courageous sports journalist for the black newspaper *Pittsburgh Courier*, and explains how he struggled against prejudice to get Robinson a Major League contract. Smith's story goes beyond the baseball diamond and reveals how he himself helped break down racial barriers in print journalism.

Finally, no book on 1947 would be complete without a discussion of transformations in technology and popular culture. Chapter 7 examines how economic and social realities of 1947 affected popular music. It chronicles the career of Stan Kenton, whose experiences with the music business and the mental breakdown he suffered presaged a transition from big band swing dances to other, more economical forms of performance. Similarly, Chapter 8 addresses how new technologies and advances in manufacturing revitalized the American television industry after the war's end. As manufacturers produced more and more television receivers, the social role of broadcasting itself came under scrutiny.

In the United Kingdom, television would soon be nationalized, but in the United States, television was undergoing something of an identity crisis. Was television simply a tool for entertainment, or could it have applications in the marketplace? Might it possibly revolutionize the public's buying habits? Chapter 8 focuses on Irene Murphy, then a 23-year-old television personality who took part in a cross-country tour to assess whether there was a future for television in retail commerce. Her experiences expose how this new technology, coming on the heels of the demobilization of troops from the armed forces, opened up new jobs for women that might otherwise have been dominated by men.

CHAPTER 1

The "Reluctant Spring"

How the Winter of 1947 Affected Europe's Historical Trajectory

Twenty months after the end of the most destructive war in history, Europeans still struggled to comprehend the enormity of the catastrophe. Demographically, the war cut a swath through an entire generation in a population already depleted by war and disease only twenty years earlier. War-weary survivors had to endure the privations attendant to the destruction of dwellings, the disruption of urban infrastructure, the lack of food, and the decline in energy production. At least the armed conflict that had pitted nations against each other was over. But now, at the end of 1946, former battlefield adversaries had to wage war against a common enemy, one that came from the skies much like the aircraft that had rained down bombs on cities and towns. This enemy, however, owed allegiance to no flag and did not ascribe to any ideology. It indiscriminately struck at everyone in its path, showing no favor to any one locality or nationality. It refused to negotiate, yield to reason, or consider appeals for mercy. That enemy was the weather.

The winter of 1946–47 proved to be one of the most disruptive natural catastrophes in twentieth-century Europe. The onslaught began in the autumn of 1946, as massive high-pressure areas anchored over Scandinavia pumped frigid arctic air out of the steppes of Russia onto the rest of the continent. Temperatures started to fall in October and by early November had reached unseasonably cold levels. In northern Germany, for example, daily temperatures ranged from a high of 37°F to a low of 27°F, and winter still had not officially arrived.[1] In mid-December, the arctic blasts intensified. During the daytime, the highs remained below freezing. Nighttime temperatures plummeted to between 23°F and 10°F, and even lower in some locales.[2]

The frigid air wreaked havoc all over northern Europe, bringing fresh hardships to civilian populations still struggling to cope with the aftermath of war. The situation was perhaps worst in Germany, where a collapsed infrastructure, an occupation by foreign armies, and internal political disunity all exacerbated the postwar economic stagnation. Large urban centers fared the worst. Apartment houses and family dwellings still bore the scars of wartime damage, making effective heating next to impossible. Those who had working stoves or fireplaces at least had the means to get warm, but they rarely had enough coal or kindling to put them to good use. For others, portable electric heaters provided some relief, but their effectiveness was limited by governmental restrictions on energy consumption. The city of Munich, for example, outlawed space heaters because of the danger of fire but also because they used up a great deal of electricity.

Like many other large cities, Munich opened "warming rooms" in hotels or restaurants, providing the public a place to get warm and procure a small amount of hot water.[3] During the worst of the crisis, as many as seventy such rooms were in operation, with a total capacity of about 50,000 people. As the Christmas season approached, most Germans found themselves wishing only for warmth, food, and continued health. When one's survival is at stake, simple things take on added significance.

During January 1947, German citizens had to endure another protracted period of intense cold with daily high temperatures that remained below freezing for weeks at a time. But the inhospitable weather had repercussions that went far beyond personal discomfort. The ever-present tandem of frigid temperatures and accumulated snow combined to produce a series of bottlenecks that crippled the still-struggling German economy. Heavy snows hampered coal mining efforts, exacerbating already existing shortfalls. To make matters worse, much of the coal that had been mined remained undelivered as rivers, canals, and ports became clogged with ice.

Drifting snow made road haulage extremely precarious. Rail transport fared little better, as the extreme cold damaged the boilers of locomotives, froze switching devices, and heaved up tracks.[4] The subsequent dearth of coal idled the turbines that created electricity, thus creating power shortages that curtailed manufacturing. Industrial plants had to contend with only four hours of electricity to run machinery, and only if they were lucky. Many factories were forced to close for weeks at a time.

The experiences of the inhabitants of Hamburg illustrate the dramatic effect that this inhospitable weather had on everyday life. Hamburg, a port city that normally benefited from more moderate temperatures coming off the ocean, was ill-prepared for the crisis. In December, the waterways froze, making the delivery of coal from the Ruhr difficult to impossible.

Chapter 1. The "Reluctant Spring"

As the weather got colder and the demand for energy increased, the city's reserve coal stocks dwindled, leaving only a scant eight days of supply at one point. Without much electricity, workers furloughed from closed manufacturing plants had little to do but stay at home in the dark and try to survive with little heat and meager food rations.

That assumes one had a home. For families whose domiciles were damaged or destroyed during the war, the best they could do was huddle in basements to preserve warmth. In the absence of anything better, Nissen huts provided some relief.[5] Unfortunately, the cheap, quickly assembled structures were never intended to house large numbers of people and they tended to fill up quickly as the displaced and homeless sought refuge wherever they could. For many, life had become a daily struggle just to stay alive.

The quotidian routines of normal life disappeared as these unbearable conditions persisted. Shivering laborers went to bed with their work clothes on. Not only did that afford them a little extra retained body heat, but it also made getting up for work the next day much easier. One inhabitant who had endured a tour on the Russian front applied the lessons he had learned there to survive in his native Hamburg. "Every two hours we got up and did calisthenics so that we wouldn't get numb from the cold. And if one of us didn't want to get up anymore, we shook him for a long while until he also took part."[6] Needless to say, these abject conditions took a toll on the health of the citizenry. By January 8, city hospitals were seeing an increase in frostbite cases, and the extreme cold had already claimed 17 lives.[7] By the thirteenth, the death toll had reached 26.[8]

The tragedy Hamburg experienced played out in countless other locations across occupied Germany. It is important to note here that the deep freeze of 1947 was not the cause of the hardships and deprivations; it exacerbated an already-existing crisis brought on by the destruction and defeat of war. If there is a bright side to this tale of deprivation and misery, it is the fact that by this time most Germans were accustomed to life in crisis mode and had devised clever ways to adapt. In this environment of perpetual shortages, survival depended upon one's ability to forage. Ever since the end of hostilities, young Germans spent much of their time scavenging for anything useful.

The practice was so commonplace that new words found their way into the general lexicon to express this hand-to-mouth subsistence. Foraging—particularly for food—became known colloquially as "*hamstern,*"[9] and the collection process, which often involved travelling into the countryside on trains, trucks, or private vehicles, the "*hamsterfahrt.*" When foraging proved insufficient, one might resort to *klauen* (looting). Besides food, heating materials were prized targets for "*hamstern.*" Rail yards were particularly susceptible as desperate individuals who could no longer heat their homes resorted to the theft of coal to survive ("*kohlenklau*"). Foraging was a particularly popular activity with young adults as it combined excitement with an element of danger. Looking back on that time, Günther Kammeyer recalled his experiences on the *Kohlenklau* that winter.

> We heard on the street, "Coal train, Ohlsdorf." And so we joined a group headed in the direction of the Ohlsdorf train station.... We thought the five or six of us would be the only ones that would show up. But at dusk there were whole masses of people on the tracks and the embankments, waiting for the coal cars. Our hearts were in our throats, because we couldn't imagine that we would be able to get to the wagons. But then things went really fast. We saw a shaded area, men jumped on the cars, leaned over the side, and threw down sacks filled with coal. Others tried to break down the side doors of the cars with bars since the train was moving slowly—someone had smeared green soap on the tracks and wheels spun. And soon coal came flying down from the wagons—I can still see it, how the coal lay in the snow, everything became black. And we grabbed what we could get with our bare hands and filled our sacks.[10]

In and around Cologne, the new word "*fringsen*," or the theft of commodities for the sake of survival, found its way into the *kölsch* dialect. The origin of this curious term resides in a sermon delivered by Cardinal Josef Frings, the Archbishop of Cologne. In his New Year's Eve message, Cardinal Frings stated, "We live in times where the single individual, in his need, ought to be allowed to take what he needs to preserve his life and health, if he cannot obtain it through other means, work or bidding."
The population soon interpreted Frings' startling comment to mean that one could suspend the seventh commandment when survival was at stake. That interpretation, though faulty,[11] came as welcome relief for those in danger of sickness or death since it freed them from whatever moral constraints they might still have left about stealing.

The cold penetrated everything. Private homes, which even in the best of times were not well insulated, quickly succumbed to cold air leaking through the broken windows and wall crevices. The only available defense was to stuff balled-up paper in the gaps, but that tactic provided scant relief. Damp air seeping through cracks quickly condensed and froze, turning interior walls into sheets of ice as smooth as glass.[12] Sleep provided a brief respite from the cold, but to obtain it one had to sacrifice privacy for communal beds, generally located in a single bedroom. Stacking children three or four to a mattress in order to share body heat became a common practice.

By mid-January, Germans had endured almost three full months of

Chapter 1. The "Reluctant Spring"

Germans take to the rails on the "hamsterfahrt" to forage for food or fuel, ca. 1946 or 1947 (Interfoto/Alamy stock photo).

miserable, bitingly cold weather. Then at the end of the month, as if to add further insult to injury, a third deep frost struck that would last through all of February. One inhabitant of Göttingen recalled the brutality of that month quite well. "The cold was barbaric and we only had enough wood for the cooking stove. So in the morning everyone congregated in the kitchen, but that wasn't very comfortable. The grownups got provoked and reacted angrily if the kids played or got loud. Many times, after eating lunch, I crept back to bed with a book. With muffs and gloves on, it was fine to stay there."[13]

It is hard to imagine the toll that constant cold and hunger took on the average person's psyche. Günther Kammeyer described his own inner struggle against the elements. "I have experienced that hunger and cold create pain. Internal pain, deep inside the body and soul. From the tip of your hair to the small toe, penetrating pain, not just momentarily, but one is permanently tormented by the hunger and crippled by the cold. One feels … you have reached the point of life or death."[14] The elderly and the sick suffered inordinately, and indeed death was the only release for many.

It is difficult to reach conclusions about how many people died as a direct result of the weather, since determining an actual cause of death was not a simple matter. Malnutrition also played a role, as did the decline in hygiene that attended the broken pipes, sewer disruptions, and the absence of usable water. In Berlin alone from December 1946 to January 1947, authorities attributed 76 deaths to the cold. Another 200 succumbed in February. By the time this frightful winter subsided, the Berlin state public health office fixed the total deaths from cold or frostbite at 390 souls. Another 1,000 individuals succumbed due to hunger.[15] And even in death, the last ignominy of this terrible winter was that coffins were in short supply and the frozen ground made a proper burial impossible. Corpses had to be stored until March when the arrival of the spring thaw allowed digging. In some cases, families had to wait four months before interment could take place.[16]

* * *

The miserable situation in Germany did not go unnoticed in the United Kingdom. The British can usually sympathize with those suffering bad weather since they often have to deal with it themselves. However, as 1947 approached, no one in Britain had much cause for complaint because they had been spared the bitter cold that struck central Europe months before. In fact, November's weather was dominated by a series of low-pressure areas coming out of the Atlantic Ocean that had brought fairly mild temperatures (albeit with typically gloomy British skies) and a good deal of rainfall. In mid-December, however, those systems gave way to the same high-pressure area that brought the bitter cold to Germany, and with it came clearer skies and more seasonably cold temperatures. The first major snow fell on the night of January 5–6, resulting in a brief but substantial disruption of transport services in the southeast. The snow continued on the seventh, but the effect was softened by a brief moderation in temperature that turned most of the previous snow cover into puddles of slush.[17] For the next 10 days, the United Kingdom experienced an unusual snap of mild weather with high temperatures reaching 57°F in some locations,[18] as a low-pressure area parked over Iceland covered most of the northern Atlantic.[19] It proved to be the calm before the storm.

Britain and Ireland's turn with the frightful weather of 1947 began on January 18, as a stationary Scandinavian high-pressure system drove low-pressure areas from the Atlantic Ocean south along a track that took them over the channel and continental Europe. The result was a wind-tunnel effect bringing fierce, frigid Siberian winds westward toward Britain. Temperatures plummeted all over England. The first region to get clobbered was the Southeast when, on the 23rd, up to six inches of snow fell in the counties surrounding London including Essex, Sussex, and Somerset. This storm was the vanguard of a much more intensive assault that began in earnest on the 26th, the day the London *Times* called "one of the wildest days of the winter."[20] As much as nine inches of fresh snow brought traffic all over southern England to a standstill, blocking roads and isolating villages. The dense snow cover was bad enough, but the accompanying gale-force winds along the straits of Dover and Folkestone drove the freshly fallen snow into massive drifts, some as much as 10 feet high.[21] The storm continued on the 27th, dumping snow in varying amounts on most of the rest of England. East Yorkshire was covered with six-foot drifts, the Isle of Sheppey in Kent was cut off from the mainland by eight-foot drifts, and some areas of Devon experienced drifts up to 10 feet.[22] Seven inches of snow covered the Isles of Scilly and Lizard Point on the western coast, two locales that usually do not experience much snow at all.[23]

The same weather pattern struck Ireland with equal ferocity. Temperatures dipped into the 20s on January 24, producing a massive snowstorm that blanketed the emerald island with a sheet of white. At first the snow added a lovely patina to the picturesque Irish countryside, but the continuing cold soon made everyone forget about the scenery. The mercury continued to fall and temperatures approached 9°F to 7°F by the end of the month. Factoring in windchill, skin temperatures dropped well below zero. All of Ireland was shivering.[24]

The great winter storm of January 1947 was the start of four weeks of the worst weather Great Britain had ever endured. Overcast skies took over, casting a dull pall over the entire English south and midlands that would last for three weeks.[25] Fresh snows fell in the southeast on the 28th as temperatures continued to drop. Accumulating snow now caused delays to the Piccadilly and Central lines of London's Underground. Even Big Ben, London's iconic landmark, succumbed to the ravages of the frigid weather when the clock chimes malfunctioned, sounding only one solitary chime at midnight.[26] The next night, temperatures dipped to near-record low levels, prompting the London *Times* to sum up the crisis succinctly with the headline, "All Britain Freezes."[27]

Southern Britain got a brief respite from the snow as temperatures moderated a bit during the first few days of February, but the rest of the island and Ireland remained locked in a wintery nightmare. As low-pressure areas from the Atlantic moved eastward pushing warmer air higher up into the atmosphere, the latent moisture condensed and returned to earth in the form of more snow. Gale-force winds produced blizzard conditions over Ireland on February 2 and soon the English north and north midlands were also buried in snow. Drifts, at places reaching heights of 10 to 12 feet, isolated large sections of the Lake District. Transportation in Northumberland ground to a halt with drifts as high as 15 feet.[28] On February 3, heavy snowfalls covered Yorkshire and the surrounding counties.

Near the town of Newbald, drifting snow trapped 78 women returning from Leeds in buses. Had it not been for the heroic efforts of one motorist who walked four miles to get help, the incident might have turned fatal. The women eventually had to abandon the buses and walk to the village of Market Weighton, a distance of over four miles, where the locals gave them food and shelter. Another party suffered a similar fate near Lockton.[29] These were not isolated incidents; travelers all over England abandoned their vehicles as they got stuck in the snow. On the road connecting Grantham to Stamford, 600 vehicles were caught in a traffic jam that extended for miles.[30]

On February 4, the London *Times* published an article, optimistically entitled "Cold Spell Ending," which gleefully reported that milder winds had brought a thaw to much of Britain. Sadly, the respite lasted only five days. More snow fell on the London environs on the 8th. A brief but welcome warming returned a few days later, prompting many to hope that a spring thaw would indeed arrive shortly. But a return to freezing temperatures, accompanied by a forecast that the cold would linger for some time yet, quickly dispelled all hopes.

For the rest of the month of February, snow fell somewhere in Britain every day, and it would have been challenging to find any spot of ground on the island not covered in snow. In Ireland, where the supplies of coal were critically short, farmers resorted to cutting down trees for fuel to heat their homes. In cities like Dublin, the inhabitants took to stripping wood from buildings just to have a minimal amount of warmth.[31] Except for the occasional mild turn, frigid temperatures retained an icy grip on both Great Britain and Ireland for another four weeks.

The snow was not the only threat. Much of Britain's and Ireland's coastal regions were lashed by the severe winds that accompanied the storms. The January gales along the Sussex coast played havoc with transportation across the English Channel, disrupting the loading and off-loading of cargo on the docks. In February, gales crippled the small fishing villages in Devon and Cornwall. High seas and rough surf continually washed over the beaches onto the roads, as storm surges exacerbated by high tides flooded homes with seawater, sometimes up to a depth of three feet. In Devon, near Slapton Ley, ocean waters surged up over the shore and flooded the coastal roads, depositing tons of sand and an odd assortment of items left over from the war, including barbed wire, parts of a landing craft, and tank traps.[32] While the interior of Devon and Cornwall contended with snowdrifts, coastal roads were covered with ice. March brought no relief from the storms; 12 more gales struck Devon and Cornwall that month.[33]

From January 23 to March 16, 1947, the weather had accomplished

Chapter 1. The "Reluctant Spring"   19

what the German Luftwaffe had failed to accomplish in 1940: Britain lay on the verge of economic exhaustion and psychological breakdown.[34] The effects of the snow, cold, and wind are almost too extensive and horrific to recount adequately. The sector most directly impacted was transportation. As highways disappeared under blankets of snow, local governments did the best they could to open thoroughfares cluttered with abandoned buses, automobiles, and trucks. There were not enough snowplows and workers to meet the demand, and crews that were available were taxed to the limit.

The situation was no better on the rail lines. The inevitable delays threw both commuter and commercial train schedules into chaos disrupting the entire grid. Engines fitted with snowplows could make some headway, but when they confronted snowdrifts as high as telephone poles, little could be done. Dire necessity led to some novel experiments in snow removal. In one case, railroad work crews used flame throwers to melt mounds of snow but soon abandoned the effort when they discovered that the melt water froze to the lines, making a bad situation worse. Another approach was to mount jet aircraft engines to tanks, in the hope that the high-speed exhaust would blow snow out of the way.[35]

Shoveling often proved the only method that worked, and towns often had to rely on the military to mobilize armies of workers, including German prisoners of war still incarcerated in England, in an attempt to avoid total isolation. Calling it "the worst winter in living memory," officials of the Ministry of Transport estimated that the cost of snow and ice removal across Britain would approach three million pounds.[36]

As also happened in occupied Germany, the dislocation of rail transport and truck haulage had cascading effects on other sectors of Britain's fragile economy. The most disruptive consequence was the impact on the fuel supply. Coal mines could not work at full capacity, and stockpiles languished at the pit heads because there was no transportation available. One estimate contends that in the height of the crisis during the first two weeks of February, industrial plants received less than half of the total amount of coal needed to keep production going.[37]

Birmingham's industries struggled mightily against energy shortages. The Austin motor works shut down its plants due to lack of energy, sending 14,000 employees home (their employment was terminated a few days later). Dunlop's rubber plants closed as well and the Goodyear plants at Wolverhampton followed suit. Imperial Chemical Industries (ICI) had to send home 6,000 workers during the first week of February and Cadbury's had to close its Bournville plant and lay off over 8,000 workers for over a week.

Textile manufacturers were particularly hard hit. Mills around Blackburn in Lancashire shut down, sending home approximately 30,000

Men working to clear snow from the train tracks between Appleby and Kirkby Stephen in Westmorland (Cumbria, U.K.) during the severe snow of winter 1947 (Chronicle/ Alamy stock photo).

workers.[38] They joined textile workers from the south who had already suffered a work slowdown several weeks before. In all, over 250 textile mills closed their doors in early February, causing the ranks of the unemployed to swell from 10,000 to 57,000 in just two weeks.[39] Such dislocations became more the rule than the exception, as factories all across Britain had to contend with little or no energy. As a result, applications for unemployment benefits skyrocketed. Estimates suggest that the number of workers receiving benefits quadrupled as a result of the weather, from 400,000 in mid-January to 1.75 million one month later.[40]

The coal shortage also exacerbated the supply of electricity available for domestic consumption. Demand had already risen that autumn, and the need for coal to power the electricity generators had jumped by 38 percent before the new year had even begun.[41] Already in early January, long before the worst of the storms hit, the Central Electricity Board (CEB) had warned of electricity cuts over much of the country unless consumers voluntarily cut back usage. The CEB eventually made good on its threat. The amount of the cut varied by location, but in general, consumers contended with disruptions between the hours of 8:00 a.m. to noon and again in the late afternoon between 2:00 p.m. and 4:00 p.m.

After the initial snowfall and frigid temperatures in late January, suppliers cut electricity deliveries in southern England by 20 percent and in other areas 10 to 15 percent.[42] In the southeast, where the severe weather had struck first, the CEB instituted cuts of 25 percent and implored everyone to increase conservation efforts or face potential blackouts lasting for a full 12 hours each day.[43] On February 10, the government took emergency action. At midnight, electrical service to the industries across most of the island ceased entirely, bringing an unwanted mid-winter vacation to millions of workers.[44]

The shut-down affected other services as well. Theaters and dance hall venues either reduced or cancelled their afternoon shows because of a paucity of energy.[45] The Ministry of Fuel and Power ordered newspapers and other periodicals to curtail publication and rationed newsprint. Phonograph recording came to a halt, and the British Broadcasting Corporation (BBC) reduced its broadcasts as well.[46] These emergency orders remained in place until they were lifted on February 24 in the midlands and on March 3 in the southeast and northwest. Still, restrictions on electricity use continued well into March.

The food supply was an ever-present concern, even before the crisis.[47] As the winter storms halted transportation, deliveries of foodstuffs trickled to a bare minimum. Remote towns were hit the hardest, and isolated villages frequently resorted to sending out "rescue parties" to trek through snowdrifts in order to procure enough food for the inhabitants to survive. The experiences of localities in East Yorkshire Wolds exemplify what small villages had to endure. In Huggate, the early February snowstorms produced five-foot-high drifts and clogged the town's main street, rendering it completely impassable. Outside of the town, the snow drifted to heights approaching 15 feet. Drifts frequently buried smaller cottages and movement from home to home could be accomplished only after intense digging or tunneling. As the stocks of bread dwindled, the townspeople pooled their remaining supplies in an effort to ration consumption.

Facing the possibility of at least another week of isolation, those who still had phone service made frantic appeals for airdrops of food.[48] It took a cooperative venture from the British army and the Royal Air Force (RAF) mountain rescue service to get them assistance. Twelve soldiers, each carrying thirty pounds of provisions and guided only by compasses, had to trek two miles on snowshoes through a blizzard to reach the town. The journey took three hours, and four of the six men were near exhaustion when they finally arrived.[49] A second onslaught of storms isolated Huggate again two weeks later.

Huggate's experience may sound extreme, but similar stories of isolation and deprivation can be found in towns all over Britain. When the tiny community of Oughtershaw in Upper Wharfedale was cut off from the rest of the world, relief wagon loads could not make it to the hamlet, forcing the inhabitants to trek out through the snow for about one mile to retrieve the supplies. Other townspeople walked up to twelve miles to a nearby town to obtain provisions.[50] In the worst cases, the RAF had to drop food by parachute.

The situation was not much better in Ireland, where a late-February storm piled three to six feet of additional snow on top of the mounds that were still lying on the ground. Eventually, the surface of the snow cover froze over to a thickness that allowed for foot travel, thus giving children the eerie sensation of walking above treetops and telephone poles.[51] In this surreal winter landscape, life was anything but ordinary.

The sheer volume of snow and the tremendous drifts proved catastrophic for agriculture. Milk production became a particularly vexing problem. Farms managed to continue producing raw milk but there was no way to get it to the cooperatives for processing; hence, a good deal of it was wasted. Farms that raised sheep, especially in Ireland, Wales, and northern Britain, were devastated. The speed and severity of the storms caught the animals outside without shelter, burying entire flocks under a shroud of snow. Bill Alderson, from Upper Teesdale, remembered the horror that shepherding families had to endure:

> The sheep were way underneath the snow and you could sometimes see the breathing hole where hot breath had come up through it. The farmer had to set to and dig them out. A lot died—a hell of a lot. I think the Sandersons lived at Valance Lodge. I think they were running a thousand sheep at that time and they lost half of them. And we were over at Ashgill. We were over there, I think it would be in May or June, and there was still snow in the bottom, and stinking, dead sheep. The place stank where they hadn't been able to get them all. It was a big job, cleaning up afterwards. There were dead sheep everywhere.[52]

Sadly, the Aldersons' experience was common. Welsh shepherds had to watch helplessly while their flocks perished. "They are dying like flies," one shepherd lamented.[53] Scavengers, themselves deprived of food sources by the advancing snows, found the herds of weakened sheep too good to pass up. Murders of crows descended onto the fields in search of carrion, and the hungriest among them attacked their victims even before they had perished. Skulks of starving foxes reacted similarly, as shepherds could do nothing to keep the attackers away. At Dolgoch, in the western uplands of Wales, 80 percent of the sheep stock succumbed.[54] In total, the United Kingdom may have lost up to four million heads,[55] constituting about half of its entire population of sheep.

Chapter 1. The "Reluctant Spring" 23

* * *

Another storm hit the south and Midlands on March 4 carrying with it an additional two inches of snow, but when combined with the ever-present winds, even that small amount made transportation precarious. Fortunately, this latest round of snowstorms turned out to be the last ones for the south. In London, rising temperatures turned the snow into sleet and rain. The Midlands and Wales were not as lucky, however. In the West Midlands, a blizzard packing gale-force winds deposited snow in drifts up to 16 feet. Railroads and highways that had been cleared weeks before were once again impassable. In some locales, the snow was so frozen solid that one could stand on top of it and walk above the signposts and hedgerows.[56] More snow fell on sixth and ninth. Transportation across Britain was again disrupted and in some places it came to a total halt.

The British Automobile Association declared that snow had "virtually cut England in two"[57] leaving no thoroughfares to get from south to north. On March 7, the London *Times*, which usually is not given to hyperbole, reported that conditions were the "worst ever known," as 30-foot-high drifts buried homes and forests.[58] The onslaught continued on March 13, this time attacking Scotland, which had somehow managed to dodge most of the snows that had blanketed the south and midlands. Just as everyone began to expect the imminent arrival of spring, fresh snowstorms blanketed the Scottish Highlands with drifts as high as 22 feet.

But for southern Britain, the weekend of March 8 brought sunshine and warmer temperatures to a grateful populace. As roads started to clear and coal shipments increased, the Ministry of Fuel and Power eased up on some of its controls on energy. On the tenth, warmer air from the Atlantic wafted over Devon and Cornwall and gradually swept inland, reaching Wales and the Midlands within a day or two. By the 13th, southern England and London registered temperatures in the low 50s. Apparently, spring had arrived, if reluctantly, ending the most vicious winter in contemporary memory.

Unfortunately, the catastrophe was not yet over. The milder temperatures brought rain showers and melting snow, but with the ground still frozen, the water had no way to percolate into the soil. Consequently, creeks and rivers soon swelled with run-off waters and within days England and Wales experienced epic floods. On March 12, the Thames River rose at the rate of one-and-a-half inches per hour and quickly broke through its banks. Roads that not long before were impassable because of snowdrifts were now impassable because of flooding. The Medway, Trent, and Avon Rivers soon broke their banks as well, inundating cities and towns from Bath to Bury St. Edmunds.[59] Despite massive levee efforts and sandbagging, landowners were helpless to stem the rising waters that enveloped their homes. The best many could do was move to the upper floors and wait for the floods to recede. The London *Times'* special correspondent described the scene in the Thames Valley:

> There is a grim monotony in the flooded landscape, dotted here and there with houses, bungalows, inns, and hotels—their signs only 2ft or 3ft above the water. In many places along the Thames Valley it was confusing to define where river, roads, and fields began and ended. The water raced under the bridge at Windsor, beyond which day and night work continues to keep the water from breaching the protective clay wall. Eton's High Street was flooded. The tops of the goal-posts marked the playing fields, a boat was seen being rowed over the rugger pitch, and the water lapped the walls of the college.[60]

The situation deteriorated rapidly in the Fens, a region of low-lying farmland reclaimed from the sea. Flood banks and dikes constructed to contain the river waters normally served the region well, however this spring the thaw proved more than the system could handle. Despite the heroic efforts of companies of sandbaggers, tributary rivers of the river Great Ouse broke through their banks in several places on March 18. The flow of the Great Ouse, which had an estimated peak capacity of 7,700 cubic feet of water per second, was recorded at over 10,000 cubic feet per second, and may have even gone substantially higher.[61]

Rising flood waters covered the low-lying countryside, laying waste to thousands of acres of Britain's best farmland. The dire situation prompted a visit from the Duke of Gloucester, who had to travel around the city of Ely by amphibious vehicle to inspect the flood-ravaged areas. Similar devastation reached the northern and upper midland sections of Britain less than a week later. In Yorkshire, 70 percent of all the homes in the town of Selby flooded, forcing some 20,000 people to seek help from makeshift field kitchens and rest centers.[62] In Nottingham, as many as 3,000 homes and 85 industrial concerns were destroyed or damaged.[63] It is difficult to estimate how much damage was done across Britain, but one source claims the final tally of properties flooded in 1947 probably exceeded 100,000.[64] In area, over 100 square miles of countryside was under water, resulting in a loss of about 600,000 acres of arable farmland.[65]

Then, as if to impart insult to injury, mother nature unleashed the most ferocious of all the storms yet encountered. On Saturday, March 15 a freakish gale swept in from the Atlantic bringing a day's worth of rain punctuated by two hours of snow to Ireland, just in time to ruin outdoor St. Patrick's Day preparations. The storm produced torrential rains driven by winds clocked at 65 miles per hour, turning streets into rivers and making projectiles out of anything that was not securely fastened to the ground.[66] As the storm system moved eastward, violent, hurricane-like winds slammed into Britain's western coastal regions. Pembrokeshire, on the Welsh coast, reported wind gusts approaching 100 miles per hour. The Midlands sustained persistent gale force winds of up to 66 knots that persisted almost 12 hours.

Over the next few days, anemometers spun all over Great Britain as the storm advanced across the island. London reported gusts of 77 miles per hour, and similar speeds were recorded in Leicester, Bath, and Birmingham. Scores of people were injured by flying debris, and several deaths resulted from dwellings that collapsed under the onslaught of the wind and rain.[67] Towns and cities that once had to contend with desperate isolation now had to clean up uprooted trees and repair damaged shingles, decking, and toppled telephone poles.

It is extremely difficult, if not impossible, to place a monetary value on the destruction brought about by the winter weather. At the very least it was, as Tom Williams, the Minister of Agriculture, explained in a House of Commons briefing, a "disaster of the first magnitude."[68] An estimated 70,000 acres of wheat were destroyed and over 80,000 tons of potatoes were lost.[69] In cabinet meetings, Williams placed the total financial loss in terms of current production at a minimum of 16.5 million pounds. If we add the losses to future production, the sum might easily reach 36.5 million pounds.[70] Williams was quite right; this winter was an economic disaster of the first order. The resulting paucity of production meant that the United Kingdom would have to continue to import grains and foodstuffs from the Americas and from Denmark, exacerbating the deficits in the country's balance of payments. An end to rationing was nowhere in sight.

* * *

By the time the winter of 1946–47 had run its course, meteorological records had fallen all across Europe. As bad as the temperature had been in the United Kingdom and Ireland, it was much worse on the continent, and it got progressively worse the farther east one went. The winter of 1947 was the coldest in Holland since 1849 and the coldest in Dresden since 1830.[71] Single digit temperatures were common in Paris and Brussels. In Austria, temperatures frequently dipped below zero, causing the Danube River to freeze, isolating Vienna from its environs. In the Soviet Union, February temperatures varied between -10°F to -20°F from Leningrad to Moscow and occasionally dipped near -30°F.

When considering the atmospheric record on a continental scale, this winter was on par with the worst ever recorded.[72] It was truly a catastrophe, made even more devastating by the bad timing of coming on the heels of destructive war. Europeans employed the imagery of battlefield conflict to describe what was happening to them, perhaps because those images had dominated their consciousness for so long. Germans often called 1947 "the eighth war year." A Dublin newspaper referred to the snow as "the white enemy." Germans preferred a more severe sobriquet, referring to the snow as "the white death" (*weisser Tod*).

All across Europe, shovelers were organized into "armies" that "attacked" the snow. A "siege mentality" again crept into the consciousness of towns and cities isolated by snow drifts, forcing them to revert back to the practices that helped them survive the war. That mentality was visually reinforced by the military personnel (including prisoners of war) mobilized to combat the elements. For those who had survived both the war and the 1947 winter, the two events remained psychologically and physically linked.

The year 1947 proved one of the strangest weather years of the twentieth century, not just in Europe but across the globe. In North America, a huge mass of frigid air swooped southward from the Arctic on February 5 and 6, engulfing much of the continent in sub-freezing temperatures. In Saskatchewan, snows that had already begun in December of 1946 culminated in one of the worst blizzards ever recorded over two weeks from January 26 to February 9, crippling the capital of Regina, burying railroads and highways, and devastating the surrounding towns with a lack of food and fuel. One report quotes the average temperature in the first two weeks of the year at -45°F.[73]

In the United States, a massive cold front that originated in the Midwest extended all the way down to Florida, where sub-zero weather lasting up to eight hours a day ruined fruit and truck crop production resulting in losses as high as $50 million.[74] Two more cold waves swept across the United States in March. A snowstorm in the beginning of the month crippled Pennsylvania, New York, and the New England states, where snow accumulation totals from one storm alone approached 50 inches. Oddly enough, as if to underscore the insanity of the weather that year, Iceland had one of the mildest winters it had ever experienced. And then, as if to atone for the severity of the winter months, nature bestowed upon Europe one of the hottest and driest summers in recent memory. The same year that saw record-breaking cold temperatures and snowfall accumulations could now also claim record-breaking high temperatures. For Vienna and Frankfurt, that summer was the hottest on record since 1859; for Prague, it was the hottest since 1868. The year 1947 will stand as one of extremes, one that produced some of the greatest temperature differences in Europe over a 12-month period.[75]

The winter of 1946–47 left behind a wake of economic dislocation and infrastructure disruption across Europe, but especially for the United Kingdom and occupied Germany, this natural catastrophe could not have come at a worse time. Coming off the heels of an expensive and destructive war, both countries had reached critical junctions in their history. For financially strapped Great Britain, the cleanup from the catastrophe drained the treasury of cash that might have purchased foodstuffs, supported industry, or financed the transition to the welfare state.

The sudden expenditures forced bureaucrats to rethink budgets and prioritize expenditures, thus raising a critical question: Which was more important, the social welfare of the citizenry or the maintenance of empire? There would not be enough resources to manage both. Moreover, at a time when government was taking over control of much of the private sector, the harsh winter undermined the public's faith in the government's ability to get things accomplished.

Conservative critics wondered how the government could administer the mines, public utilities, and road haulage if it could not even manage to clear roads and rail lines of snow efficiently. Prime Minister Attlee's Labour government would continue in office for another four years, but the perceptions of government inefficiency and incompetence that began with the weather emergency dogged its efforts to institutionalize and broaden the welfare state.

For Germany, the horrible winter of 1946–47 pushed an already tired and demoralized population near the breaking point. As one American reporter cabled to his home office, the sentiment among locals in Frankfurt was, "We'd rather be fat and happy Nazi pigs again than hungry and freezing democrats."[76] The last thing the western Allies needed was to see their democratization efforts in western Germany fail, considering that Communism loomed just across the zonal border as a viable alternative to Capitalism. As the populace grew ever more discontented with their living conditions, the success or failure of the occupation depended upon how well the Allies responded to this natural crisis. Military governors and policy makers back home in their respective governments had some serious soul searching to do.

It seems ironic that nations ripped apart by six years of war and another 18 months of wartime privation should be united by a common natural catastrophe. But the cruel winter of 1947 was just what Europe needed to drive home the notion that cooperation, not competition, should motivate the relationships between nations. At least it is safe to say that the winter of 1947 forced nations to reassess priorities, and that reevaluation had effects that rippled across the globe. Looking at it metaphorically, it is as though the snow and ice were washing away the cinders and ashes that had accumulated over eight years of war, hardship, and privation. A new era was about to begin.

CHAPTER 2

"Sustaining Virtues"
Herbert Hoover and the Rehabilitation of Germany

By the end of March, moderate temperatures finally swept across northern Europe, releasing millions from the icy grip of the interminable winter. Those who had survived could now leave their shelters and prepare for the arrival of Easter only a week away. On March 28, an estimated 80,000 inhabitants of Düsseldorf in Germany's Ruhr Valley took to the streets, not to enjoy the spring thaw but to demonstrate against the military government. All across the city, workers put down their tools, shops and schools closed, and public transportation stopped in support of a mass demonstration planned for that day. Placard-carrying demonstrators began their march at the Hofgarten and then proceeded through the streets peacefully, but that was not the case everywhere in the city.

Several blocks away, a smaller crowd approached a building used by the British occupation authority and pelted it with rocks, then turned on a car carrying correspondents of the press. Elsewhere, a group of disaffected youths or possibly communist party agitators unceremoniously tossed an unoccupied military government vehicle into a lake.[1] At the culmination of the demonstration, delegates from the trade unions approached the town's *bürgermeister* with a list of demands,[2] which included the dismissal of Dr. Hans Schlange-Schöningen, the food minister in the British zone, and other administrators they deemed incompetent. They also argued for an intensification of the denazification process, an end to zonal authority, and an economic reunification of Germany.

The Düsseldorf march was the latest demonstration[3] in a series of uprisings that started a month earlier, when work stoppages in Leverkusen and Wuppertal quickly spread to Dortmund, Gelsenkirchen, and Braunschweig. Other strikes and demonstrations broke out in Solingen, Hagen, Bielefeld and other major cities all across northwestern Germany. These incidents were tangible manifestations of the deep current of discontent flowing in the population of the Ruhr. Given the number and magnitude of the demonstrations, Bizonal authorities took notice. The success of the occupation was clearly in jeopardy.

The workers' complaints ostensibly focused on structural economic and political change,[4] but in truth the primary motivational force behind their discontent was hunger. Food issues often topped their lists of grievances, and for good reason. For the past year and a half, Ruhr miners and industrial workers and their families had to exist on rations that were barely enough to keep them alive, let alone allow them to work. Average consumers who were supposed to receive 2,000 calories per day to maintain their health had to contend with about half that amount, which, by any definition, was a starvation diet. Deliveries of food had slowed due to the lack of reserve stocks and the transportation problems attendant to the horrible winter weather of the previous months.

Most households had to rely on potatoes cellared for the winter but they consumed those stocks so quickly that they eventually were forced to consume even the rotten ones. Short of purchasing food of questionable quality at exorbitant prices on the black market[5] or going out on the *hamsterfahrt* to forage or steal, there was little anyone could do to augment their diet. Motivated by empty stomachs and with little to lose, the demonstrators threatened more work stoppages and demonstrations unless the occupation authority procured additional food supplies soon.[6] As the German news magazine *Der Spiegel* put it, "the famine currently sweeping over almost all the British zone accomplished what a lot of Nazi underground movements didn't"—it motivated the citizenry to defy the British occupation authority openly.[7]

After two years of British and then Bizonal occupation, the economy of the Ruhr, like most other locales all across Germany, was still broken down. Without sufficient agricultural production to keep pace with demand, urban Germans lived a hand-to-mouth existence, reliant upon food exports from charitable nations to keep from starving. How did this situation get so out of hand? The terrible harvests of the past two years, and the breakdown of transportation were certainly a large part of the problem. However, German farmers themselves also bore some responsibility. Many farmers in Bavaria and Württemberg resented sending their crops to cities in the industrial northwest, so some flouted military government regulations by growing the least nutritional crops (like oats) and feeding valuable grains to livestock.

One major part of the problem was something out of the Germans' control. There was still a feeling among the victorious Allies that the Germans, as the perpetrators of the recent war, should be left to their own devices and not given any better treatment than any of the populations they had once subjugated. This was a potent argument since Germany was not the only country suffering; the entire world was still reeling from a famine that began in 1946. However, the stakes were highest in occupied Germany, where both Democracy and Communism competed to win over the hearts and minds of the population. The persistent food crisis and the inability of the British and American authorities to solve it made many Germans question the value of western democracy.

In this particular instance the Allied authorities responded quickly by promising to rush recently imported food stocks to the towns of the Ruhr, thereby averting a crisis. Their actions were at best only a stop-gap measure, however. A permanent solution to the food crisis required a revival of Germany's economy *in toto*, and that in turn required the Allies to rethink their overall approach to governing Germany. This chapter describes the critical policy course corrections the western Allies took during 1947 that turned a potential catastrophe into an unqualified success. But this chapter is not just about international politics, it is also a story of personal redemption. In the process of saving an entire nation, a discredited ex-president of the United States (who, like the Germans, knew something about being a pariah) became a hero to millions of people and in the process rehabilitated his own public image and his legacy to history. To understand these two transformations and how they intersected in 1947, a brief look at the evolution of U.S. policy toward Germany and the postwar realities that threatened the success of the occupation is in order.

* * *

By the end of summer 1944, the successful D-Day landing at Normandy and the advances of both the western allies in France and Soviet troops in the east assured that victory over the Nazi war machine was just a matter of time. Policy makers needed to finalize plans for the military occupation of foreign territory, so experts gathered into "country units" to collect information about the countries about to be liberated or, in the case of Germany and Austria, conquered. The initial strategy envisioned that as Allied troops conquered hostile territory, specially designated civil affairs units would do most of the work restoring public services, administering local government, and maintaining law and order in the civilian populations.

But once the Allies began their advance into Germany proper in 1945, the rapid collapse of the Third Reich took many by surprise. Ground forces captured a great deal of territory quickly, and the civil affairs units that were supposed to establish control were either overwhelmed or unavailable, leaving combat units to do much of the quotidian civil affairs tasks. Therein lay the conundrum. The army's primary mission was conquest, not civil administration; thus, it needed guidelines on what it should and should not do with the captured populations. By April 1945 the war was clearly nearing an end but the U.S. forces still had no official statement of policy to govern the conquered German populations.

A basic blueprint for the administration of Germany after the Nazi surrender finally emerged at the Yalta Conference in February. There, the "big three" agreed on a curious compromise. Each victorious army would be in control of a "zone of occupation" and an Allied Control Council, comprised of representatives from the Soviet Union, the United States, and the United Kingdom, was empowered to reach policy decisions and then enforce them uniformly across the entirety of occupied Germany. In that way, the Allies would each have a share in the administration of the conquered territory but make decisions in common.

In April of 1945, with victory only weeks away, the U.S. government finally issued directives to guide the work of the occupation armies. The document, known as JCS 1067, embodied the spirit of Yalta decisions but was intended to be in force only for a transitional period until a more formal policy statement could be devised. The foundational motivation of JCS 1067 was to ensure that Germany would never again threaten world peace, and so the country was to be disarmed, denazified, and decentralized.

Military governors were instructed to be "firm but aloof" when dealing with the conquered populations, and fraternization between soldiers and civilians was strictly prohibited. Germans were to enjoy no better standard of living than that of the nations they had subjugated during the war. Accordingly, the Allies were to take no steps to import supplies or provisions to occupied Germany except those required to forestall "disease or unrest." Similarly, the document strictly controlled industrial production. Anything that might be used for war purposes, including "iron and steel, chemicals, non-ferrous metals (excluding aluminum and magnesium), machine tools, radio and electrical equipment, automotive vehicles, heavy machinery, and important parts thereof" was prohibited.[8] In its instructions to the commander of the United States zone, JCS 1067 forbade any steps "looking toward the economic rehabilitation of Germany, or designed to maintain or strengthen the German economy."[9]

It is understandable that JCS 1067 would reflect wartime animosities and be predicated on the sentiment that the Germans ought to be punished for their wrongdoings. The most famous expression of that spirit was the Morgenthau Plan,[10] a proposed policy to de-industrialize Germany by removing all heavy industry from its economy and recast Germany into several agricultural states. Although in retrospect the plan seems overly harsh and economically short sided, Morgenthau's vision, which had been expressed many months before the Nazi surrender, still garnered a great deal of sympathy in high policy circles in Washington.[11] Many of its tenets found expression in the Yalta and Potsdam agreements, particularly those that called for the dismantling and removal of industrial plants as reparations. But more dispassionate observers knew that a complete destruction of Germany's industrial infrastructure was not only undesirable but, in fact, impossible. Hence, the Allies needed to craft a more permanent policy that would incorporate the spirit of the Morgenthau Plan while accepting the reality that Germany's industrial economy should be retained.

The "Level of Industry Plan" of March 1946 fulfilled that need. In a rare moment of multinational agreement, the Allied Control Council devised a complicated schedule of ceilings for German industrial production, ranging anywhere from 11.4 percent to at 50 percent of 1938 production levels. The plan also prohibited or severely limited an entire class of heavy industry. Steel production, for example, was limited to a production of seven million tons, or roughly 25 percent of prewar capacity. In general, the overall effect was to reduce Germany's industrial production to 50 or 55 percent of 1938 levels. That figure gave the occupation authorities justification for the dismantling and removal of plants or equipment deemed "excess capacity" as reparations.[12]

Considering the stated goal was "to enable [Germany] to maintain herself without external assistance," the Level of Industry Plan seems economically stultifying and overly restrictive. However, a general revival of the German economy was not possible at that time anyway, even if the will to do so had existed. The Level of Industry Plan accepted the Yalta decision that Germany should be treated as a single economic unit, but that unification never really happened. The Allied Control Council, now (with the addition of a French component) comprised of four nations' representatives, proved ineffective in reaching or enforcing decisions across all of occupied Germany. Consequently, the occupation zones evolved into semiautonomous units something akin to "fiefdoms" where commanders had a good deal of latitude in governing. Quadripartite decision making became difficult if not impossible. Hence, in the absence of multilateral policy, JCS 1067 remained the policy basis of the U.S. occupation authority.

The wisdom underpinning JCS 1067 came into question in 1946 as famine swept across Europe and much of the globe. Food experts had predicted the crisis, but its severity caught many governments by surprise. Wartime ration controls had to stay in place and in some cases strengthened as populations everywhere struggled to produce enough food. As food stocks in Germany diminished, the United States and British zones proved especially vulnerable. Most of western Germany's food had come from areas that were now under Soviet or Polish control and, in this milieu of scarcity and distrust, those occupation authorities were loath to share.

Faced with possible mass starvation, the United States soon had to export stocks to Germany under the "disease and unrest" provisions of JCS 1067. Those shipments cost a great deal of money that the occupation forces themselves, and by extension the taxpayer back home, had to pay. The lack of interzonal cooperation was proof enough that four-power control over Germany was not working. Many within the Office of Military Government for the United States (OMGUS) already by spring of 1946 urged a revision of JCS 1067. In an attempt to get the wheels of change moving, Lt. General Lucius Clay sent a report on conditions in Germany to the State Department in May of that year. In the cable, Clay pointedly described the reality of the German economic picture:[13]

> After one year of occupation, zones represent air-tight territories with almost no free exchange of commodities, persons, and ideas. Germany now consists of four small economic units which can deal with each other only through treaties, in spite of the fact that no one unit can be regarded as self-supporting.

His report argued for the creation of a provisional indigenous government that could oversee German economic recovery in the broadest sense. Then, prophetically, Clay concluded that

> If agreement cannot be obtained along these broad lines in the immediate future, we face a deteriorating German economy which will create a political unrest favorable to the development of communism in Germany and a deterrent to its democratization. The next winter will be critical under any circumstances and a failure to obtain economic unity before the next winter sets in will make it almost unbearable. The sufferings of the German people will be a serious charge against democracy and will develop a sympathy which may well defeat our other objectives in Germany.[14]

Clay's dire warning got swift attention. After the Soviet press repeatedly misrepresented American policy using Morgenthau Plan imagery for propaganda purposes, U.S. Secretary of State James Byrnes decided to set the record straight. In September, he addressed an audience of occupation officials and German civilian personnel in Stuttgart. In his speech, Byrnes blamed the lack of improvement in the German economy on the Allied Control Council's failure to achieve common policy. More importantly, he spoke in favor of "changes in the levels of industry agreed upon by the Allied Control Commission if Germany is not to be administered as an economic unit as the Potsdam Agreement contemplates and requires."[15] The speech implicitly blamed the Soviets (and to a lesser extent the French) for obstructing four-power decision making and thereby perpetuating Germany's economic troubles. One point was becoming very clear. Communists were rapidly replacing Nazis as the preferred objects of scorn.

In fulfillment of the promises Byrnes made at Stuttgart, the United States and Great Britain agreed to merge their zones into one larger administrative unit, regardless of French and Soviet reactions. The inauguration of Bizonia in January of 1947 was a big step toward economic unification, but there was still no official revision of JCS 1067 or the Level of Industry Plan to accompany the new administration.[16] Instead, just as Clay had predicted, the winter of 1946–47 proved to be the driving force behind change. Germans who had to contend with food scarcity during the previous year again faced months of hunger. As transportation breakdowns crippled the distribution of imported food, the suffering increased. Body weights fell precipitously due to malnutrition, especially among city-dwellers. Diseases such as typhus, tuberculosis, and rickets, affecting particularly the elderly, the infirm, and children posed a serious public health crisis.

While it is true that the rest of Europe also had to suffer through the severe weather and the scarcity of food, the situation was most dire in Germany.[17] Responding to pleas from the occupation authorities, Tracy S. Voorhees, special assistant to the Secretary of War, met with Lt. General Clay in December of 1946 and learned that Germany would need to import an additional 300,000 tons of food each month just to ensure the population's survival.[18] The potential financial drain on the U.S. treasury was staggering.

In an effort to stay on top of the impending crisis, the State Department sent a memo to the White House dated January 16, 1947, suggesting that "an authoritative survey of the food requirements in the bizonal area in Germany and also in Austria by a person whose conclusions would command the confidence of everyone, including the leadership of the new Congress, would certainly be most helpful."[19] One person stood out as the clear choice to head this crucial mission. All agreed that this was a job for Herbert Hoover.

Many remember Hoover only as the president who failed to combat the Great Depression, but a closer look reveals a man who devoted his entire life to public service in pursuit of humanitarian causes. His biographies all describe how his Quaker upbringing informed his commitment to aiding others in times of distress.[20] After graduating from Stanford University with a degree in geology, Hoover made a personal fortune working as a mining engineer for several corporations. His first foray into humanitarian service was in 1915, when he arranged financial help for Americans trapped in Europe by the outbreak of the First World War.

A few years later, serving as the director of the U.S. Food Administration, he coordinated relief efforts to ship food to starving Belgian children; an effort that probably helped save tens of thousands of lives. In the 1920s, Hoover entered the Republican administrations of Presidents Harding and Coolidge as secretary of commerce, where he distinguished himself by organizing the relief effort in the states stricken by the disastrous Mississippi River flood of 1927.

His record as a cabinet secretary, plus the strong economy, helped elect Hoover to the White House in 1928. Unfortunately, the stock market crash of 1929 cast a pall over his entire presidency. His previous accomplishments receded in the memories of workers who blamed him for chronic unemployment and financial ruin. Defeat to Franklin D. Roosevelt in 1932 effectively ended his political career and he spent most of the next 12 years out of the limelight, during which time his name became a metaphor for anti-progressive policies and economic stagnation.

All that changed at the end of the Second World War when the new president, Harry S. Truman, decided to invite Hoover to the White House to discuss the key issues of the day.[21] Hoover admitted to his friend Edgar Rickard that the President's invitation pleased him, speculating that it might portend an offer to work within the Truman administration. In truth, Hoover had no expectation of what might come of the meeting or the discussion.[22] If nothing else, it would be a small step out of the political shadows and back onto a national stage.[23] Their first meeting took place on May 28, 1945, and over a 55-minute discussion the two men developed a good personal relationship; one that kindled a lifetime friendship that transcended party loyalties and ideological differences.

When the international food crisis became acute in 1946, Truman asked Hoover to serve as honorary chairman of the newly-created Food Emergency Committee. As part of his duties, Hoover embarked on a fact-finding mission that took him and a team of experts around the world on a three-month tour of 35 countries. Suddenly, Herbert Hoover the humanitarian was back in his element, working to save lives around the world. More importantly, the appointment marked the return of Herbert Hoover the politician, giving him influence and voice in shaping policies that could ameliorate one of the postwar world's toughest problems.

As the food crisis in occupied Germany and Austria worsened during the winter of 1946–47, Truman again turned to Hoover to lead another fact-finding mission. However, when Secretary of War Robert Patterson first approached him about taking the assignment, Hoover balked. First, he felt that such a study could be accomplished without requiring another trip to Europe and second, he felt that such a request ought to come directly from President Truman himself. When Truman got word of Hoover's hesitation, he reacted almost immediately with a cordial request in writing.

> Dear Mr. President:
>
> Last year you made a trip around the world at my request to report on food needs at a time of critical shortage. The result was most helpful in meeting the acute problems which confronted us.

World conditions this year are not nearly as threatening, but a serious situation in food still exists in certain areas, particularly those in Europe occupied by our forces and for which we, therefore, have a direct responsibility. I believe a food survey by you of these areas would be of great benefit to us in determining our policy in supplying food or funds for its purchase. The recent merger of the United States Zone in Germany with the British Zone for economic purposes makes the food conditions in the British Zone also of interest to us.

I should, therefore, like to ask you to undertake this economic mission as to food and its collateral problems, and report to me upon it. It is hoped that methods can be devised which will release some of the burdens on the American tax payer.[24]

Hoover responded affirmatively, but politely suggested a mission with a broader mandate.

My dear Mr. President:

I have your letter of yesterday. I, of course, wish to be of service. I feel, however, that such a mission, to be of real value and helpful to you and the country, should be somewhat broadened out. It will come as a great shock to our people that the American taxpayer for a second year must expend huge sums to provide food for the enemy peoples. Therefore, it seems to me that this mission to accomplish its purpose must also include inquiry into what further immediate steps are possible to increase their exports and thus their ability to become self-supporting; what possibilities exist there are of payment otherwise; and when charity can be expected to end. Without some such inclusive report, the Congress and the taxpayer are left without hope. I trust this suggestion will meet with your approval.[25]

It was presumptuous of Hoover to put conditions on his participation. Indeed, there were those, including Secretary Patterson, who urged Truman to reject Hoover's stipulations. "Food is much more urgent than other phases of the German economy," Patterson argued.[26] But securing Hoover's participation was now more critical than ever. Republicans controlled both houses of Congress and were already clamoring for belt-tightening and budget reductions. Any lasting solution to the food problem would surely require a lot of money. If increased spending was inevitable, it seemed wise to have the appropriations recommendations come from an elder Republican statesman rather than from Truman.

Hoover and Truman met on January 22 to discuss the mission. Before departing for Washington, Hoover confided to Rickard that he would demand "complete freedom to express his findings" and believed Truman would not agree to such a stipulation.[27] Much to Hoover's surprise, Truman accepted. However, by mutual agreement, his carefully worded charge described his task as an "economic mission directed to food and its collateral problems." That clause was sufficiently vague to allow both Truman and Hoover to interpret it as each saw fit. In a press conference later that day, Hoover wasted no time in describing his interpretation: "The ability of the Germans to feed themselves and restore their productivity is probably two or three years away," Hoover opined, "so my mission is not so much a question of determining their needs for the next two or three months as it is a long-range study."[28] Whether Truman privately agreed with that interpretation is an open question, but he made no public attempt to contradict it.

The mission almost collapsed before it even got started. Truman's staff failed to inform the State Department of the content of the personal discussions between the two presidents, so it drafted a dossier briefing Hoover on the limits of his mission and the restrictions that would be placed on his activities. Incensed, Hoover nearly resigned on the spot, but he decided to call the White House first to lodge a verbal complaint. Wisely, Truman told him to forget the State Department instructions and proceed with the work as he saw fit.[29] That satisfied Hoover. With some initial reluctance, Hoover packed for yet another trip abroad. He admitted to Rickard that this would be "his last public job."[30]

Not everyone agreed with Truman's choice of Hoover to undertake yet another mission on behalf of the government. Letters of disapproval flooded into the White House just as they had with the previous appointment. Many complaints focused on petty party loyalties. Other critics chastised Hoover for his efforts to build up Germany after the First World War. All that effort achieved, they contended, was another war. A common complaint was based on Hoover's shortcomings as president during the Great Depression. (He didn't mind if Americans starved in the 1930s, why should we trust him to feed Europeans now?) As might be expected, the biggest number of complaints had nothing to do with the choice of Hoover at all; instead, they chided Truman for helping former enemies. Why should Americans spend money and effort to feed a people who had killed our sons on the battlefield? That was inescapable logic for many. Tax moneys could be put to better use at home than abroad.[31]

Yet for every negative letter or telegram, there were others praising Truman for his decision. Pro or con, the choice of Hoover was a shrewd political move. Hoover, the one-time mining engineer, was convinced that the only way to see Germany out of its economic stagnation was to help it restore its balance of trade, and the best way to accomplish that was to revive its industrial base. Without such a revival, Hoover contended, Germany might never earn the credits it needed to purchase its own food, and thus it would be perpetually dependent on the largesse of other nations. Consequently, Hoover publicly criticized the Morgenthau Plan's push to de-industrialize Germany. Truman's administration welcomed such sentiments and they were music to the ears of those in the Bizonal administration who (like Lt. General Clay) had for months been urging steps toward the economic unification of the zones. Hoover's agreement gave those goals (at least) a patina of bipartisan support.

In preparation for the mission, Hoover hand-picked a team of experts to assist him. Most of the men he chose were either friends or trusted advisors who had served on the 1946 Food Emergency Committee trip. Accompanying him was Hugh S. Gibson, the former ambassador and career diplomat who had helped Hoover coordinate the food relief efforts for Belgium. Tracy Voorhees also signed on. Rounding out the team were Louis P. Lochner, former Associated Press bureau chief in Germany, the Austrian-German economist Gustav Stolper, Dr. William H. Sebrell of the United States Public Health Service, Colonel Frank E. Mason (Hoover's friend and public relations advisor), and Dr. Dennis FitzGerald of the Department of Agriculture, an expert on food distribution. Another of Hoover's trusted friends, Hugo Meier, agreed to be secretary for the trip. Several other assistants also joined the team.

The entourage left New York City on February 2 for Bermuda, where the rainy weather spoiled what might have been a pleasant stopover. The next leg of the trip took them to the Azores. The long flight brought them in at night, and since the tight scheduling had them heading on to Germany, the quick turnaround afforded the men little sleep. After the stop, they continued to Frankfurt, landing in frigid temperatures during the afternoon of February 4. Hoover and his party were greeted by an honor guard headed by General Joseph T. McNarney, the military governor of the American Zone, his adjutant Colonel Hugh Hester (head of the U.S. Food and Agriculture Program in Germany), and several of his staff.

The entourage proceed to their quarters at the Victory Guest Club, a sumptuous resort located in Königstein about ten miles outside of Frankfurt, where the group spent what was left of its first day resting from the trip and engaging in informal discussions. The next morning brought a fresh layer of snow and the first full day of serious work, primarily focusing on how to deal with the masses of refugees and displaced persons. Discussion ended in late afternoon as the party boarded a train to Berlin.[32]

Hoover's group spent the next four days in the frigid confines of the former Third Reich's capital city. It was here that the team linked up with Lt. General Clay (Deputy Military Governor), his deputy Maj. General Frank Keating, Brig. General William H. Draper (head of the Economics Division of the Allied Control Council) and the technical specialists that would accompany their discussions, fact-finding sessions, and conferences. The talks here were substantive, spanning a broad range of topics with Hoover seeming to take a genuine interest in each one. The displaced persons issue again received much attention, but it was the discussions about denazification that really grabbed Hoover's interest.

Even though removing Nazism from German society was a key objective of the occupation, the arrest and removal of former Nazi party members was having a deleterious effect on civil government and the economy. Capable administrators who happened to have minimal Nazi involvement were being removed from office and replaced with "untainted" but less competent functionaries. Although German courts had by now taken over much of the denazification effort, they were proving inefficient at best. Eventually, Hoover concluded that denazification itself was part of the reason for Germany's troubles. In one meeting, he stated that the "bad eggs" should have been dealt with quickly and then the remainder—many of whom were professionals who had been forced to join the Nazi party or risk losing their jobs—should have had their "slate(s) wiped clean" and allowed to start their lives afresh.[33]

The discussions focusing on economic matters proved especially productive. The hottest topic was the recent Soviet and French suggestion to separate the Ruhr from Germany and put it under a four-power administration; a suggestion motivated at least in part by their suspicions of the recent merger of the American and British zones. Hoover agreed that

Discussing food and agriculture problems in occupied Germany, 7 February 1947. From left: Mr. Dennis FitzGerald, Secretary General, International Emergency Food Council; Lt. Gen. Lucius D. Clay, Deputy Military Governor for Germany (U.S.); The Honorable Mr. Herbert Hoover, and Brig. General William H. Draper, Jr., Director, Economics Division OMGUS (NARA, 260mgg268-4).

separating the Ruhr would be disastrous for the German economy and would set back revival for years. The discussion then shifted to the scarcity of food. At that point, the official average consumer's food ration was only 1,550 calories per day; a figure well below the 2,000 deemed necessary for retention of health. In truth, actual consumption was far less than that.[34]

Recognizing the danger that near-starvation diets posed, Hoover urged the authorities to find a way to raise the caloric intake value to 2,000 calories per day (a figure which later was changed to 1,800). Hoover's team suggested that this could be achieved by figuring out how much the U.S. and UK governments could contribute. The rest would have to be "squeezed" out of indigenous sources, particularly by increasing production.

Although that seemed easier said than done, there were two ways to accomplish such a feat. First, the zones suffered a shortage of fertilizer[35] so even though more fields were under tillage, crop yields were not as high as they might have been. Provide more fertilizer and German farms could be more productive. Second, the attitudes of German farmers had to change. The men quipped that Germans had a "mystical attachment" to the pig, and so food crops that might have been used to feed humans were being squandered as fodder.[36] The group agreed that a stricter enforcement of crop utilization regulations would increase food stocks. Even if these steps proved successful, they could not eliminate food shortages entirely. The occupiers still needed imported stocks, and they carried a hefty price tag. Quick calculations revealed that the American contribution alone would cost taxpayers $560 million.

Drawing from his experience with the Belgian relief effort decades before, Hoover realized that any attempt to raise ration levels for all consumer groups was destined to fail. Instead, he suggested that the occupation authority should at least try to raise the intake of school children, the elderly, and the infirmed. His suggestion was not without precedent. Similar emergency relief efforts had already begun under the auspices of agencies working within the Council for Relief Agencies Licensed to Operate in Germany (CRALOG) but that program, which was dependent mostly upon private contributions, had floundered.

Hoover urged prioritizing this feeding program and urged the Bizonal authorities to search for army surplus food stocks to apply to the effort. Lt. General Clay was initially doubtful that Hoover's plan would succeed, but once Colonel Hugh Hester, Chief of OMGUS Food and Agriculture Branch, expressed his support for the idea, he changed his mind.[37] The challenge would be to find enough comestibles to make the nutrition supplements meaningful.

After four days of intensive work in Berlin, the entourage left by train for quick visits to Hamburg (on February 10) and Stuttgart (February 11).

In Hamburg, the team endured the coldest weather of the trip. Hugh Gibson made especially keen observations about their discomfort. Conference rooms, he recounted, were "as cold as the inside of a fish." His description of the Germans he encountered is particularly vivid.[38]

> The people look pretty miserable; most of the women wear ski trousers and heavy boots, sometimes with an incongruous get up of skiing equipment from the waist down and fancy hats and fur coats from there up. Apparently, the thing that gets them down more than anything else is never being able to get warm, day or night.

The cold only exacerbated the negativity already present in the population. In briefing Hoover's team on local public opinion, military government intelligence officers concluded that the inhabitants blamed the British and Americans alike for their situation. Some citizens attributed the problems to incompetent management, but others went so far as to say that the democracy itself was to blame. After two years of being lectured about the virtues of free markets, they were still no better off. One intelligence officer estimated that a staggering 40 percent of the voting public would choose a totalitarian party again if doing so would alleviate their misery.[39] This was sobering news for Hoover and his team, but it accurately described the latent discontent that spilled out onto the city streets in the form of demonstrations and vandalism just weeks later.

After a stop in Stuttgart, most of Hoover's team travelled to Vienna where they spent three days of fact-finding in more frigid, snowy weather. Instead of travelling with them, Hoover and Gibson flew to Rome for a scheduled audience with the Pope. After a day of discussions at the Vatican, Hoover and Gibson flew back to Berlin to rendezvous with the Vienna contingent arriving by train.[40] Once reunited, the team conducted three more days of discussions and conferences before concluding their work. On Thursday, February 20, the Hoover mission departed Berlin for London.

The stopover in London, made at the request of the British Ambassador to the United States, Lord Inverchapel, gave the Hoover team members an opportunity to discuss their findings with officials of the Labour government. Hoover was scheduled to meet with Foreign Secretary Ernest Bevin but Bevin had taken ill, so he met with Minister of State Hector McNeill instead. During the brief meeting, Hoover outlined the essential points of what he would soon report to President Truman in detail. Their discussion focused on common occupation problems, such as how to keep the Soviets from infiltrating the German economy through the take-over of industries and how to reform the denazification program.[41] After a briefing with Prime Minister Attlee,[42] Hoover and his party prepared for the return flight to the United States. The three-week mission ended as their plane touched down in New York on Sunday February 23 after a relatively uneventful flight.[43]

Back home, Hoover began the tedious process of organizing the information and shaping it into a coherent presentation for President Truman. It is a testament to his work ethic that Hoover tendered his report on food and agricultural requirements only three days later. Over the span of 21 pages,[44] Hoover described the horrific conditions that most Germans in the western zones had to endure. He admitted that the target 1,550 calories was insufficient and noted that although the bizonal authorities had agreed in 1946 to raise rations by 250 calories, they were unable to comply. As a substitute, Hoover recommended his school feeding program to provide emergency rations for 3.5 million endangered children and adolescents.

The plan envisaged setting up soup kitchens in schools to provide an extra 350 calories of food to every child who needed it. The extra food was to be derived from a cache of surplus 10-in-1 rations[45] that the army was sending to Germany and about 40,000 tons of other food, including some that had been slated to go to displaced persons camps. In addition, Hoover recommended slaughtering five million heads of livestock held by zonal farmers, not only to augment the ration but to cut down on the wasting of cereal grains. He further suggested that the United States should immediately export 250,000 tons of seed potatoes to Bizonia.

The school feeding program could begin almost immediately, but the supplies needed to raise the rations of adult normal consumers would have to be purchased with money raised in emergency appropriations. Hoover's report made clear that this effort was not charity; all expenditures would be charged to future reparations payments. That was a welcome suggestion, since the total cost for the first six months of 1947 to cover food, fuel, and fertilizers was estimated at $384 million and the cost for the next fiscal year was estimated at a staggering $567 million. Hoover admitted that these sums might "come as a great shock" to the American and British taxpayers footing the bill, but he was prepared to justify it as an absolute necessity.

> If we want peace; if we want to preserve the safety and health of our Army of Occupation; if we want to save the expense of even larger military forces to preserve order; if we want to reduce the size and expense of our Army of Occupation—I can see no other course than to meet the burdens I have here outlined.

His concluding paragraphs summed up the situation well.

> If Western civilization is to survive in Europe it must also survive in Germany. And it must be built into a cooperative member of that civilization. That indeed is the hope of any lasting peace.
>
> After all, our flag flies over these people. That flag means something besides military power.

Chapter 2. "Sustaining Virtues"   43

Hoover's third report[46] bore the somewhat ponderous title, "The Necessary Steps for Promotion of German Exports, so as to Relieve American Taxpayers of the Burdens of Relief and for Economic Recovery of Europe," and addressed the "collateral problems" mentioned in the charge to his mission.[47] One need only to read the introduction to see that this report presaged a major shift in Allied attitudes toward Germany. "The productivity of Europe cannot be restored without the restoration of Germany as a contributor to that productivity," Hoover wrote.

The rest of the text dispelled any lingering doubt about Hoover's opinion of the Morgenthau Plan. "There is an illusion," Hoover wrote bluntly, "that the new Germany ... can be reduced to a 'pastoral state.' It cannot be done unless we exterminate or move 25,000,000 people out of it." He continued, "The overall illusion is that Germany can ever become self-supporting under the 'levels of industry' plan within the borders presently envisioned for New Germany."

Hoover skillfully dismantled the logic that had guided economic policy in Germany and urged that current regulations be either changed or scrapped entirely. "To persist in the present policies will create, sooner or later, a cesspool of unemployment or pauper labor in the center of Europe which is bound to affect her neighbors. We can keep Germany in these economic chains but it will also keep Europe in rags."

The report contained several specific recommendations. First, Hoover urged the occupation authorities to free industrial production from the restraints imposed on it at the war's end, while retaining oversight in the form of a control commission. That presupposed a second goal; namely, halting the dismantling of industrial plants and ending denazification and decentralization efforts. Finally, Hoover urged the zonal authorities to protect German industry from encroachment by foreign ownership (particularly Soviet) and argued that the Ruhr and Rhineland should remain integral parts of the German state.

In assigning responsibility for Germany's economic morass, the report pulled no punches. "The Russians and French have failed to carry out the provisions of the Potsdam agreement for economic unity in the four zones," Hoover blasted. Their violations "warrant our ignoring all agreements for level of industry," and he suggested that Bizonia should go ahead with reforms even without French and Soviet cooperation. In a separate communication with Truman, Hoover could not resist summing his mission up using Christian imagery drawn from his Quaker upbringing. He wrote:

> We can carry on the Military Government of Germany by the tenets of the Old Testament of a tooth for a tooth and an eye for an eye, or we can inaugurate the precepts of the New Testament. The difference in result will be the loss of

millions of lives, the damage of all Europe, and the destruction of any hope of peace in the world. I prefer the New Testament method.[48]

Hoover's conclusions were dramatic but not unprecedented; there had been calls both within the government and outside for changes to JCS 1067 and the Level of Industry Plan for months. His report gave increased legitimacy to those calls for reform—but would the Truman Administration accept and agree with his findings? Over the course of two face-to-face discussions, Truman revealed to Hoover that he supported much of Hoover's conclusions and agreed to move ahead immediately with the suggestions that needed no legislative approval (like the remedial school feeding program).

Truman's reaction to the third report, however, was more reserved. His letter of thanks bore none of the enthusiasm that his earlier missives did (he called the report "a most interesting document"), possibly because the report contained an implied criticism of Truman administration policies up to that point. Some of Truman's staff also criticized the report, contending that there would be a political price to pay should the United States abandon its agreements with other nations as Hoover suggested. Others, still suspicious of a resurgent Germany, felt that allowing a revival of German industry without sufficient oversight was a serious mistake.

By March 12, even before the issuance of report No. 3, Hoover had already begun to lobby Congressional leaders about his plan, going as far as to propose specific amendments to appropriations bills. In May, he testified to a House committee on the need for even more money for relief. In June, newspapers published a letter Hoover wrote to Senator Styles Bridges, chairman of the Senate Appropriations Committee. The lengthy missive concluded with a list of policies Hoover wanted adopted—a rather bold thing to do, considering that Hoover's mission was advisory only. Skeptics interpreted Hoover's actions as an "end around" official Truman administration efforts. But in the final analysis, his efforts worked. Two aid bills passed; one for $300 million dollars for fiscal year 1947 and for $600 million for fiscal year 1948.

In the ensuing months Hoover continued his lobbying, but by autumn the Truman administration was moving in new directions that would lead to passage of the European Recovery Program (ERP), a comprehensive effort to provide Europe with appropriations in the form of outright grants and gifts, more commonly known as the Marshall Plan. Hoover, the parsimonious Republican ever critical of charitable handouts, was not in favor of the plan. He felt that it was too much of a "blank check" with too little oversight, and the resulting drain on American treasury might prove detrimental to the economy. As he put it, the United States ought not become "a competitive Santa Claus" in an attempt to "out-gift" the Soviets.[49]

Chapter 2. "Sustaining Virtues" 45

Although the State Department approached him to participate in the Marshall Plan design, Hoover declined and distanced himself from the effort. And yet, despite his misgivings, Hoover refused to attack the ERP publicly even though he had plenty of opportunity to do so. In the end Hoover acquiesced, accepting it as the best possible solution to a difficult problem. Explaining his stance in a letter to Speaker of the House Joseph Martin in 1948, Hoover wrote:

> I realize that many approach this gigantic experiment with great apprehension and a realization of the sacrifices it will mean to our people. All legislation must be the result of compromise. However, if it should produce economic, political and self-defense unity in Western Europe, and thus a major dam against Russian aggression, it would stem the tide now running so strongly against civilization and peace. The plan, if well devised and under a capable Administrator, stands a good chance of success. I believe it is worth taking the chance.[50]

Hoover the patriot won out over Hoover the partisan politician. And, as much as Hoover and Truman may have disagreed over the way to bring about a German and European revival, they remained in agreement on the key humanitarian issues. In a public statement in New York, Hoover reiterated those ideals.

> The fundamental law of our civilization is based upon compassion and charity. And compassion and charity do not ask whether the sufferer has always been good or bad, whether he has brought his misery upon himself, or is the innocent victim of forces beyond his control.... We know that the great bounty that has been placed in our keeping must not be hoarded while others starve and are in pain. We dare not, even in this age of gross and abject materialism, forget that our consciences were forged by tender women and strong men who have built for themselves a world to their liking, always setting aside a mite for the charity that they knew God enjoined upon good people.[51]

* * *

What was the overall effect of the Hoover mission on the United States' policy toward Germany? It would be a mistake to attach a direct causal link between Hoover's recommendations and the actual changes that took place in 1947. However, those conclusions that coincided with Truman administration policy were welcomed and acted upon fairly quickly. And while it is true that Hoover's Republican affiliation silenced many would-be critics, the real value lay in the fact that Hoover was not officially tied to the Truman administration. He could therefore be blunt and state publicly what many people in the State Department were already thinking in private. It was a subtle but effective way the Truman administration could lay blame for the German situation on other foreign authorities (particularly the Soviet Union) without facing any diplomatic consequences. Any backlash from foreign governments could easily be deflected by Hoover's status as an "independent expert."

In the months following publication of the reports, many of Hoover's recommendations came to fruition. At the Moscow Foreign Ministers' Conference in April, the secretaries agreed that it was time to transfer all responsibility for denazification to the German *Länder* (state) governments. By October 1, the regulations went into effect, thus accomplishing one of Hoover's main goals. More importantly, On April 18, Secretary of State George Marshall and Foreign Secretary Bevin privately agreed in principle to revise the Level of Industry Plan for Bizonia. Their staff got to work devising new plans and managed to produce a new document by early July. Just as Hoover had concluded, the plan admits that an economic revival in either the bizonal area or the entirety of Germany was not likely under the prevailing policies.

In an attempt to make the territory self-supporting and cognizant of the changing geopolitical conditions, the new Level of Industry Plan proposed that the bizonal area should be allowed close to 100 percent of 1936 levels of general industrial production. Metals and machinery production that had heretofore been severely curtailed could now rise to 85 or 90 percent of 1936 levels. These new levels fell short of the complete removal of controls that Hoover had advocated; it was a compromise that would allow industrial growth in Germany while still holding out the possibility that some plants might still be removed as reparations.

In short, this was an expedient way to allow the Truman administration to chart its own policy course and nevertheless claim that it was not in violation of the Yalta and Potsdam accords. The State Department delayed publication of the document long enough to allow the French to weigh in on the proposals.[52] It was finally issued in late August.[53]

In July, coincidental with the first drafts of the New Level of Industry Plan, the Truman administration rescinded JCS 1067. The new policy, designated JCS 1779, was based on the premise that "an orderly and prosperous Europe requires the economic contributions of a stable and productive Germany." To achieve that stability, JCS 1779 stipulated that the level of industry "should not permanently limit Germany's industrial capacity." It goes on to say that the German people "should not be denied the right, consistent with continued disarmament, to develop their resources for the purpose of achieving higher standards of living."[54]

Additionally, JCS 1779 allowed the Germans to create national political parties, state governments, and eventually a central government. While the new policies put Bizonia on a developmental path independent of the French and Soviets, it reiterated that quadripartite supervision over those activities was still a priority and encouraged the two other zones to participate through the Allied Control Council. Nevertheless, the bizonal authorities held fast that "no other country will have any vote, veto or power of decision as to the bi-zonal level of industry."[55] By the end of summer, two more impediments to German rehabilitation were gone. A general revival of Germany's national political and economic infrastructure, using Bizonia as its nucleus, was now possible.

Hoover kept abreast of these developments through personal correspondence and reports. General Clay (now the new Military Governor) wrote to him on June 8 about the planning for the new Level of Industry Plan, in part to solicit his public support. "While this revised level of industry will not meet in full the view which you have expressed in your report, it will go a long way toward doing so,"[56] Clay wrote. Gustav Stolper kept Hoover briefed on even the most confidential parts of the process and wrote him a detailed five-page report in July.[57] Hoover's ability to influence the reform effort was limited, however. Despite lobbying legislators for their support, Hoover could now only sit back and watch as his suggestions were recrafted into Truman administration policy.

Food procurement, the single most important humanitarian effort in Hoover's recommendations, received immediate attention from zonal authorities. On March 17, Secretary Patterson announced that the Hoover emergency food program was already being conducted by the War Department, specifically the procurement of seed potatoes and an increase in nitrogen production for fertilizers.[58] Emergency foodstuffs helped to elevate caloric rations to levels minimally sufficient to keep nutrition from slipping any further, but they were still insufficient to reach the 1,550 target. The emergency assistance could not have come at a better time, for food production was about 20 percent lower than the previous year's, and it would only get worse thanks to one of the worst droughts in recent memory, both in Europe and in the United States.

Despite the below-average harvests globally, America had an impressive surplus of 470 million tons of wheat, but even that was not enough to meet the 570 million tons that Germany needed.[59] Only a concerted effort of food conservation at home could save the situation, so in September, the Truman administration created the Citizens' Food Committee. In an effort to reduce American intake of food, the committee launched a public campaign to encourage conservation. Catchy posters and slick advertising called for meatless meals and other voluntary restrictions on the diet. The effort even went so far as to curtail whiskey production in order to save grain. Americans were once again sacrificing for the sake of a people who had formerly been their enemy.

The soup-kitchen feeding plan for German children turned out to be Hoover's *tour de force*. The army 10-in-1 ration stocks arrived in Germany in late March, and the program kicked off shortly thereafter. Success lay in the fact that the Germans administered most of the program themselves. Once the occupation authorities delivered the food to the appropriate states, local German food and agricultural (or educational) ministries took over and supervised the distribution. Schools were required to submit regular reports tallying the numbers of children receiving food, describing the types of meals served, and demonstrating that every child received at least 350 additional calories per day.[60] Committees comprised of parents and school officials watched over the process to make sure that cooks acted properly and efficiently.[61]

Meals consisted of pea soup or oatmeal porridge made with skim milk, fat, sugar, and sometimes tinned meat, along with some bread and a glass of milk. Occasionally, students received a drink made from cocoa added to powdered milk and sugar. Children from farming families were often excluded from the program since they could augment their intake from their own production. For the remainder, there was a small charge of up to 25 cents, but any child who could not pay received the extra meal for free.

The effort, known across Bizonia as the *Hooverspeisung* (Hoover feeding program), was not only a noble humanitarian gesture but a wise investment in the future. After one year, Bizonal authorities proudly reported that more than 3.5 million school children had received supplemental rations, and that figure rose to 4.25 million at the start of the second year. Hence, there is no exaggeration in claiming that the *Hooverspeisung* helped an entire generation of children back to nutritional health. The Germans themselves certainly thought so, as the reports from local authorities attest.

The author of one summary, submitted in 1948 from the state of Hesse, said that the *Hooverspeisung* was an "act of true humanitarian, Christian sentiment and love for the fellow man [that] has in the first twelve months of operation kept countless children healthy, promoted new strength, and perhaps even saved their lives."[62] Another report from Hessian medical authorities wrote that "in general, doctors and lay persons refer to the *Hooverspeisung* as a true blessing for our school children."[63] Messages of gratitude sent to both Hoover and Truman bear witness to the impact of this program. A letter received at the White House described what one German schoolchild thought of the feeding program.

> Dear Americans: We were happy when we heard that there was a school feeding program in a few cities, because we all hoped that we would soon get the program too. When we came to school one morning we were all surprised, because our teacher said "Today you are going to get a bar and a half of chocolate." That was just the beginning. Then a big pot came into our school kitchen and Frau Heller cooked a strong soup for us normal consumers every day. We could hardly wait until lunchtime came.

Chapter 2. "Sustaining Virtues"   49

It always tastes so good and mother was happy that she could save some of the breakfast toast.

Every fourth Saturday we get weighed and measured. We can see that we have gained a few kilograms. We want to thank the Americans for the good children's food program!

For the 5. Klasse of the Dudenhofen school, Willi[64]

Letters such as this one, sent to Hoover by a young girl named Rosemarie, describe what this program meant on a personal level far better than any statistics can. Using her best English, she wrote

> Sir: A little German girl with blew [sic] eyes and fair hair will thank You for Your great kindness to spend lavishly to so many hungry pupils the wonderful Hoover-food. To-day we have got the fine soup for the first time and so I must thank You immediately.... I have lost my father in this war. I was born in the forests of Ostpreussen *[East Prussia]* and I am twelve years old. Now my mother with my brother and my sister and me are living in Pyrmont. We all are poor fugitives. All German childrin [sic] will remember your name in thankfulness forever.[65]

History shows that Rosemarie was correct. Millions of German children would remember *"Onkel Hoover"* and the American largesse that helped them survive the most difficult period of their lives.[66] The school feeding program convinced Western Germans that the United States and Great Britain sincerely wanted them to recover from the hardships of war. It may

German school children receiving supplemental rations, ca. 1949 (Herbert Hoover Presidential Library and Museum, NARA [31-1949-27]).

have been the single most important action in turning wartime enemies into peacetime friends.

By the end of 1947, the necessary structural and psychological foundations for the ultimate revival of the West German economy were in place. Building on the creation of Bizonia at the start of the year, U.S. and UK occupation authorities moved toward the single economic unit envisioned at Yalta and Potsdam, even if the decision alienated their other two allies. The revocation of JCS 1067 and the first Level of Industry Plan removed impediments that had kept the western zones in economic purgatory for so long. That is not to imply, however, that a complete recovery was quickly forthcoming. The summer droughts again ruined the harvests, and with the food stocks still at dangerously low levels, Germans would have to endure another winter of deprivation in 1947–48. Fortunately, the next year's harvests recovered sufficiently so that the threat of famine diminished, and the currency reform of 1948 removed the last major obstacle to the economic unification of the three western zones.

During 1947, the western allies made a dramatic *volte face* in their attitudes toward Germany. Even casual observers now realized that the immediate postwar policies that governed the occupation had not worked. Clearly, success depended on the allies' ability to set aside wartime animosities in search of a more promising future; i.e., retreat from previous policies of retribution and advance toward a policy of rehabilitation. Abandoning the hatreds that had grown over many years was not an easy task, but "Nazis" were slowly becoming "Germans" again in the minds of the west. That critical transition was the key to the success of the occupation.

Success came at a price, however. By acting bilaterally, the United States and the United Kingdom widened the political rift with the Soviet Union. Even if they did not say so openly, most western leaders understood that the new "menace" in Europe was the communist east. Even before 1947, despite mounting evidence that interzonal economic cooperation was not going to work, the western Allies nevertheless paid lip service to the spirit of Yalta-Potsdam by dismantling and removing plants for reparations payments to the Soviet Union. It was in 1947 that the Allies openly acknowledged the fiction of quadripartite control and stopped placating the Russians.[67]

That decision cost Germany its unity. The Soviets, provoked by the West's actions, took parallel steps toward making its zone self-sufficient including the creation of a different currency, a separate constitution, and a single party communist government. The end result was the bifurcation of Germany into two nations kept apart by rivaling political ideologies and Cold War animosities. It took fifty years and the collapse of Communism in Eastern Europe to undo that division.

How does history interpret Herbert Hoover's role in this critical time? Hoover's Republican detractors condemned him as a traitor, duped by a Democratic administration into cooperating with it in an attempt to garner Republican sympathies. They contend that Hoover was more than willing to participate, since doing so gave him the opportunity to rehabilitate his own image and, more importantly, get back into the political limelight. Hoover's post-report lobbying efforts fit well into such a cynical interpretation as evidence that Hoover was simply trying to stay in the public eye.

For Democrats, Hoover's attempts to influence legislation were a mixed blessing. Hoover's lobbying, however intrusive, helped swing critical Republican votes. Evidently, the administration was willing to put up with a little "meddling" in foreign policy if it meant that the critical appropriations bills could get passed. However, his continued involvement prompted Truman's detractors to question who was actually driving American foreign policy. Additionally, co-opting Hoover in this way put the Truman administration in a difficult position. Having sanctioned the mission, Truman had to acknowledge and act on his recommendations while simultaneously asserting his own foreign policy identity. The Marshall Plan proved a suitable compromise. It could incorporate many of Hoover's recommendations for Germany while casting them in a framework for general European revival that was purely "Truman."

A more benevolent interpretation focuses on the personal sacrifices Hoover made in lifelong service to others. Here, Hoover's legacy is undeniable, powerful, and lasting. Those who accompanied him on the Germany/Austria trip saw firsthand the dedication and determination he put into his work. Louis Lochner related how Hoover possessed an energy that belied a man 72 years of age. In defiance of the extreme cold, Hoover frequently met with officials wearing an overcoat and wrapped in a blanket. "The Chief" (as he was known to his close friends) often worked long hours writing personal reflections about the day's activities, digesting statistical information and planning his reports. Upon awaking in the middle of the night, he passed the time by reading and jotting down notes on what he learned from the previous day's meetings.[68]

It was to his credit that Hoover included men like Stolper and Lochner on his staff, since they had the ability to gather information directly from the German people, and thereby come closer to the reality of the situation than military government sources and statistical analyses could. His greatest strength lay in his ability to organize larger tasks into smaller, more manageable pieces. And he was a wizard with information. His uncanny ability to "tease fact from fiction" allowed him to sift through mounds of detail to get to the crux of any problem. Given the complexity of his assignment, the reports that bear his name are remarkably concise and to the point.

For Herbert Hoover, 1947 was—as Edgar Rickard wrote—"not a fruitless year."[69] That was quite an understatement. That year, Hoover became a political actor again and continued on the path toward rehabilitation that had begun the year before. His rehabilitation was not without some concomitant suffering, however. Looking back on the trip, Hoover admitted to Rickard that he was "never warm at any time."[70] The punctured eardrum he suffered on the return flight affected his hearing for months. Toward the end of the year, he contracted shingles and lost the use of an arm for a while.

Despite the hardships, Hoover could take pride in the final outcomes, even if they were not precisely the ones he hoped for. Truman was sufficiently impressed with Hoover's efforts that he would draft him into service once more later that year to direct an effort to reorganize the executive branch of the government. Reflecting back on his experiences, Hoover admitted to his friends that Truman's invitation to him "was a great stimulant in his life" because it gave him the chance to do something constructive for his country. He believed it may have added as many as ten years to his life.[71]

The fairest assessments of Hoover's role come from those who worked closest to him. General Clay developed a lasting admiration for Hoover. Writing about the child feeding program, Clay admitted that Hoover's efforts "did more to convince the German people of our desire to recreate their nation than any other action on our part."[72] In a later interview, Clay repeated his conclusions. Recalling Hoover's efforts and Truman's support for emergency food requisitioning, Clay said "If it hadn't been for this, we would have had mass starvation."[73]

For his part, President Truman was forever grateful for what Hoover had done. Even though he was not above using Hoover's name pejoratively in the 1948 elections, Truman considered Hoover a close friend, and their friendship lasted for the rest of their lives. In recognition of Hoover's contributions, Truman signed the bill to restore Hoover's name to the Grand Coulee Dam. That was a nice tribute, but it hardly suffices when one considers the scope of Hoover's humanitarian accomplishments. As one newspaper editor put it, "His permanent monument is his patriotic help to mankind.... He extended the one world of humanity without ever prejudicing his devotion to his own country."[74] Right-wing columnist George Sokolsky commented in an opinion piece:

> History has its own way of determining where greatness truly is. And it takes its own time to weigh in the balance the virtues that are eternal. Those virtues are never in words or voice or beauty of person or even in the acclaim of the

moment. The sustaining virtues of history are always measured by the accomplishment of an individual in his services for bettering the life of his fellow men. In that realm, Herbert Hoover stands a colossus in our age.[75]

One may question Sokolsky's objectivity or his ability to comprehend the dynamics of history, but the sentiment he expresses is reasonable enough. Herbert Hoover personified the best of those "sustaining virtues." The tens of thousands of lives he saved over five decades of service to humanity serve as ample evidence.

CHAPTER 3

"A Stitch in Time"
Arthur Vandenberg and the Truman Doctrine

In the early afternoon of March 12, 1947, President Harry S. Truman climbed into his limousine for the short trip to Capitol Hill to address a joint session of Congress. White House staffers had already briefed Congressional leaders that the speech would concern American foreign policy and the rise of Communism in the near east, and that Truman intended to discuss "the whole situation" that day. As Truman entered the hall, the traditional pomp that normally accompanies a presidential address was noticeably absent, replaced by an air of solemnity and seriousness reminiscent of December 7, 1941, when his predecessor asked Congress for a declaration of war against Japan.

By one account, Truman looked "drawn" and "glum" as he exchanged greetings on his way up to the speaker's platform.[1] With a seriousness of purpose befitting the occasion, Truman opened the folder containing his speech and proceeded to ask Congress to approve an immediate aid package for Greece and Turkey, two countries of "vital interest" that were threatened by Communist insurgents. After outlining the present danger and advancing his arguments why the United States should aid the two countries, Truman uttered the line that has ever since defined his presidency. Reading calmly from the text, Truman asserted "that it must be the policy of the United States to support free peoples who are resisting attempted subjugation by armed minorities or by outside pressures."[2]

With this one statement and the elaboration that followed, President Truman committed United States to a new course in foreign policy and world affairs. The "Truman Doctrine," as this policy statement became known, laid the intellectual foundation to justify the United States taking on the role as the guardian (at least in principle) of the interests of democratic governments wherever they were threatened.

How the United States came to adopt that mantle, at a time when a war-weary electorate had clearly begun to turn inward again, is a complex

Chapter 3. "A Stitch in Time"   55

story of cooperation and consensus building on a grand scale, the likes of which have rarely been seen since. It is the tale of two unlikely political bedfellows—a world-wise Missouri Democrat and a business-minded stalwart Republican from Michigan—who found a way to set aside partisanship and work together. Although the scope of Truman's appeal caught many by surprise, the events that compelled this change in policy had been brewing for quite some time. As fate would have it, the focal point of this struggle for democracy was the birthplace of democracy itself, Greece. How did this tiny country become the epicenter of a global dispute?

Greece's experience in World War II was, like that of many other nations, a story of occupation and resistance. In 1940, Mussolini's fascist armies invaded the Greek mainland as part of a general attempt to spread Italian influence throughout the Balkans. At first the Greek people rallied to hold off the invasion, but Hitler's *Wehrmacht* ultimately intervened to help the Italians subjugate the peninsula. By April 1941, Athens had fallen and the entire country was occupied. The Greek people responded by taking to the mountains to conduct a guerrilla war against the invaders. Out of their efforts emerged the resistance organization called the EAM (*Ethnikó Apeleftherotikó Métopo*, or National Liberation Front) and its armed military wing the ELAS (*Ellinikós Laïkós Apeleftherotikós Stratós*, or Greek People's Liberation Army), both dominated by Greek Communists.

However, there was a republican counterpart to EAM known as the EDES (*Ethnikós Dimokratikós Ellinikós Syndesmos, or* National Republican Greek League), comprised mostly of non–Communists who supported the Greek government in exile. Initially, these two organizations found ways to cooperate despite their ideological differences in an effort to defeat the invaders. Unfortunately, the two factions had very different visions of what a post-occupation Greek government should be like. As the war continued, the two resistance groups stopped cooperating and by the end of 1943, Greek partisans were not only fighting the Nazi occupiers, they were also fighting each other.

The Greek resistance movement, particularly the communist elements, received a shot in the arm when the Soviet armies that had already retaken much of Poland and Romania advanced toward Bulgaria in the autumn of 1944. A Soviet victory, combined with the advances of communist-led resistance in Yugoslavia under Marshal Tito (Josip Broz), threatened to cut off the southern Balkans from the rest of Europe, thereby making the Nazi military position in Greece untenable. Faced with the possible isolation of German forces, Hitler ordered a general troop withdrawal from Greece in October of that year.

In anticipation of the power vacuum that the Nazi retreat would create, British Prime Minister Winston Churchill quickly sent troops to

Greece, ostensibly to bolster the British garrison already in Attica (there had already been a token force sent there to assist the rebels) but more importantly to "insulate" Athens from any direct attacks by the communist ELAS. In essence, the Greeks had traded one occupation for another, and the end result of British intervention was a stalemate between the EAM and the EDAS, neither of which was able to establish its legitimacy.

The Nazi surrender in May 1945 brought only a modicum of solace to the Greek people, for their country had sunken into a brutal and bloody civil war that showed no signs of a quick resolution. By December, Greek Communist leaders agreed to reorganize their disparate bands of resistance fighters into one "democratic army" in order to present a united military opposition to the British-supported national government. By now, communist control over the entire Balkan peninsula had been fairly well established with Albania, Yugoslavia, Romania, and Bulgaria all well on their way to becoming satellites of the Soviet Union.

Throughout 1946, support for the "democratic armies" (i.e., the Communists) poured into northern Greece from these neighboring communist states, with Tito even allowing ELAS fighters sanctuary in Yugoslavia following raids into Greece.[3] Already by summer, elements of the democratic army had taken over large sections of northern Greece, thanks in large part to the guerrilla war they waged in the mountains. Their tactics proved so effective against Greek National Guard troops that the government invoked martial law there.[4]

The presence of the British occupation forces complicated this political morass. The British could justify their occupation by proclaiming that their sole interest was in seeing a truly democratically elected government emerge in Athens. Even though they did provide stability, their presence was a propaganda gold mine for the communists who could castigate them as an example of western interference in the internal affairs of another sovereign nation. Under the watchful eyes of the British, the Greeks conducted free elections in 1946 that Greek communists boycotted. The results were therefore predictable; the conservative victory led to the establishment of a right-wing government under Prime Minister Constantinos Tsaldaris that included many officials who had collaborated with the Nazis.

A subsequent plebiscite (that many, including some non–Communists, felt was rigged) resulted in an invitation to King George to return from exile. Given that the Communists disputed the validity of both the election and the plebiscite, the new government had to take draconian measures in order to maintain its extremely tenuous hold on power. Tsaldaris' government established a special security commission reminiscent of the Nazi Gestapo that rooted out suspected Communists and deported them without due process of law. Greek police were granted extraordinary powers to search homes and arrest individuals. Courts-martial awaited those accused of criticizing the government, and the penalties for a guilty verdict included death.[5]

To enforce its will, the new government armed civilians and organized them into local militia units, thereby deepening the conflict and intensifying the slaughter. In time, even its own supporters came to the realization that the Tsaldaris government was at best incompetent and at worst rotten with corruption. But despites its failings, Tsaldaris' administration continued to function as the "legitimate" government of Greece, thanks in large part to the British armies backing it.

This was clearly a no-win situation for Prime Minister Clement Attlee's government in London. By February of 1947, the United Kingdom was stuck supporting a corrupt Greek government that was embroiled in a nasty civil war with no end in sight. Propping up Greece would be expensive even in the best of times, but when the brutal winter destroyed much of the farm crop that the United Kingdom was relying upon to get them through the first months of 1947, it became more and more difficult to justify the cost of stationing 40,000 troops there.

A government white paper on the economic state of Great Britain, published on February 21, 1947, made it painfully clear that the drain on the treasury meant continued economic privations including continuing food and energy rationing. Supporting the Greek state now seemed an expensive luxury. Bowing to the inevitable, the Labour government concluded that British aid to Greece would end on March 31.[6] The same day the white paper was published, UK ambassador Lord Inverchapel[7] arrived in the United States carrying a communiqué stating officially that the United Kingdom would "no longer be able to continue acting as a reservoir for the financial and military support of Greece and Turkey."[8]

The communiqué caught no one by surprise. The contents of the white paper were known in private governmental circles in Washington and the State Department had been studying the Greek predicament for several months. Long before Inverchapel's arrival, diplomats were already dropping subtle hints that the United States might be willing to assist the British occupation effort with military and monetary support. Some worried, however, that sending aid could give the appearance that the United States approved of a brutal monarchical government imposing its will through martial law. For public opinion to accept such aid, Greece would need to prove that it was indeed working toward democracy and that the present civil war would not devolve into a perpetual right-wing dictatorship.[9]

For its part, the Greek government did what it could to show it was serious about establishing a democracy. Following an attempted reorganization of the government to include all political parties, Prime Minister Tsaldaris journeyed to the United States to address the United Nations in December 1946. In his speech, he told the assembly that Greece desired only peace and justice but was prevented from achieving those goals by an unjust war forced upon them by Communists and supported by outsiders.

Taking full advantage of the trip, Tsaldaris stopped off in Washington for a four-day visit with State Department officials during which he discussed how American help in the form of loans and grants would help keep Greece from political collapse. Tsaldaris pressed his case, but the State Department would not commit to any specific assistance until Paul Porter, chief of the American Mission to Greece, could finish his special report on Greece's financial situation. Unfortunately, Porter's conclusions agreed with those of most other observers. Things were actually much worse than they appeared. Greece's economic collapse seemed imminent.

Porter's sober assessment and the British declaration to quit Greece kicked the State Department into full gear. Given all their advance preparation, the State Department managed to get all the relevant agencies to weigh in on the issue, pull together a statement on the crisis, and assemble a list of recommendations all within one week.[10] Deciding on a course of action was easy; getting Congress to appropriate funds was another matter entirely. This was an inopportune time for the Truman administration to be asking for more money. Supporting Greece financially would entail a huge increase in government spending at a time when the Republican majority in Congress had already called for deep cuts in President Truman's budget proposal. A request for an additional $400 million ($250 million for Greece, $150 million for Turkey) would certainly not go over very well with a Republican party that was always looking to shrink the size of government.[11]

In addition, Herbert Hoover had just returned from his fact-finding mission to Europe to study the food crisis, and his report speculated that it might take billions of dollars to forestall another humanitarian catastrophe in Germany and all across the continent. Truman understood that he needed Republican votes to pass an aid bill for Greece and Turkey but to get them, he had to convince the Republican leadership to put partisanship aside in the overall national interest. He needed a powerful Republican to champion the cause. The most likely candidate to play that role was Arthur Vandenberg, the senior senator from Michigan.

Arthur Vandenberg may have been the stereotypical United States senator, both in his appearance and demeanor. He was a tall and imposing figure, fairly heavy set, who sported a comb-over of (what was left of) his gray mane in a futile attempt to hide a balding head. When walking, he evinced a self-confidence that one writer characterized as a "strut resembling that of a pouter pigeon."[12] On the floor of the Senate, his oratory had a flourish that aroused the admiration of his colleagues and accusations of political theatrics from his detractors. Dean Acheson, then Undersecretary of State, wrote that Vandenberg "would often be carried away by the hyperbole of his own rotund phrases."[13] Sometimes, when dealing with a topic he considered boring, his attention wandered and he occupied himself making pencil sketches or chomping on a cigar.

Outside of the halls of Congress, Vandenberg developed an interest in the life and political career of Alexander Hamilton and penned three volumes extolling his virtues. At home, he was comfortable telling jokes or long-winded stories based on his experiences and often utilized his booming baritone voice to sing to his friends or anyone who would listen. Despite his idiosyncrasies, he was known as a deep thinker who liked to seek what he called "the common denominator."[14] In other words, he could reduce difficult issues down to a few key principles that both parties could agree on and then build on those principles in order to achieve change through consensus. This complex man would become the Senate's most influential Republican during the Truman years and played an instrumental role in the formation of U.S. foreign policy in the immediate postwar period. Yet, his path to prominence was anything but direct.

Arthur Hendrick Vandenberg hailed from Grand Rapids, Michigan. He was born on March 22, 1884, the only child of Aaron Vandenberg, a leather worker whose family had originally emigrated from the Netherlands. His mother, Alpha Hendrick, came from a much more influential family. Her father was a local physician who had been active in the newly created Republican Party and had attended the nominating convention that put forth the candidacy of Abraham Lincoln.

His father Aaron's leather business was practically ruined during the Great Depression of 1893 and, as he watched his dad struggle to make ends meet, young Arthur decided that the hard times were the fault of Grover Cleveland and the Democrats. That determination, plus his maternal grandfather's political legacy, convinced him to become a Republican. Having learned about business from his father, the young Arthur decided to help out his family by working at petty jobs. He proved to have a knack for earning money, and his early experiences as a young businessperson imbued him with a firm belief in the efficacy of free markets, entrepreneurship, and unrestricted competition.[15]

Vandenberg's high school experience was like that of many others. Although he had friends, he never really fit in with the popular cliques, possibly because he was beginning to show exceptional academic talent. He achieved some measure of fame during a public speaking contest wherein he argued (of all things) that America should get involved in the

Hague Peace Convention of 1899 as a way to further chances for world peace. The second prize he took from the competition belies the importance of this speech, in that it was the beginning of his lifelong interest in foreign affairs and the idea of collective security. Following his graduation, Vandenberg decided to matriculate at the University of Michigan and he took a job with the *Grand Rapids Herald* as a staff writer in order to raise money for his tuition and expenses. Unfortunately, the expense proved too dear and he had to withdraw from the university. His attraction to journalism continued unabated, however, and he took a full-time job as a reporter for the newspaper. In 1906, he became its managing editor.[16]

Although his political upbringing landed him squarely in the Republican camp, Vandenberg nevertheless also believed that governments have a role to play in promoting the general welfare of its citizens. Thus, he initially identified with the Progressive movement and supported workplace safety legislation, laws to protect women and children factory workers, and the idea of creating a federal welfare agency. As his political beliefs spilled over into his journalism, Vandenberg's first articles for the *Herald* exhibited a curious mixture of traditional Republican Party values and the Democratic Party's social activism.

All that changed, however, with the election of Woodrow Wilson in 1912. Vandenberg believed the income tax provisions of the Sixteenth Amendment went too far. In one of his columns, he called the graduated income tax "grossly un–American, un-democratic, and unfair."[17] His dislike for Wilson softened somewhat once the Great War broke out in Europe, as he agreed with and supported Wilson's attempts to keep America out of the conflict. But once the news of the Zimmerman Telegram[18] broke, his belief in pacifism took an abrupt turn. In his editorials, Vandenberg blamed the war on German aggression and criticized the neutralists and pacifist groups he had once been a part of. In the process, Vandenberg transformed himself into one of America's most notable war hawks.

The Versailles peace settlement of 1919 became more fodder for Vandenberg's editorials. He liked the idea of creating a League of Nations to ensure international peace, but he was concerned that the United States would have to surrender too much of its national prerogatives to be an effective member. Vandenberg struggled with this conundrum, at times announcing his support for the idea of collective security while simultaneously advocating that every member nation should have the freedom to pursue its own interests. When it came time to vote on the United States' entry into the League, Vandenberg's editorials urged the Senate to oppose the League Covenant but vote to join the organization anyway. More importantly, he attacked Wilson for not doing more to create a "partnership" between the Senate and the executive branch in reaching foreign policy decisions.[19] That belief would become his mantra in later life and the cornerstone of his legislative philosophy once he arrived in Washington.[20]

Vandenberg got his entrée into national politics in the spring of 1928 upon the untimely death of Michigan's Senator Woodbridge Ferris. Vandenberg (who had decided to run for the Senate that year anyway) was nominated to fill the seat for the remainder of the term. That November, voters elected him outright. Upon arriving in Washington, Vandenberg's political agenda exhibited the tenets that would become the hallmarks of the Republican Party over time, including reducing government, cutting taxes, eliminating waste, and paying down the national debt.

However, he was still mixing his conservatism with a healthy dose of progressive thinking. In a *Herald* column, he wrote that "we need men who are progressive enough to meet our new emergencies with new methods, and who are conservative enough to remember and to profit by American political and constitutional history."[21] He quickly caught the attention of Republican party leadership. Vice President Dawes thought him to be a "man of strong convictions and unusual aggressiveness, he has ability, patience and judgment."[22] Those qualities, combined with his penchant for foreign affairs, landed him a seat on the Senate Foreign Relations Committee.

The early 1930s proved a terrible time to be a Senate Republican. The Great Depression had sunk the party's chances to dominate Congress, and Vandenberg found himself confronted with a myriad of expensive New Deal proposals designed to curb the ravages of the slump. True to his tradition as part-conservative, part-progressive, Vandenberg supported many of them but only where the legislation could be "softened" to make it more palatable to fiscal conservatives. In foreign policy, Vandenberg became a staunch isolationist. He supported neutrality legislation and held firmly to the conviction that America should stay out of European affairs. His reelection in 1934, while many of his fellow Republicans went on to defeat, afforded him even more notoriety and stature within the party. That fame as a "rising young star" resulted in his being asked to run for vice president on the 1936 ticket with Alf Landon. He turned the invitation down.

By 1941, Senator Vandenberg had forged an identity as an archetypical isolationist. That identity came into question on December 7 as the Japanese attack on Pearl Harbor thrust America into war. Vandenberg owns the dubious distinction of giving the only speech in the Senate before the vote on the war declaration. In it, he fired one last salvo at FDR's foreign policy, but ended up pledging his full support to the war effort. As he wrote in his personal papers, "I felt it was absolutely necessary to establish the reason why our non-interventionists were ready to go along—making it plain that we were not deserting our beliefs but that we were postponing all further argument over policy until the battle forced upon us by Japan is won."[23]

As the war continued into 1942 and 1943, the Roosevelt administration discovered just how valuable having Vandenberg on its side could be. In September 1943, Vandenberg helped convince skeptical Republicans to approve a statement that international cooperation should be a hallmark of the postwar settlement. The Mackinac Charter,[24] as it came to be known, became a plank in the Republican platform in the 1944 elections and provided a common ground whereupon Republicans and Democrats might jointly explore the topic of postwar international peacekeeping. In an address that September, Vandenberg enunciated what would become the foundational principle guiding the rest of his career.

> The wise voice of American intelligence and enlightened American self-interest which [says] that a bad world for others cannot be a good world for us, and which reliably intends to do its full cooperative share in helping to sustain peace and progress in a happier world. So long as both of those objectives remain inseverably linked we can *unite* America on foreign policy. When they are divorced we inevitably fall apart.... A rational, tolerant meeting of patriotic minds upon wholly compatible philosophies of action which complement each other ... spells dependable *unity*. It is the only source of *unity*.[25]

In 1944, as the European war drew closer to conclusion, Vandenberg served as a member of the "subcommittee of eight" that was charged with devising plans for possible postwar international organizations. Vandenberg took his appointment seriously and played an instrumental role in forging a consensus on international peacekeeping at the Dumbarton Oaks conference in Georgetown, Washington, D.C., in August of that year. Those negotiations led to concrete proposals on what would become the United Nations and the United Nations Relief and Rehabilitation Agency (UNRRA), both eventually approved with bipartisan support.

As the 79th Congress convened its first session in January 1945, everyone knew that foreign policy and the impending end of the war with Germany would dominate the legislative agenda that year. When Arthur Vandenberg rose to address the assembly on January 10, few could have anticipated that he was about to utter one of the most historic speeches in Senate history. Stepping up to the podium, Vandenberg confessed that he had had a personal and political epiphany.

> I have always been frankly one of those who has believed in our own self-reliance. I still believe that we can never again—regardless of collaborations—allow our national defense to deteriorate to anything like a point of impotence. But I do not believe that any nation hereafter can immunize itself by its own exclusive action.... I want maximum American cooperation, consistent with legitimate American self-interest, with constitutional process

Chapter 3. "A Stitch in Time" 63

and with collateral events which warrant it.... I want a new dignity and a new authority for international law. I think American self-interest requires it.[26]

Some called it "the speech heard around the world." Vandenberg, once the inveterate non-interventionist, now admitted that isolationism no longer served the United States' best interests. For those pundits who had watched Vandenberg over the years, the speech came as a major shock. Newspapers and magazines jumped on it, interpreting it as something of an "instant conversion." In truth, this was no sudden transformation. "The whole world changed ... with World War II, and I changed with them," Vandenberg later recounted.[27]

Many newspapers reported the speech favorably. The *New York Herald Tribune* hailed it as "an indication that honest minds, to whatever party they may belong ... can, if they are willing to face the facts, come together upon a firm and common ground."[28] Indeed, most political observers respected Vandenberg's conclusion that he had been wrong in the past and agreed that the United States must go through a similar conversion in order to meet the realities of changing times. Whatever his motives, Vandenberg's confession was a truly remarkable admission that carried with it enormous consequences for American foreign policy in the postwar world.

As the importance of his speech sank into the American public consciousness, the reaction was no less remarkable at the White House. Suddenly, the man who had once been FDR's chief critic was holding out the olive branch of cooperation. More importantly, he was laying down a challenge to his own Republican party to abandon obstructionism and collaborate with Democrats to forge a foreign policy consensus. Despite the unusual opportunity, Roosevelt's team was slow to capitalize on Vandenberg's "conversion," in part because of ongoing preparations for the Yalta Conference (scheduled for February) and in part because of FDR's failing health. As something of a token reward, the administration named Vandenberg to the UN conference delegation scheduled to meet in San Francisco that April. However, subsequent events prevented any further reconciliation between Vandenberg and Roosevelt; two weeks before the beginning of the San Francisco conference, FDR was dead.

As Harry S. Truman stepped into the White House for the first time as president, Senator Arthur Hendrick Vandenberg was among the first to wish him well. "Good luck and God bless you," read the brief note the new president received. "Let me help you whenever I can. America marches on."[29] The two men were no strangers to each other, having both served in the Senate as senior senators from their respective states. In fact, they may have had more than a little professional admiration for each other. Truman later recalled one poignant moment in the Senate chambers when

Vandenberg asked him to weigh in on an issue. After Truman had completed his remarks, Vandenberg commented, "When the Senator from Missouri makes a statement like that, we can take it for the truth."[30] It was a compliment Truman valued greatly and never forgot.

The members of the new Democratic administration understood and appreciated what having a powerful Republican ally like Vandenberg might mean, so they consciously involved him in as much of their foreign policy decision making as they could reasonably allow. Secretary of State James Byrnes was more than happy to have Vandenberg accompany him on foreign policy missions and frequently approached him for advice on diplomatic matters.[31] Vandenberg's presence on those trips allowed Byrnes to assert that they were agents of "American policy," not Truman administration policy, thereby giving an appearance of solidarity at a time when a

A foreign policy jaunt to Germany, 5 September 1946. From left, Senator Tom Connally, Secretary of State James F. Byrnes, Senator Vandenberg, Lt. Gen. Lucius D. Clay (NARA, 260-MGG-959006).

unified approach to foreign affairs was crucial. It also sent a message that America's postwar policies would remain unchanged, even if the electorate shifted in favor of the opposition party.[32]

However, Senator Vandenberg's cooperation came with a price. Byrnes's detractors poked fun at him as the "junior partner" in this foreign policy partnership. Indeed, Henry A. Wallace (FDR's third-term vice president who was dumped from the ticket in favor of Truman) complained bitterly that "Jimmy Byrnes ... was under the control of Vandenberg" and Vandenberg had "veto power" over him.[33] Despite getting along well with Byrnes as a travelling companion, Vandenberg was becoming increasing disenchanted with what he perceived to be Byrnes's "soft" approach in dealing with the Soviets.

By late 1946, Vandenberg had rethought his role as Byrnes's sidekick and announced in December that he would stop travelling to conferences and devote his time to his duties back home in the Senate. He was quick to point out, however, that his decision had nothing to do with Byrnes. "I am for him 1,000 percent," he told reporters.[34] Truman, however, was not as happy with Byrnes and eventually accepted his resignation.[35] Truman's choice to succeed him was none other than General George Marshall, the former chair of the Joint Chiefs of Staff. Vandenberg had always respected Marshall, and he promised his support for getting Marshall's appointment swift Senate approval.

Truman, Vandenberg, and Marshall would soon become one of the most influential triumvirates in the history of American foreign policy. With the crisis in Greece escalating and the British withdrawal imminent, all the principal players arrived at the White House on February 27, 1947, for the meeting that would determine the future course of American foreign policy. President Truman, Secretary Marshall, and Dean Acheson (Marshall's undersecretary of state) represented the administration. From Congress came a delegation that included Senator Tom Connally of Texas, House Speaker Joseph Martin, and Representative Sam Rayburn of Texas, among others. Arthur Vandenburg, recently elevated to the chair of the Foreign Relations Committee and Senate president pro tempore, was also in attendance.[36]

It was a meeting of high-powered politicians, each of whom had substantial political gravitas.[37] Secretary Marshall opened with a frank but lackluster explanation of the crisis, prompting some of those present to question whether aiding the Greeks would just be "pulling British chestnuts out of the fire." Sensing that the presentation had not driven home the point well enough, Acheson asked for permission to speak and then jumped in with his own take on the crisis.

Using the analogy of "one bad apple in a barrel infecting all the rest" (a variant of the more familiar "domino effect," which would later become the more standard metaphor), Acheson outlined in graphic terms what was at stake for American and European security if Greece and Turkey should fall to the Communists. Taking some license, he postulated that such a calamity could allow the Soviet Union access to the Middle East by threatening both Iran and Egypt, and that it would also strengthen the hand of the Communist parties already at work in France and Italy. With Britain's role in Greece ending, the United States was the only world power with the resources to prevent such a calamity.

At the conclusion of Acheson's impassioned explanation, Vandenberg was the first to break the silence. "Mr. President," he intoned, "if you will say that to the Congress and the country, I will support you and I believe that most of its members will do the same." With one simple sentence, Vandenberg again showed his belief that when it came to foreign affairs, domestic politics should remain "at the water's edge."[38]

Having obtained the valuable support of leading Congressional Republicans, President Truman's staff began drafting the speech that would outline the emergency to the American public. Convincing Congress to grant aid to Greece and Turkey would be difficult enough, but gaining the acceptance of average war-weary Americans might be even harder. On top of that, Truman and his staff knew that they would be attacked for pledging American support to an oppressive, monarchical government in a part of the world most Americans cared very little about. To deflect that criticism and win over public opinion, they needed to place the issue in a larger context. Suddenly, the debate became much more than whether to aid Greece and Turkey; this now became part of a global struggle to protect democracy from the onslaught of Communism.

At 1:00 p.m. EST on March 12, Truman delivered the most important address of his presidency to date; one that resonated far beyond the halls of Congress: "I believe that it must be the policy of the United States to support free peoples who are resisting attempted subjugation by armed minorities or by outside pressures.... I believe we must assist free peoples to work out their own destinies in their own way."

Thus, the Truman Doctrine was born. Not everyone in Truman's own inner circle was happy with it. George Kennan, who later became famous as the author of the famous "Mr. X" article espousing containment, felt the speech went too far.[39] The objections raised over the next two months questioned whether the United States would willingly interject itself anywhere if an ally claimed it was threatened by "armed minorities" or "outside pressures." Acheson, too, had to reassure the Senate Foreign Relations Committee that this was not a blanket promise, but that each appeal would have to be determined on a case-by-case basis.[40] Still, the gamble was worth it. The Republican Party and the American citizenry might reject the policy unless convinced that it was part of some "crusade" to support the right of freedom-loving people to self-determination.[41]

President Truman left Washington by plane shortly after the speech for a brief vacation in Key West, Florida. Vandenberg wasted no time in getting on board with Truman's initiative. Speaking to journalists, Vandenberg said

> We cannot fail to back up the President at such an hour—even though many critical details remain to be settled in consultation with the Congress. Meanwhile, we must review our own foreign policy in other directions and make it consistently effective. We must proceed with calm but determined patience to deal with practical realities as they unfurl. We must either take or surrender leadership.[42]

Vandenberg's support was never really in question; the initial discussions with Marshall and Acheson had long settled that. The more immediate issue in Vandenberg's mind was to figure out what role he personally might play in getting this critical policy directive passed. He was no stranger to the Greek dispute, having had personal discussions on Greece's financial political situation with Greek Prime Minister Tsaldaris during his visit to Washington the previous year. Vandenberg left the meeting with a renewed sympathy and understanding for the Greek predicament, so he was predisposed to granting the United States' support. But would he go along with framing the Greek crisis as part of a worldwide crusade to support democracy?

Truman's new "doctrine" fit well into Vandenberg's conception of what America's role in world affairs ought to be. Strategically, Vandenberg had hoped that Communism and Capitalism could co-exist peacefully and learn to settle their differences through consultation and mutual agreement. However, when it came to tactics, Vandenberg was less forthcoming, possibly because his thoughts were still in the formative stages. Privately, Vandenberg often criticized the executive branch for too often making policy decisions while in "crisis mode." Invoking the philosophy he had formed years before, he felt that the President should seek Congress's assistance in solving problems before they became crises. The Greek dilemma, he contended, was another instance where early consultation might have strengthened Truman's chances of getting his aid bill passed. However, such bemoaning was now water under the bridge; the danger was present and the need urgent.

Having accepted that the Greek crisis was essentially a struggle between good and evil, Vandenberg threw himself into drumming up support for the policy. In a letter to Representative John Bennett, he wrote,

> I sense enough of the facts to realize that the problem in Greece cannot be isolated by itself. On the contrary, it is symbolic of the world-wide ideological clash between Eastern Communism and Western Democracy; and

it may easily be the thing which requires us to make some very fateful and far-reaching decisions.[43]

This was another instance where politics should stop "at the water's edge." For Vandenberg, this phrase was no mindless construction. He firmly believed that Democrats and Republicans should cooperate on foreign policy, and he saw the Greek loan issue as a catalyst for even deeper cooperation. He reasoned that the security of the United States was too important to bicker over, and nothing angered him more than when such matters became politicized. In one instance, when the Democratic National Committee chairman attempted to use Vandenberg's name in appeals to Republicans to get on board, Vandenberg fumed. "Bi-partisan foreign policy," he wrote in a letter to RNC chairman B. Carroll Reece, "is not the result of political coercion but of non-political conviction.... I have never made any semblance of a partisan demand for support and I never shall."[44]

It is ironic that the man who once had been an avowed isolationist was now a primary defender of collective security. Despite his support for the doctrine, Vandenberg nevertheless had one substantive complaint. The appropriations bill made no mention of the United Nations, let alone give it any authority to oversee the aid to Greece and Turkey. This "colossal blunder" (as he put it) prompted him to draft an amendment to give both the United Nations and the President authority to terminate the program if it was no longer wanted or needed.

Acheson considered the amendments little more than "window dressing," but after an opinion poll indicated substantial public agreement with Vandenberg's stance, he accepted it as a small price to pay to keep the Senate's foreign policy expert on board.[45] Acheson's conclusion may seem a bit cynical but considering that Vandenberg had been instrumental in bringing the United Nations into existence in the first place, his suggestion made sense. The amended bill cleared Vandenberg's Foreign Relations Committee by unanimous vote (13–0).

Vandenberg's stump speeches in favor of the bill were certainly welcome but not all his Republican colleagues were on board. The pivotal moment to win them over arrived on April 8 during the Senate debates on the appropriations bill. In a carefully crafted speech reporting the Foreign Relations Committee's unanimous vote to send the bill on to Congress, Vandenberg outlined in detail the reasons why Congress should pass it. This was not just a struggle to support the rights of Greece and Turkey, Vandenberg argued, this was a struggle over human rights and fundamental freedoms; moreover, it was a way of taking preemptory action to prevent the spread of Communism. Characteristically resorting to his usual homespun wisdom, Vandenberg argued that the bill was in keeping with "the intelligent American self-interest which prefers an ounce of precaution to a pound of cure, and which believes 'that a stitch in time saves nine.'"⁴⁶ His argument continued,

> Let us be totally plain about it. It is a plan to forestall aggression which, once rolling, could snowball into global danger of vast design. It is a plan for peace. It is a plan to sterilize the seeds of war. We do not escape war by running away from it ... we avoid war by facing facts. This plan faces facts.⁴⁷

The debate over the aid package and the Truman Doctrine continued into May. Eventually, the bill passed the House by a vote of 287–107 with 127 Republicans voting affirmative, and the Senate by a 67–23 majority, with 35 Republican senators voting in favor.⁴⁸ On May 22, the legislation became law.

The Truman Doctrine became the cornerstone of American foreign policy for the rest of the Cold War. It was nothing short of a public declaration that America would now be the protector of democratic ideals worldwide, and it signaled the demise of the long-entrenched belief that Europe's problems were of no concern to the American people. Simply put,

Senator Vandenberg recording a message to the Greek people for the opening of Greek language broadcasts of the Voice of the United States of America (NARA, 469-V-1007).

the United States, once an isolationist nation, had just transitioned into the role of world policeman.

However, the Doctrine was more than that; it was an embodiment of the ideals Americans had heretofore accepted only in philosophical terms. Instead of just talking about the virtues of democracy in abstraction, the United States now showed its willingness to apply actual economic and military assistance to support imperiled democratic governments. The first half of the twentieth century demonstrated the United States' willingness to defend attacked democracies by outside powers; now the Truman Doctrine extended that readiness to cases where *internal* subversion, supported by covert assistance from outside, threatened to disrupt the democratic order.

The Truman Doctrine is not without its own contradictions, however. First, as is true with all sweeping policy decisions, the immediate issue was how broadly it would be applied. Would the United States intervene everywhere? Acheson's testimony to Congress, explaining that each case would be considered one at a time, may have calmed fears somewhat. This would not be an extension of the Monroe Doctrine and would not apply in all circumstances. But that then begs the question, which cases would the United States support and which would it not? Certainly, the United States could not act with impunity around the globe, so there would have to be a "litmus test" to help decide when intervention was appropriate.

In subsequent decades, the standard applied was the nebulous concept of "strategic national interests." This may sound reasonable, but there is a clear value judgment at work. All too often that determination is predicated on an assessment of that county's strategic location, its raw materials, or its human capital. On its face, the Truman Doctrine was a blanket statement of ideological belief but in practice, it justified intervention only where possible, when possible, and with sights on a result that would yield clear practical advantages for the United States. In the coldest days of the Cold War, the containment of Communism was a sufficient reason. Decades later, it would be the supply of oil.

A further criticism of the Doctrine questions just how much democratic ideals truly were the guiding principles. This was already painfully obvious as the support for Greece, ostensibly to protect "democracy," was actually propping-up a brutal right-wing dictatorship, leaving the Truman administration open to charges of hypocrisy. The State Department countered such accusations by claiming that the reactionary Greek government was only a temporary expediency, and that the world should not expect a country that had gone through a war, an occupation by a foreign power, and a vicious civil war to instantaneously become a paragon of democratic virtue. The Greek civil war, it argued, was only one small theater in a struggle of Democracy versus Communism, and the individual players were really not as important as the larger conflict.

But what should American policy be toward long-standing dictatorial regimes who find themselves threatened? Is containing the communist menace more important than promoting democratic values? This contradiction opened up the United States to charges of being the inheritor of fascist and imperialist thought, a charge leveled repeatedly by communist "freedom fighters" around the world in the coming decades.

A final unintended, but perhaps unavoidable, consequence of the aid to Greece and Turkey was the emasculation of the United Nations. The U.N. lacked both the monetary and military resources to do anything about the Greek conflict. Besides, even if the U.N. had the resources, there was little likelihood it would take swift action, given the cumbersome decision-making apparatus of the United Nations General Assembly and Security Council. Greece was on the verge of collapse and only immediate action could prevent a complete breakdown and takeover by Communists.

The Truman Administration's decision to intervene ironically circumvented the authority of the very institution the United States fought so hard to create two years earlier at Yalta. That decision set a precedent giving more powerful states license to act unilaterally without the approval of, or in spite of the disapproval of, the United Nations. Except for the Korean conflict, the United Nations' effectiveness as a peacekeeping agency was marginalized, and the job of protecting the status quo fell to other organizations, including the North Atlantic Treaty Organization (NATO) and the Warsaw Pact. While the United Nations did what it could to aid strife-torn areas of the world, it could not assure the kind of collective security that was available under the nuclear umbrellas of the United States and the Soviet Union.

What became of Greece and Turkey? With the bill passed into law, civilian and military advisors from the United States poured into Greece to take the places of their British counterparts. Given the size of the appropriations award, the U.S. government took on a substantial role in the administration of the money and thereby wielded a great deal of influence over the Greek government. The tide of the civil war turned with the proclamation of a rival provisional Communist government in late December 1947. The United States lodged vehement protests and, to the surprise of many, Stalin balked at granting the communists diplomatic recognition. It may be that Stalin had written off Greece to the western postwar sphere of influence long before, so he was apparently content to stay out of the affair and let his Balkan satellite states take the initiative,[49] even to the point of pressuring Tito to terminate his support for the Greek communists as well.[50] Apparently, Stalin wanted to avoid any confrontation with the West over Greece.

Nevertheless, the civil war continued to rage for two more years. Aided by weaponry, supplies, and know-how from the United States, the Greek government launched a counteroffensive in 1948 that succeeded in isolating many of the Communists in northern Greece. Government troops finally claimed victory in October 1949. Turkey, which had never been seriously threatened by insurgency, also benefited from the Truman Doctrine and became one of the West's sentinels against communist aggression in the Middle East. Thanks to the outpouring of money and supplies through the Marshall Plan, Turkey began a long process of integration with the West that would lead it to membership in the Organization for European Economic Cooperation in 1948 and NATO in 1952.

* * *

The American intervention in Greece and Turkey and the ensuing victory for democracy might not have been possible without the bipartisanship that Truman enjoyed, thanks in no small part to Arthur Vandenberg. That bipartisanship could not have come at a more opportune time. With Communism advancing across Eastern Europe and making inroads into the political structures of many western European nations, it was imperative that U.S. policy be based on consensus. By placing his considerable political clout behind the passage of the Truman Doctrine and the European Recovery Program, Senator Vandenberg played a pivotal role in achieving that consensus.

Nevertheless, Arthur Vandenberg was the object of ire among some Republicans who reviled him for "selling out" to the Democrats and for his lack of consistency in his own core beliefs about isolationism. He was thick-skinned enough to deflect those attacks, but any suggestion that he was "un–American" met with the most vitriolic retaliation. In a response to a critical letter from a clergyman from Kalamazoo, Vandenberg lashed out with a scathing reply and in the process penned one of the best and most succinct summaries of his approach to foreign policy and internal politics.[51]

> My dear friend:
>
> What interests me is your own basis for suggesting that I am "no longer interested in America"; that I am "just an internationalist"; and that you "never thought I would carry things so far." I am particularly interested because, as a Minister of the Gospel, I know you are interested in truth and tolerance. So let's good-naturedly see what it is you are talking about.
>
> 1. I believe that *peace* is the most important, moral objective for which we can strive; that in this atomic age, we cannot depend solely upon our own resources to prevent war.... Is *that* anti–American? Do you disagree?

Chapter 3. "A Stitch in Time" 73

2. I believe the world is fundamentally locked in a struggle between Eastern Communism and Western Democracy; the Western Democracy *must* strongly survive this contest.... Is *that* anti–American? Do you disagree?
3. I think the control of our atomic secrets is a vital core in our foreign policy.... Is *that* anti–American? Do you disagree?
4. Let's sum it up. I enclose herewith a reprint of a speech on foreign policy in which I have outlined my total credo.... What part of it is *anti*-American? With what part do you disagree? Be good enough to let me know. I am sincerely interested in your reactions to my *real* views. I am interested in knowing whether my *real* views, or a grotesque misrepresentation of them, is responsible for your condemnation.

Unfortunately, Vandenberg would not live to see the seeds he had sown blossom into a general European peace. Only one year after the Truman Doctrine and Marshall Plan decisions, he was diagnosed with a tumor in his lung, undoubtedly the result of the cigars he enjoyed so much. Although his doctors urged him to have the surgery immediately, he postponed it in order to devote himself to the passage of the bills creating NATO. Eventually, the operation succeeded in removing the tumor (and much of his lung), but the delay may have cost him his chances to recover fully. Upon returning to work, Vandenberg suffered headaches and body aches that sapped his strength and physically kept him away from the Senate chambers. In the spring of 1950, doctors at Georgetown Hospital discovered another tumor, this time located on his spine. Following a second surgery, he returned home to the comforts of Grand Rapids and seemed to be recovering well before suffering a relapse in February 1951. He rallied long enough to smoke a cigar in celebration of this 67th birthday on March 22.[52]

Arthur Hendrick Vandenberg passed away in his sleep on April 18, 1951. The outpouring of sentiment in the Senate eulogizing him was immediate and eloquent, delivered ironically on the same day that his idol, Douglas MacArthur, addressed a joint session of Congress to deliver his famous "old soldiers never die" farewell speech. Homer Ferguson, the junior Senator from Michigan, remarked that "when some day in the future, the world knows peace, that peace will be a monument to the architecture of Arthur Vandenberg."[53] That statement may suffer from some hyperbole, but there is truth in it. It is certainly accurate to call Vandenberg the architect of bilateral foreign policy but, as the word implies, there had to be those on both sides of the political aisle who were willing to make bipartisanship work. Equal credit goes to the wisdom of Marshall, Acheson, and Byrnes, who had the foresight to bring the opposition party into their foreign policy discussions to the extent they did with Vandenberg.

In that dramatic moment of world history, the United States needed individuals who could come to grips with the new realities of a postwar world and meet them—not by "running away," but by facing them head-on. Vandenberg was foremost among them. The most apt description of Vandenberg came from Dean Acheson who, despite being on the opposite end of the ideological spectrum, nevertheless held a grudging admiration for the senator from Michigan. "His mind was not original," Acheson wrote later, "but it was open. He was not a creator of ideas, but could use them well, a powerful advocate but no great public speaker, yet without him the history of postwar diplomacy might have been completely different."[54]

President Truman eulogized Vandenberg even more succinctly, calling him "a patriot who always subordinated partisan advantage and personal interest to the welfare of the nation."[55] That too may be a bit hyperbolic, given Vandenberg's early career as a staunch Republican and the voice of isolationism. But for the last six years of his career, that description is on point. Once he set aside his political differences to work toward a bipartisan foreign policy, Vandenberg stopped being just a senator. He became a statesman; a title rightly reserved for only a few.

History has been kind to Vandenberg. His life and career are replete with lessons worthy of intense study, as the spate of Ph.D. dissertations based on his life and work will attest.[56] Eventually, his name became something of a metaphor for bipartisanship and cooperation. President Gerald Ford, who owed his first Congressional victory in 1948 in part to Vandenberg's assistance, repeatedly brought up the name of his fellow Grand Rapids native during foreign policy debates with Democrats in February 1975. And today, visitors walking into the Senate reception room of the Capital Building in Washington, D.C., can look up to find a mural portrait of Vandenberg above the archway leading into the chambers. His likeness rests there as a memorial to all that can happen when people of conviction set aside their political differences in order to work for the common good.

Chapter 4

"Up from the Dust"
Mohammad Ali Jinnah, Masood Ghaznavi, and the Creation of Pakistan

One of the most overused clichés about history is that "the sun never sets on the British empire." However trite that phrase may be, there is no denying that Great Britain's lust for economic expansion and territorial acquisition created, over the span of three centuries of conquest, the largest colonial empire the world has ever known. Although there were British colonial possessions on six continents, its most prized possession had to be India. Ever since British armies wrested control away from the Mughals and other European nations in the eighteenth and nineteenth centuries, Conservative, Liberal, and Labour parties that normally would disagree on most everything all agreed that the Asian subcontinent should remain under the Union Jack banner. But in an address to Parliament on February 20, 1947, Labour Prime Minister Clement Attlee broke with centuries of tradition and announced his government's "intention to take the necessary steps to effect the transference of power into responsible Indian hands."[1]

The proclamation to quit India was a pivotal moment in both British and world history but it hardly came as a shock; the issue of Indian self-rule had been debated for decades and it might have come sooner had two world wars not intervened. But now, Attlee's announcement made it official and in the ensuing ten months, the United Kingdom would grant self-determination to the Indian subcontinent. Such momentous change is never easy. With the transition from colony to independence, the religious and ethnic hatreds within Indian society quickly surfaced, eventually resulting in a human catastrophe of epic proportions. Freedom was bought and paid for by the blood of hundreds of thousands of innocent people.

To understand why 1947 was a year of triumph and tragedy for the Asian subcontinent, it is necessary to understand India's tortured history. Before 1947, "India" was nothing more than an expression of geography; as Winston Churchill put it, "no more united than the Equator." British rule had arbitrarily conquered and amalgamated a wide expanse of territory stretching from the Indus River in the west to the Ganges River in the east. Within those confines resided a wide assortment of ethnic groups with an attendant multitude of languages, religions, and tribal loyalties. Hindus, numbering approximately 252 million people in 1941, comprised about 66 percent of the overall population, making it the largest religious community in India.[2] Another 92 million people (24 percent) were Muslims. Smaller religious groups, including Sikhs (approximately 5.7 million), Parses, Buddhists, Jains, Christians, Jews, and others completed the ethnographic mix.

In generalized geographic terms, the Hindu populations predominated in interior (peninsular) India while Muslim populations were more prevalent in the outlying regions along the rivers (for example, in Punjab, Balochistan, the Northwest Frontier Provinces, and Sindh in the west and Bengal and Assam in the east). This overly simplified description of Indian demographics masks the fact that Hindus, Muslims, and Sikhs lived side by side all across the subcontinent but especially so in the Punjab, Kashmir, and Bengal. Consequently, it was virtually impossible to draw distinct boundaries between religiously and ethnically disparate communities.[3]

Oddly enough, the colonizers themselves helped plant the seeds of Indian independence.[4] In 1885, the British allowed their Indian subjects to establish an advisory body to represent the interests of the Indian peoples to the viceroy and the UK home government. The body they created, the Indian National Congress, brought together Hindu, Muslim, Sikh, and other delegates from all over India. Discussions in Congress eventually suggested giving local administrative control over to the people themselves, and some of the more revolutionary members even suggested that their end goals ought to be the complete termination of the British Raj. Although those voices represented a fringe minority at first, the demand for self-determination grew considerably in the early twentieth century. As the movement gained momentum, minority religious groups across India began to consider what life might be like in an independent state where Hinduism was the predominant faith.

In 1906, an All-India Muslim League came into being. Although its published goals included loyalty to the British government and working to promote understanding between Muslims and other religious communities, the primary goal of the League was to safeguard the rights of the Muslim community within India.[5] Almost immediately, the League divided into two competing ideologies. Some of the members could foresee Muslims and Hindus working together in a large, religiously diverse and independent India. Others favored the creation of a separate Muslim country—an idea that had found expression in the middle of the nineteenth century in the teachings of the Islamic scholar and educational reformer, Syed Ahmad Khan, who once opined that Hindu and Muslim communities would never "join wholeheartedly in anything."[6]

The Great War put both visions on the back burner, but the smoldering embers of self-determination reignited during the interwar period with the emergence of two of the twentieth century's most notable statesmen, Mohandas Gandhi and Muhammad Ali Jinnah. Yet, as united as they were in the goal of liberation from British rule, these two statesmen could not have been more different from each other personally.

Mohandas Karamchand Gandhi, the father of Indian independence, is among the most well-known and respected persons of the twentieth century. His practice of *Satyagraha*, or the countering of unjust laws and governmental prejudice with nonviolent disobedience, became a model for oppressed populations all over the globe. Trained as a lawyer, "Mahatmaji" (as he was called later in life) began his crusade against oppression by fighting apartheid in South Africa before turning his attention to his native India. After World War I, he immersed himself in Indian colonial policy by organizing strikes and boycotts aimed at bringing international attention to the injustices of the British Raj. As a member and then later leader of the Indian National Congress, he fought to keep both the Muslim and Hindu populations working in concert toward a goal of a unified, multiethnic, and multireligious India free from outside interference.

His tactics repeatedly landed him in jail but over time Gandhi achieved such gravitas that even the threat of his involvement in an issue, such as leading demonstrations or going on a hunger strike, could achieve political results. World War II found him again in prison, this time for advocating that Indians should refuse to take part in the war effort unless the United Kingdom made certain concessions to home rule. He was released in 1944, however, and he renewed his efforts to keep Muslim and Hindu populations united, a goal that motivated him for the remainder of his life.

Muhammad Ali Jinnah posed a stark contrast to Gandhi. The man who would head the Muslim League and eventually become *Quaid-e-Azam* (the Great Leader) to millions of Indian Muslims was born on December 25, 1876,[7] the eldest of seven children in a middle-class family near Karachi in the Sindh region. An early biographer, Hector Bolitho, relates stories of his childhood (some of which may have been apocryphal), describing a determined young man who valued education and hard work. In one story, Jinnah refuses to play in the streets with another boy, imploring him instead to "stand up from the dust so that your clothes are unspoiled and your hands clean for the tasks that fall to them."[8]

In another vignette, Jinnah reportedly told his mother "You know

I can't achieve anything in life unless I work hard," when she suggested that he take a break from studying. In truth, he found little enjoyment in the drudgery of schoolwork. However, the young Jinnah received a rare opportunity to go to London as an apprentice and once there he developed a passion for education, especially law. In only two short years he passed his law exams and, at age 18, he became the youngest Indian ever admitted to the bar.

Jinnah's time in England thoroughly Anglicized him. He acquired a taste for fine hand-tailored suits, silk ties, and wearing a monocle. As a barrister, Jinnah developed an affinity for the English language and preferred to speak it over his native Urdu. His friends described him as hardworking and serious, devoid of both malice and passion (except for reading newspapers), and aloof to the point of having no social life. After a brief flirtation with a career in Shakespearean acting, Jinnah returned to India in 1896 to open a law practice in Bombay. His career got off to a slow start, but he soon garnered a reputation as a solid trial lawyer, in part thanks to his days as a thespian.

Those who knew him noted his facility for quick, clear thinking in the courtroom. Occasionally, Jinnah would taunt judges on legal points and soon perfected a courtroom presence that one admirer called "omnipotent."[9] To his detractors, such skills smacked of arrogance. Many described him as a "difficult" person to deal with. One thing all could agree on was that he was scrupulously honest, even to the point where he refused to take any bonuses or gifts from clients. He accepted only his fee for services rendered and not one penny more.

Jinnah's interest in politics took off when he joined the Congress in 1904. Oddly enough, Jinnah disagreed with the home rule movement; he had become too enamored with British culture (particularly its education system) and the perceived virtues it had bestowed upon the Indian subcontinent. Like Gandhi, Jinnah was a close friend and admirer of Gopal Krishna Gohkale, the famed social reformer and advocate of Indian independence. The two men traveled together extensively and over time they developed a strong personal bond. From this interaction, Jinnah (again, like Gandhi) had come to favor the idea of a creating a unitary Indian state. For that reason he delayed joining the Muslim League, claiming that it was too Muslim-oriented, but he eventually reconsidered and joined in 1913 on the condition that his membership "would in no way and at no time imply even the shadow of disloyalty to the larger national cause" that he espoused.[10] By 1916, he became president of the League and was well-known in both League and Congress circles as the "ambassador of Hindu-Muslim unity."

At the time, "ambassador of unity" was not necessarily a popular reputation to have. There were many Muslim nationalists in the League who were convinced that a partition of India was not only necessary but inevitable. The leader of this movement was the poet and political theorist, Muhammad Iqbal, who had picked up the threads of Syed Khan's teachings decades earlier. Despite their differences, Jinnah and Iqbal became close friends and associates; Iqbal supported most of Jinnah's reform initiatives, but Jinnah could not reconcile himself with Iqbal's view that Muslim nationalism should be given expression within a federated India. In addition, Iqbal also believed that the Islamic religion had a role to play in the government of any future Islamic government on the subcontinent.

That was simply too much for Jinnah, a secularist schooled in British liberalism, to accept. By the 1920s, Muslim nationalism was gaining traction as more and more Muslims adopted Iqbal's vision. Jinnah now had to walk a very fine line. As a leader of the Muslim League, he had given voice to Islamic nationalist aspirations on the subcontinent. But as a member of the Indian National Congress, he still had to work with Hindus to create a unified state. He may have reached his tipping point toward the end of the decade, when the Congress rejected a plan he had devised to keep the Muslim and Hindu political movements united. In 1930, after years of frustration and haggling within the Congress in vain attempts to foster Hindu-Muslim unity, Muhammad Ali Jinnah left India and returned to England.

Whether this "flight" to London was the product of his displeasure with Congress and League politics or a calculated ploy to distance himself from Gandhi and Iqbal and assert his own stature as leader of the Muslims remains a matter of speculation and interpretation. However, his timing was fortuitous as he arrived just in time to participate in the first governmental roundtable discussions about home rule for India and how Muslim interests in a united India could be safeguarded.

About that same time, the word "Pakistan"[11] had gained currency to express a country forged out of the Muslim-dominated western provinces of India (including Kashmir in the north). As the momentum shifted in favor of Muslim separation from Hindu India, Jinnah yielded to the urging of Iqbal and Liaquat Ali Khan (who would later become prime minister) and returned to India to lead the League. His decision was transformative. Sometime thereafter, he broke with the Indian unity camp and became a champion of Pakistani self-determination, in one form or another.[12]

With the start of the Second World War in 1939, Indians of all religions saw the chance to leverage their wartime cooperation for independence. The Muslim League passed the Lahore Resolution in 1940, a vague and inwardly contradictory statement calling for the creation of "autonomous and sovereign units" for the Muslims of India. Jinnah was undoubtedly pleased to announce and promote the document despite its lack of a specific plan of action, since doing so gave him cachet as the champion of Muslim independence. At the same time, Jinnah secretly admitted to his friends that the Lahore Resolution was a "tactical move" and that he was prepared to accept less than what he was demanding.[13] As some contemporaries put it, the crafty Jinnah "kept his cards close to his chest."[14]

The British home government acknowledged the Lahore statement but did little about it since the threat of a Nazi invasion of Britain and a Japanese invasion of India were much more pressing issues. Recognizing that some accommodation would have to be made, Churchill sent Stafford Cripps, who at the time was Lord Privy Seal and member of the wartime cabinet, to India to broker an agreement with Gandhi and Jinnah during the height of the war in 1942. The Cripps mission advanced a simple quid pro quo. In return for Indian cooperation in the war effort, Britain was prepared to reward India with dominion status after the war with the right to claim independence. According to the plan, any province could opt out of an Indian union and form a union or unions of their own if they chose. This was a clear concession to the Muslims, even though the word "Pakistan" was not mentioned.[15] Needless to say, the "opt out" provisions were anathema for the Congress unionists who wanted to maintain Indian unity at all costs.

With the war's end in 1945 and the accession of a new Labour government in Parliament, Hindus and Muslims alike expected that the United Kingdom would soon grant India home rule, possibly as a dominion within the British Commonwealth. The question then became, would that independent nation be a single entity, or would there be a partition of the country to assuage the nationalist aspirations of the Muslims? In December, Lord Wavell, the British viceroy, announced his government's intention to convene a constituent assembly for the purpose of framing an all–Indian Constitution. Local elections began at the end of the year and continued into 1946, and the process of bringing home rule to India had begun.

The situation in Punjab at this critical junction of British India's history is an especially instructive example of what the new elections meant for local Muslim and Hindu communities. At the end of war, Punjab was still reeling from the inflation and economic privations that typically accompany the return of peacetime. Farmers started hoarding their goods rather than selling them on the open market, leading to food scarcity.

As local electioneering began, Muslim agitators seized on the economic difficulties and tried to convince voters that a new independent Muslim state might be the solution to all of Punjab's problems. Their vehemence occasionally grew ugly, as League supporters (not just in Punjab, but across India) accused anyone who did not favor the creation of "Pakistan" of being less than "true" Muslims.[16] When election results were revealed on February 24, 1946, the Muslim League had secured 75 out of the 175 seats in the legislature,[17] a result that surprised the League as much as it did their opposition.

Despite its victory, the League could not convince any of the other minority parties to join with them and form a government. Instead, the Hindus, Sikhs, and non–League Muslims combined their delegations in a coalition under the returning governor, Khizar Hayat Tiwana, himself a Muslim but a member of the Unionist party. Khizar's success only reinforced the League's fears that Islamic populations would forever be a minority in a government dominated by others. For many, independence now seemed more and more the answer.

As the Khizar government took office, Punjabis picked sides in the political debate. Should they cooperate with the Khizar government, or continue to agitate for separation? Masood Ghaznavi was a 15-year-old student at the time of the elections. His family history was atypical for most Punjabis. He was born in a small village near Bahawalapur, but his family's true ancestral home lay in Afghanistan. His great-grandfather was a religious scholar who taught a "pure" version of Islam based on Mohammad's teachings that local Afghani Mullahs rejected, resulting in his eviction from the region. The family first moved to Delhi and then later relocated to the town of Amritsar, where the elder Ghaznavi became a religious leader of some renown.

Masood's large family had amassed enough respect that a section of Amritsar where the family had settled was named "*kucha Ghaznavia*" ("Ghaznavi neighborhood") in their honor. In his early life, Masood was often the man of the house. His father, who was a leader and eventual president of the local Amritsar Congress party, was imprisoned repeatedly during the war, as was his uncle. Still, the family was able to provide Masood with private tutoring and eventually send him to attend school at Quetta in Balochistan, 350 miles away. There he immersed himself in student affairs, organizing the school's first student government and serving as student president. He soon became active in politics as well. As he later remembered, "I joined the college and was reasonably active in the Pakistan movement. The way things worked I became the leader of the student movement, which was the most active part of the Muslim League movement in Balochistan anyway. Pretty soon they elected me general secretary for the whole province."[18]

The "electoral snub" of the Muslim League and the return of the Khizar government back home in his native Punjab did not go unnoticed. Ghaznavi recounted,

> I heard about this movement starting back in Punjab after the elections challenging Khizar's government, and I rushed to Amritsar [during the winter break]. I contacted my student friends who had known me so I became part of

the movement. We used to organize rallies coming out of the colleges in Punjab, and we'd take up actions demonstrating our unacceptance of the government's action in not inviting the Muslim League to form a government. The tension was there long before the election and after it as well, and the tension was all over India and Pakistan.[19]

That "tension" broke into violence in nearby Lahore on March 9, as fights broke out between Hindu and Muslim student groups, resulting in 11 wounded. The demonstrations drew the attention of the *Quaid-e-Azam* himself. At a Muslim League meeting on March 20, Jinnah infused his speech with the imagery of battle, exhorting the Punjabi Muslims to "let your sword arm play a more magnificent part in the achievement of Pakistan."[20] It was a surprising appeal to violence, made by a lawyer who had until then seemed more concerned with the legal aspects of the struggle for independence. No one at the time knew just how active that "sword arm" would become in the upcoming months.

Meanwhile, as part of the transition to local self-government, the British established a new executive council to bring together leaders of all the constituent groups into one advisory body. Gandhi and his associate, Jawaharlal Nehru, still clung firmly to the vison of a unified India. As far

Muhammad Ali Jinnah (far left) speaking with Masood Ghaznavi (left, facing Jinnah) and other Muslim college students, 1947 (courtesy Nadeem Ghaznavi).

as they were concerned, partition was out of the question. For Jinnah, the question really was no longer if a Pakistan would emerge but when. He began to ponder what shape the new nation would be and also whether it would be part of a larger federation or a completely separate state. Jinnah was of the mind that some sort of union between the two states was still a possibility. He had hoped that Pakistan and India might come together after independence to form a "super-Center" with bureaucracies designed to look after common interests.

Congress wanted the reverse; i.e., to start with a center that would address the interests of the whole and then talk about how much autonomy the regions would be allotted.[21] To assist the viceroy in devising the best possible settlement, Attlee's Labour government dispatched a special Cabinet Mission to India composed of Lord Pethick-Lawrence (secretary of state for India), Sir Stafford Cripps (author of the 1942 proposals), and A.V. Alexander (First Lord of the Admiralty). The Mission arrived in late March 1946, and from the start the two factions entrenched their positions. This left the Mission with the impossible task of having to devise a plan that would reconcile two completely opposite visions for the future of India.

After weeks of wrangling, the Cabinet Mission revealed its plan for open discussion on April 27. The Mission plan rejected the idea of a unified Pakistan as impracticable, both because it claimed too much non–Muslim territory and the fact that millions of Muslims living in central India would become an alienated minority in a foreign country.[22] Paradoxically, the Mission plan also stopped short of recommending unifying India in favor of creating "sections," each comprised of groupings of provinces, with each section free to create its own constitution. Most importantly, the plan stipulated that a province could withdraw from its appointed section if its government decided to do so, but only *after* the new constitution took effect. Any such breakaway province would then be free to join another region or assert its independence.

The Mission Plan proposal would have created a highly decentralized federal structure where the provinces would exert almost complete autonomy from the central authority except in foreign affairs, defense, taxation, and communication. Even though the Plan made no provision for the creation of an independent Pakistan, its terms were quite favorable to the Muslim minority. Jinnah seized the moment and voiced his acceptance of the proposal, provided that the six Muslim provinces he claimed for Pakistan be grouped together.

The Hindu leadership in Congress promptly became suspicious that Jinnah was only paying lip service to the idea of greater India while secretly carving out a pathway to independence. To forestall such a possibility,

Congress reasserted its demand to form a central government first before any parts of the Plan were put into effect. Now it was Jinnah's turn to question Congress's motives, arguing that the Hindus wanted to submerge Muslim aspirations into a political structure dominated by Hindus.

The executive committee, drawn from the leadership of both sides, debated the Mission Plan proposal at the town of Simla and, predictably, the delegates could not reach an agreement. Nevertheless, the Cabinet Mission moved ahead anyway and issued a statement on May 16 proposing formation of a constituent assembly constructed on the basis outlined in its original April blueprint.

For Jinnah, the Mission Plan was a step in the right direction. It was not the fully sovereign Pakistan he had hoped for, but it was the next best thing; it gave the Muslim regions of India a chance to dominate an entire provincial grouping within the framework of a weak central government. Ever conscious of his image as leader of the Muslim movement, Jinnah spoke out publicly against the plan because it did not overtly permit the creation of a Muslim nation-state. However, to everyone's surprise, he asked the League to accept the proposal anyway "in the hope that it would ultimately result in the establishment of a complete sovereign Pakistan."[23] Jinnah's statement only reinforced Hindu suspicions that he had no intention of staying within any union and would invoke the "opt-out" contingency regardless of any outcome. In truth, the Congress was not entirely happy with the plan either, since it would have forced Hindu-dominated provinces to enter into Muslim-dominated groups.

Viceroy Wavell moved forward with the plans to constitute an interim government based on the Plan outline anyway and threatened to proceed without the Hindus if necessary.[24] Disputes quickly erupted over who had the right to nominate members to the Executive Committee—in other words, over the issue of whether or not a Congress Muslim could be brought on board. Such a concession would have diminished the Muslim League's claim as the sole representative of the Muslim interests and allow for renegade or disaffected Muslims to find a home in opposition to the League. Additionally, Nehru was vocal about his opposition to the forced groupings. In direct contradiction of the wording of the Plan document, he said that the Congress interpreted the document to mean that states could opt out of groups *before* the writing of any constitutions.

Nehru's unfortunate pronouncement drew fire from many including sympathetic Congress Hindus, who pointed out that his interpretation was not only ill-advised but factually wrong. Clinging to his pronouncement nonetheless, Nehru stated that the Congress would participate in the constituent assembly "completely unfettered by agreement and free to meet all situations as they arise."[25]

Chapter 4. "Up from the Dust" 85

Jinnah's acceptance of the proposal gave the Muslim League the patina of being cooperative in contrast with the Congress's obstreperous stance. Jinnah interpreted the British government's willingness to go ahead with the interim government anyway, despite Nehru's clear misinterpretations of it, as just another attempt to mollify the Hindus at the expense of the Muslim populations. Nevertheless, Jinnah urged the Mission to make good on its threat to proceed with the plan, but his request fell on deaf ears. Finally, on June 25, the Congress changed its position, accepting the Mission Plan as a basis for discussion and agreeing to enter a provisional government. But when the Congress insisted that a non-League Muslim be recognized as one of its delegates, it was Jinnah's turn to object. Jinnah would not allow anything to jeopardize his position as "sole representative" of the Muslim community and so the Muslim League decided to boycott the interim government. The continual bickering left everyone wondering if a compromise was even possible. Even Wavell felt the strain of the repeated failures, calling the Indian politicians "disheartening to deal with."[26]

* * *

It would be pointless to attribute blame for the failure of the Cabinet Mission Plan. The Hindu-dominated Congress certainly owns its share of the responsibility for its convoluted (and overtly inaccurate) interpretation of the Plan provisions. However, the League also deserves some of the responsibility for destroying any agreement with its statement that it hoped the plan would "ultimately result in the establishment of a complete sovereign Pakistan." One can hardly fault the Hindus for assuming (probably rightly) that the League had no intention of keeping India united should the plan proceed. To some extent, the Mission was partially responsible for its own failure. At first it handed concessions to the Muslims, knowing full well that they would be unacceptable to the Hindus. Then, as if to even the score, it gave concessions to the Hindus that it knew would antagonize the League. In its attempts to keep India united and (they hoped) in the Commonwealth, the Mission tried to placate both sides but wound up satisfying neither. It discovered over time that it is impossible to reconcile what are by nature irreconcilable demands.

What is certain is that the failure of the Cabinet Mission ended any hope for a peaceful resolution of the crisis. The Muslim League had already drawn up plans for "direct action" and ten days after Nehru was invited to form a government without League participation, they set those plans in motion. There never was a clear definition of what exactly "direct action" entailed. Jinnah and the League had issued instructions that demonstrations should be "peaceful" and "disciplined,"[27] but the more firebrand activists interpreted the call as license to use violence as a means of political persuasion. In Muslim Balochistan, Ghaznavi and his fellow students took Jinnah's announcement seriously, thereby sparing Balochistan from large-scale violence and social disruption.

In other areas, however, the situation quickly got out of hand. Islamic rioting all across India resulted in approximately 5,000 deaths and another 15,000 wounded, with most of the victims being innocents caught in the wrong place at the wrong time. Naturally, the Sikhs and Hindus retaliated, and a whirlwind of death blew across the rest of India. The rioting in Calcutta was especially brutal and ended up with a toll of nearly 4,000 deaths and 10,000 wounded.[28] In the east Indian state of Bihar, Hindu reprisals against Muslims resulted in thousands more deaths. Horrific riots continued through October and into November as the subcontinent sank into a maelstrom of violence.

Such communal rioting was not new to India. In fact, small-scale rioting had been a regular occurrence in many areas for decades. However, past disturbances paled in significance to the brutality that began in mid–1946. What made the hostilities more insidious was that most were not random acts but carefully planned and systematically organized assaults on civilian populations. What began as a political disagreement had become a "civil war" in the purest sense of the term, pitting groups of armed civilians motivated by religious zealotry and ethnic vendettas against each other.

The unprecedented scale of the violence produced, in the words of historian Yasmin Khan, a "psychic break" that realigned and hardened the allegiances of the people of the Indian subcontinent along religious lines. As the violence that began on Direct Action Day escalated from Calcutta to Bihar and onward, most understood that there was little hope for reconciliation now that blood had been spilled. As Winston Churchill presciently remarked during a speech to the House of Commons in December of 1946, these riots were "only the first few drops of rain before the thunderstorm breaks."[29]

The League's refusal to take part in the interim government was a shrewd tactical move, but as the death toll rose and public opinion turned against them, it proved a strategically untenable position. Consequently, Jinnah announced that the League would join the government if the original precepts of the plan were enforced as written; namely, that the provinces could not opt out of groups before they were constituted. Eager to find a way to end the violence, Wavell agreed and pressured Congress to accept the original intent of the Plan. Once again Congress refused, thereby leaving the viceroy hopelessly stuck between two alternatives. He could not afford to antagonize the Hindus and risk losing India for the Commonwealth, but without concessions to the Muslim League there would never be any hope of compromise.

Meanwhile, the rioting continued unabated, and the world watched with horror as India sank ever deeper into an ethnic bloodbath. Eventually, Jinnah reached the conclusion that the interim government would go on without him if it had to; so, when Gandhi gave him vague assurances that Congress would not seek to appoint non–League Muslims to the government,[30] Jinnah accepted. He and five of his nominees took their places in the interim cabinet. On October 26, a new government was born that was "baptized by the bloodshed in eastern Bengal."[31]

A successful interim government might have stemmed the violence, but the chances for such success were slim from the start. Rather than working in concert, Muslim and Hindu delegates clashed repeatedly over issues like taxation. In time the two delegations divided into entrenched ideological blocs, arguing incessantly and hurling petty insults at each other to make their points. In an attempt to break through the impasse, party leaders were summoned to London to confer. The meeting did prove a victory for the League, when the UK government conceded the point about the provinces opting out only after the first elections. Invitations for the constituent assembly went out, but Muslims refused to participate unless the Hindus also agreed to the May 16 statement. Congress eventually "accepted" it but still contended that it would not be bound to the strict letter of plan's provision. For Jinnah, this was just one more example of Hindu subterfuge. Consequently, when the interim government met on December 9, it did so without the Muslim League members. Both sides felt the other had reneged on the Mission Plan.

* * *

As 1947 began, the prospects for a peaceful resolution to the crisis seemed more remote than ever. The interim government had failed and hopes for a settlement preserving the unity of India were fading rapidly. Meanwhile, much of India was in the grip of the continuing civil war. By New Year's Day 1947, Punjab was an armed camp. League forces had taken the "direct action" approach to launch a concerted, month-long effort to overthrow the Unionist ministry of Khizar. As the crowds of demonstrators grew, Khizar's government resorted to repression in order to hold on to political power. Police ransacked the League headquarters in Lahore, and a number of League leaders were arrested under Section 144 laws banning public meetings and processions. The crackdown only set off more mob demonstrations centered in and around the local mosques. On January 24, Khizar's government upped the ante by outlawing the Muslim League National Guard.[32]

For the young firebrands of Punjab, Khizar's move was another good reason to take to the streets. Masood Ghaznavi, the young student leader and political activist, was personally involved in the demonstrations:

> We were demonstrating in defiance of Section 144 and wearing the badges of the Muslim National Guard in defiance [of the ban]. So the usual beginning would be that students would gather somewhere and shout things ... and then the police would come ready for a baton charge—with sticks three to four feet long—and start beating us around, sometimes pretty bad. The general procedure was to haul off the whole lot of the [demonstrators], put them in a room at the police station, leave them there for five, six, seven hours, in a very dirty place, and then put them in a bus, take them seven, eight, nine, ten miles outside the city, and then leave them there. See, they didn't want to start a procedure [of trials] because if they did they'd never see the end of it.

But that particular day, the Punjabi authority decided to make examples out some of the more prominent demonstrators as a deterrent to further civil disobedience.

> The day I was part of the procession they started arresting some people ... and picking up the leaders of the movement and handcuffing them. They put us all in lockups and [when] they registered names and addresses, they picked out the people whom they would handcuff.... I was one of those who was handcuffed. There were hundreds who were detained at the same time, but they were released outside the town. But these few of us, I think the number in prison were about five, were chosen to be tried in court. They charged us with treason or exciting people to revolt against a legally constituted government, et cetera, et cetera.

Ghaznavi may have been singled out because his uncle, Daoud, had been a high-ranking leader in the Punjabi Congress movement who was imprisoned by the British during the war. Suddenly the young student from Amritsar found himself branded as one of the most severe agitators, potentially subject to a long prison sentence if found guilty.[33] Unbeknownst to him, this happenstance catapulted him to the status of "leader" to the crowds of demonstrators.

> The date was fixed for our appearance in the court and all five of us got ready to put on the best shine possible, wore decent clothes, and found there were thousands of people waiting outside the prison who knew we were being taken out for trial. They wanted to greet us ... and when the government saw this, they cancelled our appearance in the court and the court was brought in the prison.

The anti-Khizar demonstrations now had symbolic heroes. Ghaznavi was convicted and spent about a month in prison, but the protests continued unabated. Muslims all over India mobilized.

The uprising was so total all over the province that men women and children also participated. You see, women like to wear bangles, sometimes glass bangles ... and it is an insult to say to a man, go wear bangles ... so sometimes it would happen that women would come out in the procession and when the police started beating men, they would take their bangles off and throw them at the men [who fled].

Although Khizar's government soon lifted the ban on the Muslim National Guard, its authority with the public had clearly been compromised. His government finally fell on March 3 to the delight of the demonstrators. Ghaznavi remembered that day well. "Funny thing" he recalled, "all the poems and slogans that had been written to that point were against Khizar ... and the moment he resigned, the same people were writing 'Khizar is our brother.'" Punjabi Muslims could now put the political struggle behind them and concentrate on the wider struggle for Muslim identity and Pakistan, so even former enemies could now close ranks. But with Khizar's fall, the Hindus and Sikhs now felt threatened, and as disputes turned into confrontation, all civil authority broke down.

The local police, who were predominantly Muslims, refused to act against their co-religionists, so Hindus and Sikhs decided to take their protection into their own hands. Towns fractured into Muslim, Hindu, or Sikh enclaves cordoned off and fortified with gates and barricades. Armed civilians patrolled their areas to guard against sneak attacks. Such suspicions were entirely justified. During the worst of the violence, gangs of thugs wiped out entire neighborhoods. The fighting spared no one; Muslims, Sikhs, and Hindus alike were all victims.

In the end, an estimated 5,000 people lay dead and another 3,000 wounded. Gandhi, Nehru, and Jinnah could at least agree on the need to stem the brutality, suggesting that the British use lethal force if necessary. "I don't care whether you shoot Moslems or not" Jinnah once said, "[the violence] has got to be stopped."[34] But the British military authority, woefully inadequate to keep the peace at any rate, refused to get involved.

Punjab was only one small theater in the collapse that was beginning to play out all over the subcontinent in early 1947. Wavell had already suggested that the British make a "phased withdrawal" from India over the next 18 months, but to a Labour government struggling with postwar hardship and a full domestic agenda back home, the idea of staying in India any longer than necessary was anathema. It is in that context that the Labour government issued its February 20 statement of intent to quit India by June 1948, but the decision had been made months before. Eventually, Prime Minister Attlee removed Wavell as viceroy and replaced him with Viscount Mountbatten.

Louis Francis Albert Victor Nicholas Mountbatten cut an impressive figure both as a member of the British royal family and as a diplomat.

The young and exceedingly handsome man had much experience with India, having served as the Supreme Allied Commander of the Southeast Asian theater during the Second World War. His official charge was to work toward a united India within the British Commonwealth (if possible) and headed by a unity government—all by the deadline of October 1947. Failing that, Mountbatten was to find a way to transfer power to local authority so that the British could withdraw by June 1948.

Upon his arrival in India, Mountbatten and his wife became enamored with Nehru, and they began a close and lasting friendship. Jinnah was well impressed with Mountbatten's abilities and believed enough in his sincerity to consider him to be an honest broker. Although Mountbatten returned Jinnah's respect publicly, he loathed him personally. That animosity would figure prominently in the events that led to the British withdrawal and India's descent into a humanitarian crisis of untold misery.

Mountbatten had inherited a political mess and a humanitarian crisis of gigantic proportions. The interim government was not functioning, and the horrific violence that broke out in Punjab and Bengal was rapidly spreading to other provinces. Thus, the idea of partition, a solution that had been considered long before Mountbatten's arrival, received renewed attention as a quick way out of the morass, despite the fact that neither Jinnah nor Gandhi originally favored the idea; both men foresaw the social disruptions that such a division would create.

Discussions then turned to a plan drawn up by V.P. Menon, a Hindu civil servant and assistant to Mountbatten, which proposed a partition of India accompanied by an offer of dominion status to each part. Menon's plan, which had amalgamated ideas that had found expression in other plans, brought together proposals that both he and Mountbattan believed would satisfy both the Congress and the Muslim League. The first draft was finished in early May. On May 10 Mountbatten, acting on an "absolute hunch,"[35] gave Nehru an advance copy for his perusal. This was a prudent courtesy but one not equally extended to Jinnah.[36] Nehru's swift and profoundly negative reaction perplexed the viceroy, since most of the articles in the draft had already received Nehru's approval in earlier discussions.

At that moment, it looked as though the Menon–Mountbattan plan might be dead on arrival. Recalling the incident later, Menon wrote that the next morning Nehru's "usual charm and smile had deserted him."[37] After listening to a litany of objections, Menon set out to revise the draft. He had only several hours to do so, as Mountbattan had a strict travel schedule and wanted to get Nehru on board with the proposal before he left Simla later that day. Fortunately, Menon's revisions, which were based on the two-country formula, passed Nehru's tests and the document finally made it to the principles for initial approval on May 16, 1947.

The draft agreement stipulated that India and Pakistan could each convene a constituent assembly but that they would be governed for a transitional period by a governor-general. It also called for the establishment of a special border commission to oversee the partitioning of the provinces according to their populations. Although the agreement satisfied no one completely, both the Congress and League understood that the only alternative was continued chaos. Congress agreed to the document, but Jinnah would only give a spoken agreement in principle. Perturbed by what he perceived to be Jinnah's petulance, Mountbatten threatened to turn power over to an interim government anyway, even in the event of a Muslim rejection. But the crafty Jinnah, again playing his cards close to his chest, called Mountbattan's bluff. Jinnah calmly replied that he (Jinnah) "could not stop such a step in any case."[38] It proved to be the defining moment in Mountbatten's negotiations with the man he despised greatly. The agreement could move forward, but on Jinnah's terms.

The tenets of the Mountbatten-Menon partition plan would have the greatest impact on Punjab and Bengal. According to the agreement, Hindu and Muslim populations in each area would meet separately and decide either for or against partition. If either party voted in favor, partition would proceed. While on the surface that seems like a reasonable proposal, Jinnah again opposed it on the grounds that it would disrupt the communal fabric of those regions and most likely dislocate entire populations. Jinnah had always used this argument to support his six-province vision of Pakistan, and, of course, his assessment that major population transfers would have to take place was correct. But despite his long-standing opposition to partition, he now had to accept the innate logic of it: If Muslims could demand a division of India to give voice to their national aspirations, why not allow the Sikhs the same? Thus, the pragmatic Jinnah came to accept the idea of partition, not as a desirable option, but as a political expedient.

Although the Muslim League council also disagreed with the decision to partition those areas, it followed Jinnah's lead and urged him to accept the arrangement "as a compromise." Thus, the League could claim a victory in its battle to create Pakistan, but it had to accept the loss of East Punjab and West Bengal in order to achieve it. Congress was not happy either, and there were those in its leadership who felt that they had sold out to the British and Muslims. Gandhi had to step into the awkward position of supporting the plan, but in order to persuade the others he felt it necessary to give a veiled threat that he would resign if they rejected it. Gandhi was a figure of such gravitas that the rank and file gave in and passed the resolution. While doing so they added the caustic comment that the "false doctrine of two-nations will be discredited and discarded by all"[39] eventually.

In order to secure Congress's acceptance of the Plan, Mountbatten had held out the carrot that if India agreed to remain within the Commonwealth for the time being, the British might withdraw their forces sooner than the original June 1948 deadline. Energized by the prospect of a swift evacuation, Nehru quickly agreed[40]; therefore, the official date for British withdrawal was advanced to August 15, 1947. On June 4, Mountbatten announced the agreement and drew instant acclaim across the globe. For a brief moment, an end to the turmoil seemed close at hand. The wisest people, however, realized that Mountbatten had struck a Faustian bargain. The accelerated timetable effectively meant that there would be less than six weeks to prepare for an orderly transition of power. An entire government would have to be dismantled and rebuilt. The Indian army would have to be divided too, with officers and soldiers forced to choose which country to serve without the benefit of any clear definitions of national identity to guide them. Everything fell under the partition's axe; even furniture and books were meticulously divided.[41] The transition would prove a bit easier for India, since it would inherit most of the old British administrative and governmental infrastructures. For Pakistan, however, the changeover portended a frantic and confused drive to create new institutions where none existed before.

From a state-building perspective the shortened timetable was a monumental error, but on the human level it was catastrophic. Sir Cyril Radcliffe took charge of the border commissions for both Bengal and Punjab and was given the thankless job of deciding what territory belonged to which state. Known more as a barrister than an ethnographer, Radcliffe had little preparation for the task at hand, having never even visited India before this appointment. Thousands refused to wait for the announcement of where the lines would be drawn. Wealthier people liquidated what assets they could and moved them to banks or safe investments after purchasing airline tickets to take them to a place of relative security. The poorer people took to the streets and trains. Those in authority who had not stuck their heads in the sand could see a coming tidal wave of refugees and displaced people. There were no preparations to provide food, housing, or sanitation for the mass migrations to come.

On July 18, the India Independence Bill passed swiftly through Parliament and in August 1947, two new nations officially came into being. On the 14th, Jinnah and Mountbatten participated in a ceremony in Karachi naming the *Quaid-e-Azam* the Governor-General of Pakistan.[42] Just before midnight, Nehru announced the dominion status of the independent state of India.[43] The two nations were still a long way from stability, however. In Balochistan, Masood Ghaznavi had little time to revel in the victory of Pakistan either, as the Muslim League had still not gained control of the tribal chieftains (sardars).

Chapter 4. "Up from the Dust" 93

The big issue in Balochistan was the continuance of the tribal feudal system. Quetta was one of the few areas where there was an administration of elected people, otherwise there were no assemblies. And many of these sardars would not openly oppose Pakistan but they would not relinquish their [tribal] authority either. They were organizing ... then the students took the lead. We started our own newspaper called "The People"—I became the editor—and two or three big public rallies were held in order to counter the offensive of the sardars, because in the final analysis the question of Pakistan had to be settled by a plebiscite. So, the Muslim League leaders of national importance came to the two very big rallies we had and ... funny now when I think back...[at] both the public meetings, a hundred thousand people came to hear the speakers. The state secretary was this humble person [author's note: Ghaznavi himself] ... I had to introduce the speakers, and the state secretary was the one who begins the [rally] and ends it. So I did both.[44]

Independence celebrations ended abruptly two days later when the authorities finally revealed the Radcliffe line to the public. To everyone's dismay, the line paid little attention to the economic or social realities of the region. The result was massive confusion over what territory belonged to which nation, and angry populations suddenly found that they had become subjects of a state for which they had no kinship or allegiance. Thus, the relocations that had begun as a small trickle a month earlier rapidly turned into torrents of people, setting in motion one of the largest mass migrations in human history and unleashing intense suffering and privation on millions of innocent men, women, and children. In Punjab, random violence erupted as the different ethnic groups each laid claims to sections of territory.

The dislocations there hit the Sikh community the hardest. Although the Sikh population numbered about six million, they were dispersed throughout the Punjab. These noble people who had served the British army honorably during the past world wars now faced having their homeland carved up by the stroke of a pen on a map. Once champions of partition, the Sikhs now discovered that they would not get their own independent nation as they had hoped. Instead, the Radcliffe line intersected their homeland, and the majority of the Sikh population found itself in India while many of its sacred sites wound up in Pakistan. There was talk of rebellion against the decision, but in the end the Sikh leadership acquiesced.

Sectarian violence grew rampant as populations hurried to evict unwanted residents from their property to clear territory for incoming co-religionist refugees. Those who would not leave "voluntarily" were simply murdered. Women were captured as prizes, and the "luckier" ones became substitute wives or concubines to replace those who had been "appropriated" by the other side. Yet others suffered mutilations of their faces and breasts.⁴⁵ Rape became a ubiquitous practice, and because of the social stigmas accompanying it, some women elected to remain in a life of servitude to their captors rather than return home where they faced shame and possible death at the hands of their own family members.

During the worst of the lawlessness, indiscriminate killings reached a feverish tempo. The withdrawing British regular army troops could not be relied upon for peacekeeping. Even had the troops stayed, the Punjabi boundary force was a paltry 25,000 soldiers at most; hardly enough to keep hundreds of thousands of rioters at bay. Consequently, the only laws that existed were the internal codes of the gangs that started each day with the express purpose of annihilating each other. In their lust for blood they spared no weaponry. Rifles, hand grenades, mortars, and other military hardware down to the most rudimentary swords, clubs, spears, and rocks all saw use as instruments of death. Angry crowds frequently attacked refugee trains and massacred anyone they could find, so travel schedules were deliberately kept from the public. Gangs on execution sprees obliterated entire villages. Such attacks were not restricted to the Punjab and Bengal. The carnage spilled over into other areas with equal vehemence.⁴⁶

As autumn progressed, the subcontinent sunk into a full-blown humanitarian crisis. Expenditures on refugee needs wrecked both economies before they could even get going. For the educated and the well-to-do, the adjustment could be swift—but for the poorer and uneducated classes, partition meant increased hardship and years trying to survive as refugees. The fact that they now could consider themselves free citizens of a new independent state must have been little compensation for the privations they had to endure. Accurate figures are difficult to come by, but scholars estimate that 12 million people were dislocated,⁴⁷ a figure rivaling the numbers of displaced persons and refugees in Europe following the Second World War.

At first, both governments tried to discourage and even halt the movement of people, since the partition plans had always envisioned that the two nations would have minorities even after independence. But as the number of refugees exploded, the authorities had to step in to try to organize orderly evacuations based primarily on religious identification. By the end of 1947, three million souls resided in refugee camps, one million in Punjab alone. Many of those camps would remain in existence for years to come, and in some cases, they evolved into permanent brick and mortar settlements.

Deep in the heart of the new Pakistan, Balochistan endured only minor disturbances, possibly because there was not as large a non–Muslim population as elsewhere. Nevertheless, those non–Muslims now clamored to get out and there had to be some effort made to assist them. Ghaznavi recalled how he and many of his classmates, both boys and girls, volunteered to help relocate the resident Sikhs and Hindus. He, like many others, then volunteered to work in the transit camps. The sight of so many impoverished people proved to be one of the most indelible and horrific images in his memory. In the camp where he volunteered, Ghaznavi witnessed untold hardships, beatings, and murders of defenseless innocents. One incident remained vivid in his memory sixty years later. Hearing a loud scuffle, Ghaznavi and his friend walked over to discover a horrific scene.

> There was an old woman, like a crushed sparrow ... just a handful of bones... [His friend] asked them what...[they answered] 'she was abusing Pakistan, cussing Pakistan ... and we all got mad, and we killed her.' And he got furious. The first thing he could say was "you dogs" and "you bastards" ... and the people just melted away. And there she was lying there, just like a little ... the only thing that could come to my mind is ... like a little crushed sparrow. I'm told there were many cases like that ... people who came walking hundreds of miles, probably having lost their families, slaughtered before their eyes, probably they lost everything before their eyes. They lost their minds ... she and they lost their mind and talking all kinds of things, some abusing Pakistan at this moment. So she might have been one of that case, but that one picture in my mind—I can't erase it.[48]

Despite this vivid recollection, Ghaznavi quietly admitted that at the time he could not focus on individual suffering; the only way he could remain sane in the camps was to "stay diffused."[49] The woman he saw murdered was only one of thousands, and her horrible death was undoubtedly repeated in transit camps all across India.

* * *

For the Asian subcontinent, the year 1947 truly was, as Nehru syllogistically wrote, "a watershed dividing the past from the future."[50] The Great Partition would have repercussions long after 1947 lapsed into history. Colonial imperialism, which had once been a major motivational force in the foreign policies of European nations, was now a dead issue. Simply put, success in India and Pakistan emboldened other colonies to push toward their own statehood. For the next two decades, colonial territories all across Asia and Africa rose up against their overlords; the list of emergent nations is far too lengthy to be included here. However, it would be wrong to ascribe the beginnings of the modern era of self-determination to any instantaneous explosion. Colonialism was a process that contained within it the very seeds of its own destruction. It was the occupiers themselves who encouraged Indian political self-awareness in the nineteenth century by providing their Indian subjects with access to the finest British universities.

By the turn of the century, Indians had become well-educated and effective administrators, equally capable of running the complex affairs of government as their imperial overlords. As Britain slugged through the Great War, promises of increased self-rule had to be made in order to win Indian support for the war effort. Likewise, the economic dislocations of the early 1920s and then again during the Great Depression of the 1930s were enough to convince many that budgetary expenditures for colonial ventures could better be applied on the home front. It would therefore also be a mistake to ascribe the independence movements to the dislocations of World War II; the war with Hitler simply accelerated a process that had started long before the conflict began.

This schema of gradual withdrawal serves as a good paradigm to explain the decolonizing fever that swept across the globe in the contemporary postwar era. It is also instructive that the liberation of the Indian subcontinent was an object lesson in two very different examples of revolutionary action: Gandhi's passive resistance and Jinnah's "direct action." The outcomes suggest that passive resistance is more effective in colonial independence movements, whereas secessionist movements are better served by violence. Since both approaches proved successful, future freedom fighters had options when deciding which course of action to apply to any given situation.

The examples also show how powerful religion can be as a motivational force. Despite his avowed secularism, Jinnah was not above casting the struggle for Pakistan in religious terms, and he often used the Islamic faith to help propel his political aspirations. Consequently, Pakistan became the first postwar state to be defined by religion, with Israel following closely behind. Both examples show that nationalism based on religious principles can be a powerful tool in skilled hands. However, as subsequent Israeli-Palestinian relations have shown, religious nationalism can also arouse antithetical religious nationalism in hostile neighbors. Evidently, building nations based around religious identities can be a perilous tactic to adopt.

Another outcome of the Great Partition is the deep-seated distrust bordering on hatred between Pakistan and India that remains a reality of south–Asian politics to this day. As political disagreement devolved into outright violence, no one accepted responsibility for initiating the crisis. Instead, it was the "other side" that was blamed for the "excesses" and the atrocities that were so common in the daily lives of Hindus, Muslims, and Sikhs in 1947. It would be a fruitless exercise to point fingers now, as the damage—in the form of 200,000 or more dead and countless more wounded—has been done.

Amidst the enormity of this holocaust, history must not forget the anguish endured by 12 million innocent refugees of all faiths. The bloodbath of 1947 became the prism through which these two nations have viewed their policies toward each other ever since. As the smaller of the two countries, Pakistan has felt threatened by domination from across the border, hence it is no accident that military dictatorships have repeatedly subverted the democratic order there. India too has experienced its share of troubles as the world's most populous democracy. Part of the price it had to pay to hold on to its universalist approach to statehood is the discontent among the religious and ethnic minorities (including a very large residual Muslim population) within its borders. When there is unrest or instability in India, it is all too easy to lay blame on the non–Hindu populations.

But the most pernicious problem is the unresolved question of the disputed territories. Partition seemed a logical solution to the Hindu-Muslim-Sikh strife. But in a complex social structure like India's, geographic demarcation lines are hazy at best and a partition can never be completely accurate or fair. The Radcliffe line created lasting enmity among those who had their land "usurped." Such hatred devolved into civil violence, as happened along the Punjabi and Bengali borders in 1947. But when civil disagreements are backed by governmental power, they can turn into outright armed conflict. Within a scant two months of independence, Pakistan and India were at war over the disputed territories in Jammu and Kashmir.

Lasting over a year, the "First Kashmir War" ended with a partition of Kashmir that resolved nothing. Both sides still laid claim to the territory of the other, and war would erupt again in 1965. The Indo-Pakistani feud found new expression in 1971 (resulting in the creation of the state of Bangladesh out of what had been East Pakistan) and again in 1999. The latter conflict, although limited in scope, may be the most significant as India and Pakistan, now both armed with atomic weapons, stepped dangerously close to a nuclear war. Today, the presence of insurgency forces in Kashmir bears witness to the tenuous peace the two nations still struggle to maintain.

The Pakistani and Indian experience reveals a much more insidious trend in contemporary history; namely, how easily populations can objectify and demonize the "other." While holocausts and genocides are certainly not new phenomena, the cataclysm on the Indian subcontinent is particularly disturbing because of its relative spontaneity. The most infamous genocides of the twentieth century (Hitler's pogroms against the Jews, Stalin's starvation of the Ukrainian people, and the Armenian Massacres as examples) were all directed by governmental action. By contrast, the murderous killing sprees that engulfed India were organized and conducted by the civilian populations themselves during a period of political instability. Muslims, Hindus, and Sikhs needed little or no official encouragement to begin their rampages. Their ethnic and religious hatreds were sufficient fuel to propel them into an orgy of destruction that their leaders, despite all good intentions, were powerless to stop.

The rapes, murders, and mutilations that attended the clearing of border territories in Punjab and Bengal were akin more to what would later be called "ethnic cleansing" and provide a chilling example of what can happen when multinational or multiethnic political structures collapse. The Indo-Pakistani holocaust of 1947, like the holocaust in the former Yugoslavia during the 1990s and the more recent war in Darfur, are the detritus of ethno-religious allegiances run amuck in the absence of law.

Nationalism, which once had been considered a positive force that united peoples, now rears its head as a negative and divisive force. The failures of British India, Czechoslovakia, Yugoslavia, and the Soviet Union illustrate this transformation as ever smaller ethnic groups seek to break away from the larger nation state to claim their right of self-determination. Whether the discussion turns to Chechnya, East Timor, or Kurdistan, any study of contemporary separatist movements would do well to start with the events of 1947 and learn from the example of the partition of India.

* * *

Neither Gandhi nor Jinnah would live long enough to see how their efforts would play out. Gandhi was assassinated in January 1948 by an extreme Hindu nationalist who had thought the *Mahatma* was too conciliatory to Muslim demands. Jinnah died later that same year, a victim of chronic tuberculosis that he had attempted to keep hidden from his associates. Lord Mountbatten had three more decades to think about the decisions he made back in 1947. Although his final report to Parliament in September 1948 rationalized his efforts as the best possible result under the circumstances,[51] he admitted to an interviewer in his later years that he felt as though he had failed.[52] His life came to an end in August 1979 when a bomb planted on board his fishing boat by Irish Republican Army (IRA) terrorists exploded.

Masood Ghaznavi took a job working for the Pakistani branch of the Associated Press while finishing his studies in Quetta, and eventually broke the story of the accession of the state of Kalat to Pakistan. Thereafter he worked as a journalist, reporting on the country he had helped to found. In subsequent decades, Ghaznavi witnessed the ideals he fought for subverted by the imposition of martial law and military government. Some of his compatriots resigned themselves to it, but Ghaznavi chose to leave Pakistan for the United States. Nevertheless, the memories of his moment in history persist.

Chapter 4. "Up from the Dust"

In 1991, Ghaznavi received a National Heroes of Pakistan medal for his involvement in the epochal events of 1947. In his self-effacing and quiet manner, he could not even recall some of the things that the official citation from the Pakistani government credited him with doing. Ghaznavi explained, "In those days, we were in a daze. We didn't think about sleeping, we didn't think about eating, we didn't think about our clothes. It was one big daze … a mixture of jubilation on the one hand and of fear and crisis on the other."[53] Indo-Pakistani relations are similarly conflicted today. Whether they can stand up from the dust of their shared history to live at peace with each other or not remains an open question.

Masood Ghaznavi (third from right) receiving Hero of Pakistan award, 1991 (courtesy Nadeem Ghaznavi).

Chapter 5

"One-in-a-million"

Sgt. Paul Shimer and the Rise of the Anglo-American Partnership

The New York dockyards filled with the usual throngs of spectators on Friday morning May 23, 1947, as the *Queen Elizabeth* eased into her moorings after an uneventful four-day voyage. As the huge ship began to disgorge her passengers, a small mob of Associated Press and local wire reporters boarded the vessel to corner Nancy (Lady) Astor as she prepared to disembark. As a wealthy heir, feminist, and the United Kingdom's first female member of Parliament, the former American citizen–turned British subject was no stranger to the limelight. Although she had left Parliament two years earlier, Astor's witty and outspoken style still drew requests for her political opinions wherever she went. Today was no exception, and she willingly met with a group of journalists in the ocean liner's garden lounge.

When a reporter asked what she thought about the British government's policy in Palestine, Astor opined that "we have got to see that democratic thinking people—English speaking people—who believe in justice and mercy, prevail."[1] Her frank answer smacked of ethnocentrism, but it reflected what many people around the world were hoping; namely, that the United Kingdom and the United States would build upon the alliance that toppled Nazism and continue working in concert to find solutions to the world's complex problems. What Lady Astor may not have known is that—at least on a personal level—such *rapprochement* was already underway, even as she spoke. On board the *QE* that day was another British political figure, more famous locally than nationally, who was travelling to the United States to fulfill a promise he had made to an American soldier back in 1944. That covenant and the events that flow from it teach us lessons about duty, sacrifice, and (ultimately) trans–Atlantic friendships that would survive for decades.

Chapter 5. "One-in-a-million"

* * *

Reginald James Stranger received none of the attention Lady Astor got when he stepped onto the New York pier, despite the fact that he too had a long and interesting public life. Rex, as his friends called him, was born in 1891 on the channel island of Guernsey. Like many young boys, Rex spent much of his youth playing football or boxing and developing a passion for sport that stayed with him throughout his life. Within days of the United Kingdom's declaration of war on Germany in 1914, Stranger enlisted and eventually rose to the rank of captain in the Royal Irish Fusiliers, serving in the Balkan campaigns, in Palestine, and in France. Over the course of his military service, Stranger distinguished himself as an extremely capable officer and was awarded the Military Cross and the French *Croix de Guerre* for his meritorious service.[2]

After the war, Stranger relocated to Southampton where he became a prominent businessman and entrepreneur. His political career began in 1933 as councilor for Freemantle where, among his other duties, he worked without pay to improve the profitability of the local airport.[3] Friends described him as a man possessing a "liveliness of imagination, capacity for hard work, and a degree of moral courage by no means common"[4] who threw himself into tasks with boundless energy. Although a man of high political ambitions and an intense drive to succeed, Stranger also endeared himself to many with his "patience and understanding"[5] and his ability to bring diverse peoples together to accomplish tasks others had dismissed as too difficult.

All of these personality traits were put to the test when, in November of 1943, Rex Stranger became the mayor of the city of Southampton. It was a most difficult time to rise to political prominence. The Port of Southampton, situated directly on the English Channel and a prime staging area for ocean-going transport, was on the front lines in the war against Nazi Germany and a priority wartime target. Churchill's government closed the port to long-distance shipping after the evacuation at Dunkirk and from the summer of 1940 on, the city endured more than 50 major attacks from German Stuka and Junker bombers during the "Blitz." The worst raids, which began late in November 1940, left most of the city center destroyed.

By the end of 1941, however, as the threat of a German invasion diminished, Southampton sprung back to life as a reception port for Lend-Lease supplies and merchant marine vessels from the United States.[6] By 1944, Southampton and its sub-ports at Weymouth, Poole, and Hamble, now designated "14th Port" in the U.S. Army Transportation Corps, became major staging points for Allied troops in anticipation of the D-Day invasion of occupied France. As the city's population swelled with the influx of American GIs, soldiers and citizens were forced to deal with overcrowded conditions. Despite fears that British and Americans would not get along, the extent of fraternization amazed everyone.

Out of gratitude and a spirit of comradeship, the people of Southampton did everything they could to make the American GIs feel welcome. Local men and American soldiers often listened to music, shared a smoke, or took tea together. Women routinely cooked meals (often with food provided from Army stocks, which was plentiful) or did laundry for the soldiers who were billeted in their homes.[7] Strong personal relationships emerged, and as the H-Hour approached many families threw going away parties for their new-found friends. Considering the privations and destruction the people of Southampton had already endured, such largesse was truly remarkable. It does, however, go a long way to explain why no serious disturbances occurred during the American "occupation" of Southampton. GIs felt at home there.

Rex Stranger became mayor just as the plans for D-Day were set into motion, so it fell upon him to keep civilian government functioning during the largest buildup of military personnel in history. By all indications he did so quite effectively. Some American Army brass valued his help so highly that they eventually nicknamed him "Mr. Southampton." As Colonel Leo Meyer, the commander of the 14th Port during the D-Day build-up, remembered later, "when we needed something, he produced it … and there was no red tape or lend lease involved."[8] Colonel Meyer had firsthand knowledge of Stranger's compassion. One day, an over-worked Meyer nodded off in the Stranger's garden during a visit. When he finally awoke, he was in a nice comfortable bed thanks to the thoughtfulness of the Strangers, who had seen to it that he was carried someplace where he could rest.[9]

Average GIs soon associated Stranger with all the kindnesses they were receiving in the city, prompting Meyer to say later that if the American soldiers had been allowed to vote in local elections, they would have made Stranger mayor for life. Clearly, his personable nature, combined with a genuine desire to make the soldiers feel comfortable and safe in his hometown, made Rex Stranger a popular figure with millions of American GI's who had made Southampton their temporary home. One of those soldiers would change Stranger's life forever.

It was October 25, four and a half months after the initial D-Day landings. Stranger often made a morning trip to the dockyards to keep a watchful eye on things, but that day he was on his way to perform a most unusual ceremony. Weeks before, someone in the American transportation command had calculated just how many men had passed through the Southampton ports on their way to the European theater and determined that the one-millionth GI was about to embark. Stranger had made plans to recognize this achievement and the efforts of all American soldiers with a public display commemorating the milestone. With the permission of the U.S. commanders, he invited the military and civilian brass to participate and made sure that the press and military photographers were there to witness the event. As soldiers lined up to board the transport ship, Sgt. Murray Ley of the transportation corps, charged with counting the soldiers as they mounted the gangplank, singled out the "lucky" individual. Private Paul S. Shimer, Jr., just seconds earlier an anonymous face in the queue, suddenly became "The Millionth Yank."

Private Shimer turned out to be well-suited for the role. He was born in the small town of McConnellsburg, an agricultural community nestled in the rolling hills of south-central Pennsylvania. As a young boy in the 1920s, Paul got into the entrepreneurial spirit with his brother, John, by peddling water to beleaguered motorists struggling to have their Model T's and A's negotiate one of the many hills surrounding town. His parents were, as his sister Kathryn put it, "particular."[10] Paul Sr. was a town barber and his mother, when not busy raising eight children, made most of the clothing for the family. Paul Jr. ultimately picked up on his mother's

Mayor Reginald Stranger greeting the One Millionth Yank, Private Paul Shimer, on the docks of Southampton, October 25, 1944 (courtesy Southampton City Council).

passion for sewing and developed a taste for good clothes as he grew up. For a time, he worked for the local dry goods store where he could stock up on the latest fashions and often took umbrage when brother John "borrowed" his things without asking.[11]

With a bright future ahead of him in retail sales, Paul married Marian Mehaffey, a woman he asked out on a buddy's dare. Soon, the couple became a family with the addition of a daughter, Patricia Ann, in 1940. Paul found work with the J.C. Penney store chain, so the family then relocated to nearby Chambersburg, a city whose main claim to fame was that it had been burned down by Robert E. Lee's Confederate army retreating from the battle of Gettysburg in 1863. A year and a half later, he was transferred to a store in Salisbury, Maryland, as assistant manager. He had just taken up this promising new position when he received notice to report for induction. Paul Shimer took basic training at Camp Wolters in Texas and within a matter of weeks shipped out for Europe as an infantry replacement. Like millions of other GIs, Paul Shimer left behind a job, a wife, and a young daughter to fight in a far-off war.[12] He was 26 years old.

As Private Shimer stepped off the gangplank that October day, the organizers of the event hung a wooden sign bearing the words "The Millionth Yank" around his neck. The large sign looked a bit awkward on Shimer, dressed sharply in his uniform and overcoat, as he walked over to a makeshift stage in the middle of the pier to meet the dignitaries waiting to honor him. Present were high ranking brass from both the American and British armies, representatives of the women's auxiliary forces, and mayor Reginald Stranger. One by one, the dignitaries delivered speeches honoring the Millionth Yank. Stranger also spoke, and at the end of his address he shook Shimer's hand and presented him with a typed letter.[13] In it he had written:

> Dear Crusader,
>
> I am honoured to greet you, the millionth soldier of the United States Forces to sail from the Port of Southampton since "D" Day.
>
> As I shake your hand you are to me a symbol of the might and power of your great country. We in Southampton have witnessed with admiration, the tremendous quantity of wonderful equipment your Army has taken to France; it is the greatest build-up of military might the world has ever seen.
>
> What impressed us most of all is the spirit and soldierly bearing of your Army. You have been the best ambassadors any country could have. Your friendliness to the civilian population, your great kindness to the children (who I fear must have worried you sometimes), and your high purpose, has been a great inspiration and encouragement to us, most particularly during the period before "D" Day and immediately after, when we had every reason to expect heavy enemy action on the Town and Port.
>
> We deeply appreciate the fact that the United States did not enter this war for

Chapter 5. "One-in-a-million"

self-aggrandizement or territorial gain, but for the sole purpose of helping to free the world from oppression.

I wish you the best of luck and good health for the future. I pray God you and your brave comrades may soon be free from the dangers of war, so that you may be able to return as speedily as possible to your homes.

Yours sincerely,

R.J. Stranger Mayor of Southampton

As the event drew to a close, Stranger and Shimer found a few minutes to chat with each other directly. Although their private conversation will forever be lost to history, Stranger later recalled that they exchanged pleasantries and expressed hopes that they could meet again after the war to celebrate the Allied victory together. Private Shimer mentioned his wife and infant daughter back home and asked that the wooden plaque be sent to them somehow. Stranger told him that he would see to it. He later recounted, "I told him to come back and visit my wife and me and I would help him to start his daughter in life."[14] After assuring Stranger that he would return someday, Private Shimer walked back up the gangplank and onto the waiting transport ship. The ceremony and the conversation were over quickly; so quickly, in fact, that Mayor Stranger never asked anyone the soldier's name. He would not have gotten it anyway. For security reasons, such information was kept secret.

The war lasted another six months. In that time, hundreds of thousands more GIs left Southampton for France. Ironically, Shimer's clothing-pilfering brother, John, was on the gangplank when the "Two-millionth Yank" was feted in January of 1945. Before the war ended, a total of 3.64 million men had gone through Southampton's docks[15]—a feat roughly equivalent to transporting the entire population of President Truman's home state of Missouri.[16] The ceremony that had brought Stranger and Shimer together receded into memory as everyone prepared themselves for the impending collapse of the Third Reich. Stranger's year as mayor ended in November 1944, although he continued to serve Southampton under his successor as Deputy Mayor, the office he held on V-E Day. Private Shimer made it to France with the Third Division of the U.S. Seventh Army, a unit that had fought its way up the Rhone River valley all the way to the Alsatian border with Germany. Paul, now Sergeant, fought valiantly and earned a Bronze Star along with a purple heart for an injury he suffered in battle during January 1945. The Seventh Army then swung into Germany as part of Operation Undertone and secured the capture of the German Palatinate and Saarland. With the Reich now disintegrating and the war rapidly concluding, Paul's unit advanced into northern Bavaria. On April 14, somewhere near Bamberg, Sgt. Paul Shimer was killed by two explosions (most likely land mines) while leading his men in an attack on a strategic hill. It was only three weeks before the war ended.

Back home, Marian Shimer knew nothing about her husband's celebrity. Due to wartime censorship restrictions, news of the "Millionth Yank" had not reached the home front. The War Department finally released the pictures of the "Millionth Yank" ceremonies to the press and the local newspaper, the Chambersburg *Public Opinion*, printed them in the morning edition of April 28. In a cruel twist of fate, Marian Shimer received the War Department telegram informing her of her husband's death only one hour after she had seen his photos in the local newspaper.[17] Rex Stranger did not learn about the fate of the soldier he had met until a friend inquired with the U.S. War Department several months after the war ended. The news of his death must have affected Stranger deeply, as he recalled the promise he had made to him on that makeshift stage in Southampton harbor. "My wife and I talked about Sergeant Shimer and his family," Stranger later recalled, "We knew we wanted to visit them, but we wanted to do more than that to help show what we in England thought of the millionth Yank and all his gallant comrades in arms."[18]

No one would have faulted Stranger if he had not gone through with his pledge, uttered in the midst of a hectic day during a moment of small talk. But for Stranger, a man noted for his sense of duty and obligation, fulfilling his promise became a personal crusade. He decided to honor Shimer with a monetary gift and present it personally during a visit with his entire family in the United States. Despite the postwar privations all around England, Stranger started a trust fund (mostly with his own money) for the benefit of Patricia Ann, Sgt. Shimer's little daughter. Eventually, the fund totaled £1,000 (approximately $61,450 in 2024 dollars), but because of British treasury restrictions, he was not allowed to remove it from the country.[19] Rex had originally planned to accompany the Southampton soccer team (of which he was a director) on its trip to the United States, but when that tour was cancelled, the Strangers decided to go by themselves. Booking passage on the *Queen Elizabeth*, Councilman and Mrs. Stranger left England for the United States on May 18 to visit old friends, see the sights, and fulfill the promise he made three years earlier.

* * *

It was their first trip to the United States. The Strangers still had plenty of political connections, so news of their impending visit spread fast. William Beck, the American Consul General and good friend of the Strangers, took the liberty of mailing several contacts he had in the United States to make sure that the couple would be welcomed. The Chambersburg Town Council found out about the visit from the British Information

Service. On May 21, with only nine or ten days to go before the Strangers' anticipated arrival, the Council met and authorized William Etter, town Burgess, to organize a citizen's committee and charge it with devising a public demonstration of welcome.[20] Evidently, the citizens of Chambersburg worked fast for the committee, aptly if awkwardly named the "Chambersburg Shimer Memorial Committee of Welcome to Rex Stranger, Wartime Mayor of Southampton, England," began its work the very next day.

Fifteen of Chambersburg's most prominent citizens, including the commanders of the local Veterans of Foreign Wars (VFW) post and the American Legion, a local college president, a judge, the editor-in-chief of the local newspaper, a Chamber of Commerce representative, and a local plumbing and heating contractor, stepped up to work on the event. Claiming that the citizens of Chambersburg "consider this occasion an international gesture which merits highest official recognition,"[21] the committee sent invitations to everyone who might come. Telegrams went to Pennsylvania governor John H. Duff, General Dwight D. Eisenhower, Pennsylvania Senators Francis J. Myers and Edward Martin, Congressman Chester Gross, Secretary of War Robert Patterson, Secretary of State George C. Marshall, and even President Harry Truman himself. At Stranger's suggestion, invitations were also sent to the former commanders of the 14th Port, Colonel Meyer and Colonel Sherman L. Kiser.

The committee members set out to create a welcome ceremony befitting a visiting dignitary, one that would also acknowledge Stranger's generosity. As a counter-gesture of friendship and goodwill, the committee established a trust fund of its own that Stranger could take back with him to Southampton. Under the direction of finance subcommittee chair Horace A. Kottkamp (the local plumbing and heating contractor), four banks volunteered to serve as collection points for donations to the "Children of Southampton Fund." The target was $3,200[22]—a tidy sum in 1947 roughly equivalent to about $45,000 in 2024 dollars. They only had about a week to gather the money, so everyone went into high gear.

Charles Nicklas, the editor of the *Public Opinion* (and himself a committee member), urged his readers to contribute. "The appeal of a child is strong at any time; the appeal of a child in distress is irresistible, and there are many children in Southampton … in distress," Nicklas wrote in an opinion piece. "Give promptly. Give generously."[23] And the community did. Car dealers and repair garages chipped in for $450. Town merchants put together almost $250. Chambersburg's industries managed to contribute $500. The local Elks Club pitched in $50. Within days, this small community had raised $2,500 of the target amount. By the time of the ceremony, the fund totaled $3,000.

Kottkamp deserves much of the credit for marshaling so much money so quickly. Yet, his most interesting "contribution" had nothing to do with cash. In a discussion with Robert Frecon, a local fruit grower (most likely to solicit him for a donation), Frecon suggested that the community might actually donate fruit instead of cash. At the meeting of the fruit growers' cooperative that Monday night, Kottkamp introduced the idea to the membership. He argued that such a gift would be particularly appropriate, since Franklin County (where Chambersburg is located) was at the time the second largest apple-producing county in Pennsylvania. Looking beyond county borders, Kottkamp added that such a gift might also "increase understanding between the people of the United States and England and thus strengthen the foundation of world amity."[24] The idea apparently went over well, for the cooperative agreed to donate a "carload"[25] of apples to the children of Southampton and have it shipped to them by Christmas.

* * *

As the preparations in Chambersburg moved forward, the Strangers took to seeing the sights in New York City. Although their mission to Chambersburg was their paramount objective, it was not their only stop in what would be a five-week stay in the United States. The visitors also intended to spend some time sightseeing and looking up friends across the rest of the country and some of Canada. Three days in New York allowed them to meet up with their old friend Colonel Meyer, the former commander of the U.S. 14th Port—the same man who had fallen asleep in their garden three years earlier. Ever the sportsman, Stranger even got the opportunity to kick out the first ball of the second half at a soccer match between Ulster United (Toronto) and a team of German-American all-stars being held in New York.[26]

With only about five weeks to accomplish all this travel before their return voyage, the Strangers' itinerary was extremely tight. Originally, they had planned to visit the Shimers on June 1. But, given that the main purpose of their visit was to honor a fallen American soldier, it seemed appropriate that they arrive on May 30 instead, to coincide with Memorial Day ceremonies. After a few telephone calls with the committee, Stranger managed to rearrange his schedule to accommodate the reception plans. On the day before Memorial Day, the Strangers were in Washington, D.C., to visit another wartime acquaintance. Back in Chambersburg, all of the arrangements had all been made—the programs and schedules prepared, traffic preparations set, speeches written—all in anticipation of the arrival of the dignitaries.

The weather could not have been better on the morning of the 30th;

the air was cool, but the sun shone brightly in the sky with no threat of rain. That Memorial Day morning began—as so many others had (and have) across America—with a parade complete with the requisite local high school bands, Scout troops, and representatives of veterans' organizations marching the streets to the cheers and applause of approving crowds. Rex and Trudy Stranger were not there, however. As the parade stepped off, the Strangers were at Washington's National Airport meeting a delegate from the Chambersburg borough council who would escort them to Chambersburg on board a private plane that had been flown to Washington specifically to pick them up.

About an hour and a half later, they landed at Chambersburg airport where they met Burgess Etter, chair of the Committee, who whisked them off under state police escort to the Hotel Washington in town. After a quick press conference, the Shimer family arrived for their first meeting with the man who had come to honor their son, husband, and father. After a brief exchange (the ceremonies were supposed to start at 11 a.m. and they were running behind), the entire group walked to the courthouse to begin the public ceremony, with Patricia Ann holding Stranger's hand the entire way.[27]

The platform outside the courthouse, bedecked with both American and British flags and protected by a color guard, soon swelled as the Strangers, the Shimers, and the Chambersburg council committee members took their places. Despite all of the regrets[28] that had been sent earlier, some dignitaries did show up. The local Congressman, Chester Gross, was in attendance as was Hugh McClelland, the British consul-general, representing the British Ambassador, Lord Inverchapel. Colonel Meyer also made the trip. The festivities began with an invocation, followed by Councilman Etter's introduction of Mr. and Mrs. Stranger and the presentation of the "keys to the city."

Stranger thanked him earnestly. Taking the microphone, Stranger spoke to his purpose in coming to Chambersburg. "I am here today to mourn with you one of your townsmen, Sgt. Paul Shimer, whom I knew as the Millionth Yank," Stranger explained. "He impressed himself on my memory for his soldierly bearing … one of the millions of young men who fought this war not to increase the territory of the United States of America or for their own personal gain, but for the liberation of mankind from aggression."

His speech continued with a personal assessment of what Sgt. Shimer's sacrifice symbolized on a larger scale. "I believe the peace of the world can only be maintained by the very closest cooperation, understanding, frankness and good will between the United States of American and the British Commonwealth of Nations," Stranger intoned. "We must be ready and prepared to stand side by side to stop any attempts to interfere with our free democratic ways of life. Only by such cooperation can we feel satisfied that we have done all in our power to uphold the ideals for which your men and our men fought and gave their lives."[29]

Stranger handed Mrs. Shimer a sealed envelope containing a certificate acknowledging the £1,000 trust fund held back in Southampton. In addition, the Strangers also presented Mrs. Shimer and Patricia Ann with gold bracelets as a personal gift. Mrs. Shimer accepted the gifts "in behalf of all who served in the cause of freedom; in memory of those who paid the supreme sacrifice" and on behalf of her deceased husband, the one-millionth yank.

After a rendition of "God Save the King" by a local elementary school chorus and a few more comments of thanks from Mrs. Shimer and Mrs. Stranger, Paul Swain Havens, the President of Wilson College, stepped up to the microphone. After reciting the old truism that it is the children who suffer most from war, Havens produced what he called "a gift to the children of Southampton"—namely, the envelope bearing $3,000 from the people of Chambersburg. Suggesting that the gift might be used to buy foodstuffs that were in short supply in England, Havens said that the only condition on the gift was that it go to the children. "We wish the people of Southampton and of all the United Kingdom to know that they have a stake in the United States," Havens remarked. "Particularly we desire that your children feel the warmth of friendship that exists for them here ... for in our children lies our hope. Their smiles, their happiness, their welfare know no national boundaries."[30] Following straightaway was the announcement by R.C. McDonald, president of the Franklin County Horticultural Society, of the decision to send six hundred bushels of apples to Southampton for distribution to children at Christmas. The ceremony concluded with a rendition of God Bless America, which the entire crowd joined in singing.

The Chambersburg Rotary Club organized the luncheon that followed the ceremony—a fitting choice for several reasons. Rotary International has always been, and still is, dedicated to promoting understanding and friendship between nations. Guided by the Rotary slogan, "Service Above Self," many of the Chambersburg council members were Rotarians; so too was Mr. Stranger, who had once headed the international committee of his local club in Southampton. Rotary clubs across America had sent monetary contributions to England all through the war.

The day's activities, therefore, seemed a natural continuation of that support, and the luncheon proved a perfect venue to pause and reflect upon the significance of the day's festivities. Stranger boldly suggested that the day marked "the start of a very close association" between Chambersburg

Chapter 5. "One-in-a-million"

and Southampton, and he hoped that their example would "aid in the promotion of better understanding and cooperation"[31] between Britain and the United States as well. As if to offer proof that he was correct, the Rotarians presented Stranger with yet another gift; this time a check for $100 to assist in the Southampton disabled children's fund.

The hectic pace of the afternoon activities offered the participants little respite, however the Strangers had a little down-time at the conclusion of the luncheon before their next scheduled event, the laying of the wreath in Cedar Grove Cemetery. From there, they attended a reception at a local junior college and prep school to meet with the faculty at an informal welcoming picnic. Dinner at the Hotel Washington rounded out the day's events; 157 people attended the event, emceed by Judge Edmund Wingert. In his opening remarks, Wingert expressed his dismay at war and its cost in human life. "We hope that our catastrophes are behind us," he remarked, "but the hope can never be fulfilled merely by a union of nations or by an international court of justice. Unless we as individuals put aside selfishness and follow the Christian doctrine of self-sacrifice and service, we can have no assurance of peace."

Burgess Etter then read from letters sent by some of the invitees who could not attend, including one from William Hassett, President Truman's correspondence secretary, expressing best wishes and the hope that all in attendance would "be inspired by Sergeant Shimer's bravery."[32] Then came the speeches. Mr. McClelland, reading from a message sent by Lord Inverchapel, spoke of the "universal spirit of good-will" that existed between the peoples of the United States and Great Britain, and how the citizens of Chambersburg exhibited the best qualities in humanity, including "the doctrines of one world, of the good neighbor, and above all ... of Christian loving-kindness."[33]

Rex Stranger's keynote address talked about comradeship, drawing a comparison between the hospitality he had experienced in Chambersburg and Southampton's wartime efforts to make the American GIs feel at home. In closing, he expressed his faith in the United States and his hopes that it would continue to lead in world affairs for years to come. After the exchange of a few small gifts, the participants finally brought the evening's activities to a close.

Day two was nearly as busy as the first. Sunday, June 1, was to be their last day in Franklin County, so Mr. and Mrs. Stranger drove to McConnellsburg to visit briefly with the Shimer family at their home. Returning to Chambersburg via the local historical sites, the Strangers had only one more official duty to perform; a farewell luncheon at nearby Wilson College, hosted by President Havens. Their schedule was once again tight, as they were slated to appear on the radio show "We the People" with Marian

Shimer that same evening in New York City. At 3:50 p.m., the Strangers climbed aboard the same four-seater airplane that brought them to Chambersburg to make the one-hour flight to Camden, New Jersey's Central Airport and then further by ground transportation to New York City.

The radio show hit the airwaves at 10:30 that night and, considering the amount of effort it took to get to New York, they were on the air for only a few minutes.[34] Stranger recounted the story of his meeting the one-millionth Yank, and Mrs. Shimer recalled the day she heard of his death. After learning that the trust fund would be used to pay for Patricia's education, Stranger again expressed the hope that she and Patricia would come to visit Southampton someday. With the broadcast concluded, Mrs. Shimer returned to Chambersburg and Rex headed off with his wife on their tour of the United States.

* * *

A bitter, cold wind blew across the English Hampshires on Friday, December 19. Despite frigid temperatures, 25,000 primary school children emptied their classrooms all across Southampton to receive a small "token of affection" from people across the Atlantic Ocean they had never met. The shipment of apples from the Chambersburg Horticultural Society, all 600 bushels, had arrived and were ready for distribution. At the main ceremony at Bassett Green School on Honeysuckle Road, the new Mayor Frank Dibben, along with the local MPs, education officials, and other dignitaries, joined Rex Stranger in handing out the fruit. On hand was William Beck, the U.S. Consul General, who told reporters that he wished the people of Chambersburg "could see the happy faces" of the youngsters receiving their gifts. "Every apple and every box of foodstuffs" Stranger said to his young audience, "comes to you with the love and affection of the people of Chambersburg and Franklin County."

Barbara James, an 11-year-old student, asked Mayor Dibben to "thank our American cousins" in Chambersburg for the gift and send their "love and best Christmas greetings," which he did by cablegram the same day. At a separate ceremony, a local pastor summed up the gesture in a prayer. Thankful for the friendship the two nations enjoyed, the minister asked God to "implant into the hearts of these children and the children of the United States, a desire for closer relationship, that together they may break down all that hinders the fullness of life."[35]

Those barriers did come down, even if for a brief moment, that cold December day. In the scheme of things, it was a small gesture; but for a city that still reeled from economic hardship where foodstuffs were still difficult to come by, those apples and the $3,000-worth of lard and tinned comestibles conveyed the message that they, and the United Kingdom

Chapter 5. "One-in-a-million"   113

overall, would not have to go it alone anymore. The people of the United States still stood behind them as they had done in the war.

Reginald Stranger continued on in public life as city alderman, chairman of city financial committees, and as a member of various public boards. In private life, he devoted his time to Strangers, Ltd., his family's mineral water bottling company, as a director. In 1951, he stood for election to Parliament from the Itchen constituency as the Conservative-Liberal candidate but lost to his Labour party opponent. The next year, after determining that his "business and political concerns" made it difficult to execute his duties, Stranger retired from the city council. By that time, the former mayor had made an indelible mark on Southampton and, indeed, the world. He had received many notable awards, including the French Legion of Honor in 1946, and in 1947 the U.S. Medal of Freedom with bronze palm for "exceptionally meritorious conduct in the performance of outstanding services"[36] as wartime mayor. He would ultimately even hold the *Ordem Nacional do Curzeiro do Sul* for his efforts at promoting friendships with Brazil.[37]

Given the depth of Stranger's wartime efforts and postwar political exposure, it might be tempting to write off Stranger's sojourn to Chambersburg as a minor publicity stunt, meant to garner votes and increase his visibility. However, the facts undermine such an interpretation. For one, Stranger returned to the United States, not once but twice (in 1960 and in 1971) to continue the tradition, taking part in Memorial Day services in Chambersburg and visiting his friends. During the 1960 visit, a young Patricia Ann Shimer, then 19 years old, made the trip from South Carolina where she was attending Columbia College as a first-year student, to meet with the benefactor who had made much of her education possible. Just like the first trip, Stranger participated in the wreath-laying services at the Shimer memorial. The local Rotary Club again threw him an elaborate celebration during which he was given a "certificate of honor" and named an honorary member of the local club. H.A. Kottkamp, a veteran of the first visit and now a former town burgess, interpreted Stranger's return as reaffirmation of the close ties between the United Kingdom and the United States at a time when "everything precious and worthwhile"[38] in the western world was again under threat-this time from the Soviet Union. Stranger agreed that their comradeship had to be sustained and nurtured, because "on our understanding and unity depend the peace of the world."[39] As Cold War antagonisms worsened, the Anglo-American partnership seemed more important than ever.

In his later years, Stranger devoted much of his time working as president of the Federation of Old Age Pensioners' Clubs in Hants, an organization giving assistance to the elderly. But after years of paying taxes on two residences, the Strangers decided to retire to Jersey in 1970, ending a lifetime of service to Southampton. At his farewell party, his Southampton friends described him as one who "towered among men of great stature" and as a man who possessed "a capacity for bringing diverse peoples together." Reginald Stranger, CBE, MC, died at his home in St. Brélade, Jersey, in January 1976.

Rex Stranger and wife visiting Chambersburg (courtesy Darren Boeck).

* * *

History remembers World War II as the war to rid the world of fascist tyranny, but it should also be remembered as the war that linked the United States to the United Kingdom, not only by the solid political alliance it formed but also by trans-national personal friendships it engendered. One needs only look at the record of how many British women came to the United States as war brides to see firsthand how quickly those personal relationships evolved. The ties that emerged between the British and American peoples go far beyond the bonds of spouses, however; they include the brotherhood of soldiers who trained, worked, fought, and died side by side.

Rex Stranger's personal quest serves, on a small scale, as an example of the mutual respect and recognition of the sacrifices both nations made toward the common good. But Stranger's story, as compelling as it is, may not have been exceptional. Millions of men had already proven that soldiers, when faced with a struggle to preserve their homes and their ways of life, could set aside their differences and find common ground. Already before Stranger's voyage to America, scores of military men from both countries had concluded that the wartime friendships between Brits and Yanks should be built upon and strengthened now that the war was over.

In 1946, a number of officers who had served in the joint western command under General Eisenhower advanced the idea of creating a "Fellowship of US-British Comrades" to perpetuate this spirit of friendship. The organization's mission statement announced that its goal was to "perpetuate, develop and extend the spirit and practice of British-US co-operation which began in the combined and integrated headquarters and staffs ... in which U.S. and British men and women ... worked together in the cause of freedom." Specific objectives included the publication of magazines and promotion of cultural or and social activities designed to "promote and extend understanding and toleration among English speaking peoples."[40]

Originally conceived as an organization more for the officers of the combined command, the "Fellowship" boasted the likes of Lieutenant Generals Jimmy Doolittle (of Tokyo raid fame) and Sir Frederick E. Morgan (the Operation Overlord planner) as president and vice president, and counted among their membership such names as General Dwight Eisenhower, Air Marshal Arthur Tedder, and other officers who would achieve prominence in public life in the years to come, such as Captain Peter W. Rodino (later Congressman and House Judiciary Committee Chair during Watergate) and Colonel Darryl F. Zanuck (film producer and studio head). In one month alone, the Fellowship enrolled almost ninety new members. By June of 1947, approximately six hundred officers from the American side alone were members.

It is understandable that personal friendships would emerge from military comradeship. However, it is another thing entirely for civilian populations to feel such a kinship. Southampton and Chambersburg are separated by more than just 3,500 miles of ocean; one is a major European city and seaport, the other a relatively small community in the agricultural heartland of southern Pennsylvania. Yet, despite their differences, the people of these two localities shared a long-lasting bond of friendship. Despite living in a city destroyed by bombs, the people of Southampton launched the greatest armada of weapons and personnel ever assembled in the 12 short months from June 1944 to May 1945.

Similarly, the people of Chambersburg managed to mobilize the resources of their town too, putting together an elaborate welcome ceremony for Mr. and Mrs. Stranger, amassing $3,000 in monetary donations, and procuring a pledge of a carload of apples for the children of Southampton, all within the 12 days from May 20 to June 1, 1947. Although the two events differ greatly in scope and purpose, they reveal much about the new relationship that was emerging between the United States and the United Kingdom—a relationship forged in war and perpetuated by the ties of a common language and heritage, a desire for democracy, freedom, and mutual security.

A memorial to the soldiers who fell in World War II still stands in the Cedar Grove Cemetery and it is still the focal point for Chambersburg's Memorial Day ceremonies to this day. Unfortunately, the granite memorial has withstood the passage of time better than the personal friendships and community ties that resulted from Rex Stranger's visits. Death has claimed most of the principals involved, and the personal memories of sacrifice during World War II are quickly leaving the public consciousness and receding into the expanse of history.

However, it is clear that the close relationship between the two nations not only continues but prospers. Although the Fellowship of U.S. British Comrades failed to survive beyond its first few years, the spirit of cooperation it embodied continued during the Korean War, the Vietnam Conflict, in the United States' support for the United Kingdom during the Falklands War in 1982, and more recently in the United Kingdom's resolve to stand by the United States during the 1991 Gulf War and Operation Iraqi Freedom in 2003. Rex Stranger's vision that the United States and the United Kingdom "stand side by side ... to uphold the ideals for which [our] men and women fought and gave their lives" endures.

CHAPTER 6

"Making Democracy Practical"

Wendell Smith's Crusade for Racial Equality in Sports

New York City's sports franchises have enjoyed a spirited, energetic, and intensely loyal support base in recent years. However, such was not always the case. In the 1940s, the Brooklyn Dodgers, affectionately called "the Bums" by even their own fans, were the target of fairly intense ridicule and derision thanks to their perennial status in or near the bottom of the baseball standings. Consequently, when over 25,000 fans headed to Ebbets Field on April 15, 1947, the take at the gate was impressive, but it was still nowhere near a sellout. The fans who went to the Dodgers' first home game of the 1947 season braved the blustery cold spring weather in the hopes of seeing a good game against a dreaded rival, the Boston Braves.

Pitching that day was the Braves' ace, Johnny Sain, the lanky right-hander who had won twenty games the year before. But for many attendees, the pitching matchup was not the main attraction. Batting second in the Dodgers' lineup was Jack Roosevelt Robinson, and by taking the field that day he became the first African American in modern baseball history to start a regular season Major League game. His performance that day was lackluster (he had no hits in three official plate appearances)[1]; nevertheless, it was the start of a stellar career that proved that black athletes could perform just as well as or better than whites.

More importantly, Robinson projected an air of grace and levelheadedness while ignoring the insults hurled at him from the public, his opponents, and even his own team members because of the color of his skin. Understandably, he became a hero to millions of Americans of all races and is still revered today for his groundbreaking role in the integration of America's pastime. On that day in April 1947, America took a major step toward the goal of racial equality.

Jackie Robinson's debut is one of *the* most pivotal moments in American sports, certainly as far as race relations are concerned. Organized baseball definitely thinks so. No one will ever wear Robinson's number 42 again; it has been officially retired from all teams in recognition of Robinson's role in baseball history. However, a deeper look at the history of professional sports tells a much more complex story of race in sports and dispels several common misconceptions.

For one thing, Robinson was not the first African American to receive a professional sports contract; blacks had already participated professionally in other sports—most notably in track, football, and basketball—long before Robinson took the field that day in 1947. He also was not the first African American in professional baseball. Back in the 1870s and 80s, when the sport was still in its infancy, black ballplayers commonly mixed with whites on professional teams. A final misconception emerged out all the attention focused on Jackie Robinson, the man, over the years.[2] He has become the stuff of legends—a charismatic and heroic figure who strove against the odds and succeeded despite a hostile world.

While there is certainly truth in these assertions, they obscure the fact that the campaign to integrate baseball could not have been waged by one man alone. Robinson's path to first base was blazed by countless politicians, social activists, and journalists who worked to break the color barrier off the ball diamond. While the name of Jackie Robinson is instantly familiar to most Americans, names like Sam Lacy, Lester Rodney, Shirley Povich, and those of other sportswriters who fought for the integration of baseball are much lesser known and have only recently been receiving the attention they deserve.[3] This is the story of one such person's struggle for racial equality in sport. His is an American life that progresses from the sandlot baseball diamonds of Michigan to the National Baseball Hall of Fame in Cooperstown, New York. Yet, he never played a single Major League baseball game.

Wendell Smith's name does not instantly come to mind as a sports hero, but he is arguably one of the most important figures in twentieth-century sports.[4] He was born in 1914 and grew up in an all-white and affluent section of Detroit, where his father worked as a chef for none other than the automobile magnate, Henry Ford. Smith remembered his childhood days vividly, especially the trips he occasionally took with his dad to the Ford mansion. "It was like a castle," he later recalled. Some of his most pleasurable moments involved his time with the Ford children. "I knew the kids, Edsel, Benson, and Henry. We played ball together."[5] He attended Southeastern High School where he was the sole African American student and excelled at both baseball and basketball.

At the age of 19, Smith had his first real taste of racial prejudice as an adult. Playing for his local American Legion baseball team, Smith pitched magnificently in a playoff game that resulted in a 1–0 win for his team. Watching the game was Wish Egan, a scout for the Detroit Tigers. After the game, Egan offered contracts to two of the white players[6] including the losing pitcher, but not to Smith. "I wish I could sign you too, but I can't," Smith recalled Egan saying. "That broke me up."[7] In an interview sometime after Smith's death, his wife, Wyonella, related that he wept that day.[8] It was the defining moment of his life. Having confronted Jim Crow directly, Smith resolved to fight back. "It was then that I made the vow that I would dedicate myself and do something in behalf of the Negro ballplayers. That's one of the reasons I became a sportswriter."[9]

Smith began his career in journalism at the historically all-black West Virginia State College, where he worked as sports editor for the college's newspaper and its liaison to the local Charleston newspapers.[10] His collegiate schedule allowed him to indulge his love for sport by playing baseball and basketball, and he was eventually named team captain in both sports.[11] Within months of his graduation in 1937 with a degree in Education, Smith took a job working for the *Pittsburgh Courier*, which at the time was one of the nation's largest African American weekly newspapers, pulling down a salary of about $17 a week. Like any new hire, he spent most of his first months at the paper doing more menial jobs and covering high school sports.[12] Soon, Smith convinced the editors to give him his own feature column wherein he could attack racism in sports. Luckily, the *Courier* and its publisher, Robert L. Vann, had a long-standing reputation for confronting Jim Crow in everything from housing policies to the way blacks were portrayed on the radio and in films, so the idea to take on organized baseball fit the newspaper's format well.

By the end of 1938, efforts to crack the color barrier in baseball were overshadowed by the rising threat of Nazism in central Europe. England and France had already come to the brink of war with Hitler's Germany over the annexation of the Sudetenland in Czechoslovakia, and for some Americans who feared an approaching war in Europe, the possible integration of professional baseball seemed a trivial distraction. For the advocates of social change, however, the rise of totalitarianism in Europe was a much-needed shot in the arm. Activists could point out that while Americans were condemning Nazi racism abroad they were nevertheless content to allow it to continue at home.

Smith was quick to seize on that contradiction too, and so he attempted to take the moral high ground in his early sports columns. He was not always subtle about it either. One article from December 1938 (which was one of the most caustic columns he ever wrote) went so far as to compare baseball to Nazi Germany. "They play the same game as Hitler," Smith snarled. "They discriminate, segregate and hold down a minor race, just as he does. While Hitler cripples the Jews, the great leaders of our national pastime refuse to recognize our black ball players." Targeting both the owners and Commissioner Kenesaw Mountain Landis, Smith pulled no punches, claiming that Hitler had at least one virtue the league owners lacked. "He comes right out and tells why he objects to Jews. He is wrong, of course, but he doesn't think he is. And he doesn't hide or refuse to answer when asked about it."[13]

Smith's tirade summarized the frustrations of millions of black Americans. For decades, baseball's color line was something everyone knew existed, but nobody knew why. Smith decided to find out. Armed with a sense of moral justification and a keenly logical mind, he set out to record what league officials felt about racial segregation. In early February, he got the chance of a lifetime when the president of the National League, Ford Frick, agreed to an interview. On Sunday morning, February 19, 1939, Smith met Frick in the William Penn Hotel in Pittsburgh for a face-to-face chat. Their discussion became the substance of an article that would have long lasting repercussions for blacks and baseball.

Frick had already gone on record (speaking to correspondents from the *Daily Worker* in 1936) as having insisted that there was no official policy barring blacks from professional baseball.[14] And now, Frick repeated the assertion and told Smith that organized baseball was willing to accept black ballplayers immediately! For Smith, Frick's statement was something akin to a divine revelation. If that were true, then why weren't any blacks playing in the Major Leagues already? Frick answered that the American public was not yet "educated" enough to accept black players as equals to whites. In addition, he stressed that there were many "social problems" that needed to be addressed (especially given the climate of race relations in the South, where most teams held spring training).

But when Smith pressed him to say how long it would be before blacks would play in the majors, Frick would not speculate. He did opine, however, that blacks would play in the majors someday. "I can not name any particular day or year, but assure you that when the people ask for the inclusion of your players, we will use them." At the end of the interview, Frick told Smith "you must keep fighting." "Never let the issue die," Frick commanded. "It may change tomorrow."[15]

Wendell Smith had just hit the journalistic equivalent of a home run, but rather than rest on his laurels, Smith went on the attack. Within weeks of the interview, Smith criticized Frick's comments, particularly the assertion that the American public was not ready to see blacks as equals. "How is it that these same Americans will pay as high as $100 to see Joe Louis, a black man, knock a white man out? [Frick] can't seem to explain how it is that they can't stand to see a Negro hit a ball thrown by a white pitcher, but delight in seeing a Negro hit a jaw owned by a white boxer."[16] Smith extrapolated from the interview that Frick believed white players opposed including blacks in the majors.[17]

Chapter 6. "Making Democracy Practical"

To test his theory, Smith tracked down 40 players and eight managers during the months of April, May, and June 1939 to ask them what they thought of black baseball players and their talent. It was not an easy task. As a black journalist in a segregated profession, Smith could not get a press card and therefore his access to sports personalities was severely limited. Smith had to resort to unorthodox methods, including subterfuge, to gather information. His favorite tactic was to wait in hotel lobbies where baseball players and managers were staying, and then corner them during their down time with questions. "I usually started off the interview by asking 'Have you seen any Negro ball players who you think could play in the major leagues?'" Smith later remembered.[18] The question was an effective journalistic tactic—non-confrontational yet probing—designed to put the interviewee at ease and get them to open up.

And open up they did. One after another, Smith's interrogations revealed that most Major Leaguers had no problem with blacks as teammates or opponents, provided they had the requisite skills. Some of the greatest names in baseball at the time, many of them still renowned as legends, spoke out in favor of blacks. Leo "the lip" Durocher, then manager of the Brooklyn Dodgers, answered Smith's question by pointedly admitting, "Hell—I've seen a million!" Bill McKechnie, manager of the Cincinnati Reds, answered that he could recall 25 blacks who were Major League material. The Giants' pitching ace Carl Hubble had nothing but praise for the Negro league greats Satchell Paige and Josh Gibson. The list of those who answered in the affirmative goes on to include the likes of Arky Vaughn, Dizzy Dean, Cookie Lavagetto, Honus Wagner, and Mel Ott.

Of course, there were those who were not as enthusiastic. Bill Terry, manager of the New York Giants, admitted that he had seen innumerable good black ballplayers but felt that they would probably never be given a chance in the majors. Paul "Daffy" Dean of the Cardinals wanted to duck the question entirely and even refused to shake hands with Smith. Smith recounted the incident in his column, claiming that Dean brushed him off, saying "Naw, I don't wanna talk to ya! Kain't ya' see I'm busy!" Cardinals' manager, Pepper Martin, interceded and finally convinced the reluctant Dean to talk to Smith. Eventually, Dean agreed that Negro ballplayers were certainly good enough and that he would not object to a colored player as a teammate.[19]

Out of these interviews came the eight copyrighted articles of the "What Big Leaguers Think of Negro Ballplayers" series, published over the summer months of 1939.[20] These articles, now carrying the byline of "Wendell Smith, Assistant Sports Director," proved a huge success for both the newspaper and the journalist personally. Indeed, Smith had made a critical contribution to efforts to integrate baseball. By bringing white players and managers into the discussion, he turned what had been a conspiracy of silence into an open debate. As ever more white baseball celebrities weighed in with their opinions, the series began to garner national interest. Soon, other black sportswriters, including Sam Lacy who later became head sportswriter for the *Baltimore Afro-American*, published similar columns in their own publications. Eventually mainstream newspapers, including the famed *Sporting News*, picked up Smith's articles from the wire services and suddenly his readership expanded beyond the confines of ethnic black communities into all of American society.

One newspaper that sympathized with Smith's campaign was the Communist publication, *Daily Worker*. The *Daily Worker*, and its sportswriter Lester Rodney, had also taken up the issue of sports segregation, and eventually the two newspapers became allies in the fight to integrate the Major Leagues. Smith and Rodney even developed an informal working arrangement to help each other out with information and stories.[21] This liaison was a marked departure from the *Courier*'s more measured approach in the early 1930s that had emphasized passive persuasion rather than direct confrontation. Despite the potential backlash that cooperating with Communists might bring, Smith continued and encouraged the association while discreetly keeping his distance from communist politics. For the *Courier* editors, Smith's columns were starting to generate national interest, and that translated into increased circulation for the paper and a steady influx of cash. For anyone struggling to survive the Great Depression, those were two very welcome commodities.

Armed with the evidence from the "What Big Leaguers Think" interviews, Smith decided to take the debate directly the owners. In a letter to the Commissioner of Baseball, Kenesaw Mountain Landis, Smith and a team of prominent black personalities, including the famed singer Paul Robeson and *Pittsburgh Courier* business manager (and eventually president) Ira Lewis, asked for permission to make a presentation to the owners at a meeting sometime in 1939. Surprisingly, the league office agreed and Smith's entourage made its way to the Roosevelt Hotel in New York City to plead the case for integration. The men made a brief presentation, but there was little interaction with the owners and no discussion. A follow-up letter sent to Landis went unanswered.[22] The meeting was not completely fruitless, however. One man seemed interested in what the group had to say—the general manager of the St. Louis Cardinals, Branch Rickey. Smith recalled later that Rickey was "very gracious" to them even though he said nothing on their behalf at the meeting.[23] It was a fateful first encounter between two men who together would change baseball forever.

The German invasion of Poland on September 1, 1939, pushed the issue of integration to the back burner. By either accident or design, the

Courier retreated from confronting team owners in print and stayed relatively mum about the color ban for the next two years.[24] Wendell Smith also softened his crusade somewhat, but he continued to counterpunch with jabs against the owners' hypocrisy in the occasional feature story.[25] In one notable article from May 1940, in the midst of Congress's efforts to root Communist and Nazi subversives out of government, Smith branded baseball owners as "fifth columnists" and urged the Dies Committee (a precursor to the House Un-American Activities Committee) to investigate them for their discriminatory practices. "They're as un–American as any Nazi that ever raised his right paw and shouted 'Heil Hitler,'" Smith wrote.[26] Despite such hyperbole, there were signs that American society was slowly warming to the idea of racial equity. In March, the New York Trade Union Athletics Association circulated a petition to allow blacks into baseball. A few months later, they took their appeal to the New York World's Fair, holding rallies in the stadiums there to raise awareness of their cause.[27]

The attack on Pearl Harbor and the United States' entry into the Second World War inadvertently provided fresh impetus to Smith's and the *Courier*'s crusade to bring blacks into the Major Leagues. As ever more men volunteered or were drafted for military service, the pool of talent available for baseball teams dwindled. What a better solution than to tap the talent in the Negro Leagues? Additionally, the Soviet Union was an ally now, so any repercussions from Smith's association with the *Daily Worker* could be deflected, at least for the time being. As America's involvement in the war increased, so too did Smith's journalistic agitation.

During August of the 1942 season, Smith approached Bill Benswanger, the owner of the Pittsburgh Pirates, to see if he would be willing to give black baseball stars a tryout with the club. Surprisingly, Benswanger agreed to assign some of his scouts to check out some of the Negro League players and hold a tryout. Unfortunately, after repeated unsuccessful attempts to arrange a time and place, Smith gave up. Looking back on the incident years later, he opined that Benswanger apparently "got cold feet,"[28] possibly because he had gotten similar requests from the communist paper *Daily Worker* and wanted to distance himself from any association with them.

One positive result from the Pirates' failure to hold tryouts was that many mainstream newspapers picked up the story, bringing the issue of racial hatred in baseball back under the scrutiny of a wider audience. The increased attention may have forced owners to take the issue more seriously, so they put integration on the agenda for the first time at their meeting on Friday, December 3, 1943.[29] Wendell Smith was there with another delegation of notables and again made a presentation in support of integration. Smith got the chance to speak directly with Commissioner Landis, Ford Frick, and William Harridge (the league presidents). All three men admitted to Smith the presentation was impressive, but they refused to predict when the situation for black ballplayers might change. None of the owners would give official statements.[30]

Looking back on his experiences, Smith recalled that during the latter years of the war, the country "was turning fairly liberal" and an ever-growing segment of the population was paying attention to issues of racial injustice. Contemporary events outside of sports confirm his assessment. In March of 1945, the New York State legislature overwhelmingly passed the Ives-Quinn Act, making it illegal for employers to discriminate in hiring on the basis of race, religion, or color. When Massachusetts considered a similar law, Smith saw a chance to turn up the heat on team owners. Smith happened upon a short newspaper article about Isadore Muchnick, a Boston Councilman and proponent of integration. Muchnick was, as the Boston journalist Howard Bryant describes him, a "classical East Coast Liberal." Having been trained in law at Harvard, Muchnick, a Jew who had himself seen his share of social injustice, had championed many progressive stances including equal pay for female government employees—stances that often put him at loggerheads with his more conservative colleagues on Council.

For about a year, Muchnick had corresponded with Eddie Collins, general manager of the Red Sox, complaining about baseball's treatment of black athletes.[31] After receiving nothing but platitudes and empty promises, Muchnick decided to force the issue by threatening repercussions if the Braves and Red Sox continued to refuse blacks a tryout with the teams. As a city councilman, he was in a position to make good on this threat since, in that era of Sunday blue laws, both teams needed unanimous approval from the council to hold Sunday baseball games. All Muchnick needed to do was withhold his approval and both teams would lose a good deal of their income. After reading about the incident, Smith called Muchnick to offer himself as an ally, promising to deliver black ballplayers to Boston for any tryouts the Braves and Red Sox might schedule.[32] Eventually, Muchnick succeeded in browbeating the Red Sox into a tryout, and they set a date for April 12.

Smith then needed to pick the right men for this rare opportunity. He passed over two of the Negro league's biggest stars, Josh Gibson and Satchel Paige; Gibson, because he could not get permission from the owners of the Homestead Grays, and Paige, because he felt he was too old. Smith finally settled on Marvin Williams, second baseman for the Philadelphia Stars, Sam Jethroe of the Cleveland Buckeyes, and Jackie Robinson, the well-known, all–American football player from UCLA who also played shortstop for the Kansas City Monarchs. Temporarily suspending their disbelief, the four men packed their bags and headed for Boston. When they arrived, they found that the Braves and the Red Sox were engaged in a five-game city series.[33] The April 12 tryout never took place[34] so Smith and Muchnick worked with Red Sox leadership to reschedule it for the 16th. Accompanied by Smith and Muchnick, the three athletes showed up at 10:30 a.m. at Fenway Park ready to perform.

Smith gave a fairly sensationalized account of the session in his column later that week but in reality the tryout was disappointing, if not insulting. The Red Sox had brought in mostly high school and minor league players that day, and the three great stars of the Negro leagues were reduced to shagging fly balls and hitting substandard pitches. Collins, who had reluctantly agreed to go ahead with the tryout the day before, deliberately stayed in the stands to watch the exhibition, leaving it up to two of his subordinates, Hugh Duffy and Larry Woodall, to run the event and deal with the players and Smith personally.[35] Both were favorably impressed. "There is no doubt that they are ballplayers," one of them told Smith. "They looked good to me."[36] The entire exhibition lasted only a little over an hour. The coaches handed the men application cards to fill out with a vague promise that they would hear from the team again. The men then retired to a restaurant on Tremont Street where they vented that this "tryout" was just for show. Over dinner, they joked that would probably never hear anything from the Red Sox again.[37] They were right.

Smith tried to coax some response by writing a very cordial follow-up letter 10 days later, asking point-blank if the team would let him know of any decision on signing any of the players.[38] Collins did write back, but explained that Manager Joe Cronin's recently broken leg "threw everything out of gear" and that he (Collins) could not reach a decision in the near future. Collins' well-crafted response contained what reads like an escape clause. The last paragraph warned Smith that organized baseball had to avoid interfering with Negro league contractual arrangements. In a cruel twist of rhetoric, Collins wrote that he was loath to "tamper with anyone else's property."[39] Smith had every reason to be angry, yet in retrospect he never held a grudge against the Red Sox or Collins. "I should say the reception was fine," he later admitted. "They did what they said they would." Nevertheless, the event was a disappointment, personally and professionally, for Smith and the three athletes. The excursion to Boston was not a total loss however, for Wendell Smith had one more card to play. He gambled that Branch Rickey, the man whose graciousness he remembered from the owners' meeting several years earlier and who was now the owner of the Brooklyn Dodgers, might be interested in hearing about the tryouts.

Wesley Branch Rickey cut a curious figure as a sports maven. Born to a farming family in rural Ohio, Rickey was brought up in a strict Methodist tradition, taught to be fearful of God and mindful of the needs of others. He might have stayed in farming had it not been for his brother, Orla, an avid baseball fan who taught Branch how to play.[40] As a young man, he worked alternately between teaching and coaching baseball and managed to earn a college degree before setting out on a professional baseball career as a catcher with the Cincinnati Reds. Throughout his professional career, he never strayed far from his religious upbringing and made a name for himself by refusing to play baseball on Sundays.[41] Rickey eventually earned a law degree and aligned himself with conservative politics while identifying with any number of social causes, including such disparate movements as Prohibition and the social crusades of Jane Addams and Jacob Riis. Something of a perfectionist with a penchant for punctuality, Rickey developed a business style characterized by a curious mixture of capitalism, evangelism, and social responsibility. If anyone in baseball would be receptive to integration, it would be him.

Smith had heard rumors that Rickey was planning to start a third Negro League (eventually called the United States League) and was sending his scouts to evaluate and recruit black talent for a "Brown Dodgers" team.[42] With little to lose, Smith called him on the phone to see if he was interested in hearing details about what had transpired in Boston. Naturally, Rickey was intrigued, so he invited Smith to come to Brooklyn for a meeting. Smith arrived at Ebbets Field the next morning, and while relating the events in Boston he mentioned that Jackie Robinson was one of the players he had selected for the tryout. Invoking the name of Jackie Robinson, the already well-known, all–American football player, caught Rickey's attention.

At the time, Smith had no reason to assume that Rickey's polite invitation was anything more than an attempt to satisfy his curiosity. In reality, however, Rickey had pretty much decided years before that he would someday integrate the Dodgers, but his intentions were known to only the closest of his friends and advisors. In subsequent conversations, Smith sensed that there was more to Rickey's interest in Robinson than a possible place on his new Negro League team, so he pressed him with direct questions about Robinson's chances for a spot in Brooklyn's system. The cagey Rickey would not reveal his hand, at least not right away. "He was evasive," remembered Smith. "He didn't say yes and he didn't say no. But I had the definite impression there was more behind it than the Brown Dodgers."

Writing in 1947, Smith claimed that Rickey made the fateful decision on May 8, 1945. He recalled being in the Brooklyn Dodgers' office with Rickey as New Yorkers and all of America celebrated V-E Day. Looking down on the revelry in the streets below, Rickey turned to Smith and

Chapter 6. "Making Democracy Practical"

asked, "You know what this means, don't you?" Smith answered by predicting a speedy victory over Japan, but Rickey had things other than the war on his mind. "It means more than that. It means I can sign Jackie Robinson without a bit of worry."[43] When Smith reacted with a puzzled look, Rickey elaborated. According to Smith, Rickey said

> Well you see ... this means that Johnny will come marching home after four long years of war. He's been fighting to preserve democracy, and he's been through Hell.... He's certainly coming back convinced that every man in this country deserves a fair chance to make an honest living. He isn't, for instance, going to let anyone tell him that a man can't play the great American game of baseball just because the color of his skin is black. You see, he went into this war to make sure that all Americans could play baseball, as well as other sports. Johnny's going to solve this problem and I'm glad he's coming home.[44]

Their discussion returned to Jackie Robinson's suitability so Rickey decided to put his best scout, Clyde Sukeforth, on the job of scoping out the young athlete. That summer, Wendell Smith informed Robinson of the Dodgers' interest in him, but kept to himself his suspicion that this might lead to a spot on the Dodgers' Major League roster. "I didn't want him to tighten up" recalled Smith.

Over the next year, Rickey got the chance to meet Robinson personally and draw his own conclusions about his "suitability" for the task at hand. Rickey was well aware that whomever he picked to integrate the Major Leagues had to be a special individual; the wrong personality or volatile temperament could set back the effort for years. In time, Sukeforth's positive scouting reports persuaded Rickey to offer Robinson a contract with the Montreal Royals, the Dodgers' best farm team. Robinson's signing and his first year in the minor leagues have been well documented.[45] Robinson went to Venezuela to play ball with the Royals, all the while corresponding with Wendell Smith and providing him with game scores and insights from his experiences with the other players. Smith, concurrently, was in regular telephone contact with Rickey to let him know how Robinson was faring. In one conversation, Smith offered to help with preparations for spring training scheduled to begin March 1 in Daytona Beach. Rickey accepted his offer and asked Smith to arrive in Daytona ahead of time to find housing for Robinson. In a private letter to Rickey (who was in the hospital recuperating from an illness) dated January 14, Smith promised to find accommodations both in Sanford for the preliminary training camp and in Daytona Beach. Smith's missive intimated that he was ready to deepen his involvement in the project.

> I want you to feel as though the publishers of the *Pittsburgh Courier* and I are a distinct part of this undertaking. We do not want you to take all of the responsibility with regards to help to strengthen these boys spiritually and morally

for the part they are to play in this great adventure. For that reason I want you to feel free to call upon me for any cooperation which you think I may be able to render.[46]

Rickey decided to make his arrangement with Wendell Smith official, and so he hired him as an employee of the team. Technically, Smith's duties included scouting African American ballplayers but because of his "special assignment" in proximity to Robinson he soon became, in the words of baseball historian Jules Tygiel, "an integral member of Rickey's strategy circle."[47] Rickey had three good reasons to bring Smith on. First of all, there would be one other black, the right-handed pitcher Johnny Wright, travelling with the team once spring training began, so Smith could be a companion to both men. More importantly, Smith could help Robinson and Wright mitigate or, better yet, avoid the inevitable backlash that would accompany their appearance in white-only stadiums and communities. Lastly, Smith was Rickey's eyes and ears on the scene. At the first sign of trouble, one phone call from Smith and Rickey would have all the information he would need to intervene.

For Wendell Smith, this was the chance of a lifetime. Rarely does a reporter have a chance to witness, let alone be a part of a history-making event. Not only could he actually assist in bringing his lifelong dream to fruition, but he would also be physically present for it, chronicling and influencing it. This was simply too good a happenstance to pass up. Smith accepted the Dodgers' offer at a salary of $50 a week, all the while staying employed at the *Courier* and feeding his readership stories of Robinson and Wright's exploits in his regular weekly column. The *Courier* was more than happy with this arrangement, paying part of his expenses and sending staff photographer Billy Rowe to create a visual record. Given that the stories would most likely see national exposure and sell lots of newspapers, these were good investments.

When Jackie Robinson arrived in Daytona Beach late in the evening of March 4, 1946, Wendell Smith was already there to greet him. Smith travelled there early at Rickey's request and found lodging at the Brock residence, a prominent local family in the town of Sanford where the Dodgers had a practice facility. Mrs. Brock had been a college acquaintance of Smith's, and the home, which by any standard was large and luxurious, proved more than comfortable. Unfortunately, the reception from the rest of the town was not as hospitable. While sitting on the porch one evening, Smith was approached by a white man (one account says he was a deputy sheriff) who claimed to be representing a group of businessmen who were displeased by the ballplayers' arrival. His advice was to leave town.[48] Smith called Rickey, who instructed him to leave Sanford immediately. Smith and Rowe knew they needed to keep both Robinson and Wright calm, so they remained silent about why they were being asked to pack up.

The two men finally learned the whole story in the car on the way to Daytona Beach. It was a cruel reminder that Jim Crow was alive and well in many Florida towns. Fortunately, Daytona Beach was not one of them. When the group arrived, they found the city and the team more than ready to accept them. Soon, spring training began in earnest with the traditional drills but given the presence of Robinson and Wright, it was hardly a typical preseason warm-up. Professor Chris Lamb has described what Robinson and Wright had to go through to play the first spring training games. Cities cancelled games rather than allow blacks to play with whites. A frequent small-town police tactic was to threaten black players with arrest, and in one exhibition game in DeLand, Florida, Robinson was escorted off the field by a policeman after crossing home plate with the first run of the game.[49]

But luckily there were no riots, beatings, or lynchings. Smith played a role in mitigating potential threats, since he and other sportswriters opted not to report about Sanford's cold reception until well after the incident was over out of fear that other communities would be emboldened to take similar steps. He continued to write stories from Florida, revealing both the excellent play of the men and the shameful treatment they got from segregationists wherever they went. Fortunately, everyone tolerated the mistreatment, knowing that spring training would not go on forever. The regular season would start soon enough.

For the remainder of 1946, Robinson played superb baseball for the Montreal Royals, batting an overall .349 average and amassing a stunning .468 on-base percentage.[50] The Royals won the championship, and Robinson was awarded the Most Valuable Player award. His performance was sufficiently impressive that when the Associated Press asked sportswriters to predict what the number one question in sports for 1947 would be, the winner was "Would Jackie Robinson be the first Negro to play in Major League Baseball?"[51] It was a reasonable question, but the crafty Rickey was not one to tip his hand early, not even to Wendell Smith. In one letter, Smith politely prodded Rickey by asking what he intended to do "with our friend."[52]

Spring training was slated for Havana, Cuba, in February 1947, which made it possible for both the Royals and the Dodgers to be in close proximity, and thus Robinson could play with either team. Smith continued to push Rickey for a definite commitment. In one such attempt, Smith again volunteered to help find lodging "if ... he [Robinson] will be training in Havana this year." Over the next few months, Smith and Rickey rekindled their mutually advantageous business arrangement. They agreed that Smith would once again travel with the team's black players as companion and advisor.

Wendell Smith (right) chatting with fellow sportswriter Sam Lacy (left) and pitcher Dan Bankhead (courtesy National Baseball Hall of Fame Library, NBL-487-98).

As 1947 began, Wendell Smith's dream was within grasp. Jackie Robinson looked like a shoo-in to take a spot on the Dodgers roster. Spring training would be different from the previous years, as Cuba was a much friendlier environment than Florida for black ballplayers. Additionally, this year Robinson would have plenty of black friends to keep him company. Roy Partlow, Don Newcombe, and Roy Campanella all got invitations to come to camp (Johnny Wright had been released in January). And of course, Wendell Smith would be there too, seeing to room arrangements, travel needs, and meals. An exhibition series in Panama went off without a hitch, and although their time in Cuba was peppered with experiences of bad food, questionable accommodations, and racial tensions, Wendell Smith managed to keep the small group of athletes reasonably happy.

Branch Rickey himself attended the games in Panama and Cuba, and kept in continual contact with Smith, who was a frequent visitor to

Chapter 6. "Making Democracy Practical" 131

Rickey's hotel room. At one meeting of the "strategy circle," Rickey finally confessed that he intended to move Robinson up to the main team by April 10.[53] Rickey's main concern now was the reaction of the other players. Would the transition be smooth? Some team members were already "grumbling" about Robinson. Obligingly, Smith's journalistic attentions turned to Robinson's teammates and coaches, and in a brutally honest article he exposed the racial biases of some of the team's most celebrated members to his readership. Smith's mission was changing. Having convinced a team owner to take the step, he now had to convince the players to do the same.

* * *

Smith broke the news to Robinson personally that he would be with the Dodgers when the team returned to New York. Both men understood the gravity of the moment. Smith admitted in his "Sports Beat" column articles that "if Robinson fails to make the grade, it will be many years before a Negro makes the grade. This is IT!"[54] The historical record is unfortunately silent on how Wendell Smith felt at the moment Jackie Robinson stepped onto the field to play first base. One can only surmise the range of emotions that Smith experienced that day. Certainly, Smith must have felt pride in playing a central role in one of the most epochal events in modern sports. It is also not difficult to imagine him feeling vindicated for the personal wrongs he experienced as a young pitcher in Detroit. One thing is certain: Smith knew that opening day was just the beginning of the struggle. Robinson still had to perform—and behave himself—for this experiment to move forward. Furthermore, it was not enough just to have Robinson succeed. This was only the initial battle in a much larger war against racial hatred and segregation. Other black players had to follow. Nothing short of the complete dismantling of segregation in baseball would do.[55]

Jackie Robinson became a media sensation and shadowing him at every opportunity was Wendell Smith. He was present when the reporters mobbed Jackie after the first exhibition games against the Yankees. He was with Robinson and his wife and child as they read the congratulatory letters and telegrams from all over the country. Those letters, of course, made wonderful copy for his "Sports Beat" column. And of course, Smith travelled with Robinson to his first Major League road games as roommate and gatekeeper, keeping Robinson focused on the game and away from the media blitz.

For the most part, the travel arrangements and accommodations were far superior to what Robinson had known in the minors. When they were not, as happened in St. Louis, Smith stepped in with pen in hand to chronicle any bigotry they confronted, no matter how minor. On their way to

Sportsman's Park for their first series with the Cardinals, Robinson heard that the management of the Chase Hotel (where the Dodgers were staying) was "not anxious to have him." Whether or not that was true, Robinson and Smith chose to stay at the Deluxe Hotel instead, which was owned and operated by a black real estate businessman. Smith made sure to compliment the hospitality they received at the Deluxe in his column, but he also ripped the shabby treatment they got at the Chase Hotel. When the owners of the Chase realized their error, they sent a message that Jackie would be welcome there on his next trip to St. Louis. Smith reacted predictably. "It is doubtful that he will accept the offer ... even though he appreciated [it]," Smith wrote.[56]

By mid-season, the volume of Smith's reporting on Robinson started to decline. Instead, Smith focused on the East-West game, the Negro league equivalent of the All-Star Game, in an attempt to pump up interest and bolster attendance. There may have been a bit of guilt motivating these columns. As more and more African Americans got Major League contracts, the pool of talent in the Negro leagues dwindled, and teams suffered financially. Long before Robinson's reputation was firmly established, Smith wrote columns supporting the black teams, believing that there was room in organized baseball for both leagues. "Some of the owners aren't wholly in support of this campaign to get more Negro players into the majors. But we'll forgive 'em and go along with 'em because they can't do anything about it anyway," quipped Smith.[57]

Still, the economic reality was not lost on him. Pittsburgh baseball fans who might have gone to see a Homestead Grays game now decided to take in a Pirates game instead. By August 1947, Negro league attendance had already started to decline. Offering his advice, Smith reeled off a list of things the Negro baseball needed to do to survive; among them, hire a publicity director, develop more stars, become more "dignified and business-like," and promote their games better. "We know that is a big job," he wrote, "but it must be done ... and done immediately."[58] Smith's command was right on target. Within a year and a half, the Negro National League had folded. Despite all his articles urging support of black baseball, Smith was stoic about the loss, comparing the collapse to a funeral with "a grave but tearless ceremony."[59] He had to realize that his own efforts to integrate the majors dealt a death blow to organized black baseball, but that seems to be a price Smith felt worth paying in order to advance his goals of a colorless sports society.

* * *

As crucial as 1947 was for integrated baseball and for the lives of hundreds of black professional ballplayers, it was also a critical year in Wendell

Smith's career. In mid–August, Smith signed on with the *Chicago Herald American*, a mainstream daily newspaper run by whites, to write a series of eight feature articles about Jackie Robinson's life. The series ran for a week under Smith's byline mentioning him as the sports editor for the *Pittsburgh Courier*, but also with his photograph—a bold move for the newspaper to take.[60] The paper hired him full time in November, and he became Chicago's first black sports correspondent. In December, Smith wrote a seven-part series on Jersey Joe Walcott for the *Herald American*, this time without any mention of his ties to the *Pittsburgh Courier*. These features were the beginning of a relationship that would eventually see Smith moving to Chicago and taking a permanent position with the newspaper writing articles on baseball, boxing, and occasionally local high school sports.

This new job was Smith's equivalent to Robinson's first days with the Dodgers: he had finally broken through the racial barrier as a journalist. As an employee with the *Herald American*, Smith could finally apply for membership in the Pittsburgh chapter of the Baseball Writers' Association of America, whose constitution limited membership to "men ... regularly employed on daily papers." This had been a source of irritation, since writers for the communist *Daily Worker* had been granted membership while Smith, a black correspondent with a weekly paper, was repeatedly denied. The Pittsburgh chapter deferred Smith's application, however, ostensibly because Chicago's chapter would have authority over his membership. Membership would have to wait, for now.

Smith had other reasons to be occupied in late summer 1947 besides Jackie Robinson and his own breakthrough in mainstream newspaper journalism. In August, the House Un-American Activities Committee began to turn up the heat on suspected Communists across the country and eventually launched the famous "Hollywood Ten" probes that resulted in the blacklisting of filmmakers and writers including Dalton Trumbo, Alvin Bessie, Ring Lardner, Jr., and others. Smith realized that his own prewar association with the communist *Daily Worker* might potentially blow up in his face, so he decided to preempt the situation.

Setting aside the fact that he and Lester Rodney had at one time supported each other, Smith now lashed out against the Communists, particularly the assertion that the *Daily Worker* had led the way in breaking the color barrier in baseball. Using his entire "Sports Beat" column of August 23, Smith claimed that he wanted to "get straight for the record ... that the communists grabbed the baseball issue because they believed it was a vulnerable point in the physical make-up of this great Democracy."

In what may have been somewhat selective memory, Smith recounted how Robinson had to duck the *Daily Worker* reporters because of the fear that conservatives in the United States would attempt to link integration with the Communism. "Like a bad penny they always turned up when least wanted," Smith exclaimed, writing about the *Daily Worker* columnists. The *Courier*, not the *Daily Worker*, had conducted the prewar interviews that exposed the hypocrisy of the ban, Smith asserted. In his concluding remarks, Smith summed up by calling the communist assertions "twisted, false and misleading" and in truth, "the Communists did more to delay the entrance of Negroes into organized baseball than any other factor."[61]

By the close of 1947, Wendell Smith's crusade to integrate black ballplayers into the Major Leagues was largely accomplished. Larry Doby had been picked up by the Cleveland Indians that year, and Dan Bankhead and Roy Campanella would soon have their own big-league contracts. They were followed by countless others as the signing of African American athletes was no longer a novelty. America's Pastime was finally becoming truly "American." Smith's reputation for assisting blacks in sports extended well beyond Jackie Robinson; he reportedly also helped Buck O'Neil and Ernie Banks get to their tryouts with the Chicago Cubs in the mid–1950s. Some might have stopped there, content to rest on their laurels, but not Wendell Smith. Throughout the decade of the 1950s and into the 1960s, Smith continued to attack racism wherever he found it. Writing with the *Chicago American* in 1961, Smith took on discrimination in spring training and was largely successful in exposing the racial hypocrisy still prevalent in many southern towns and cities.[62] That series of articles proved to be the crowning achievement of Wendell Smith's journalism career.

* * *

Given Smith's accomplishments in breaking through the baseball color barrier, it is easy to forget that Smith was a champion of integration in general, not just in sports. One of his greatest strengths as a columnist was his ability to expose the racial prejudice and hypocrisy still pervasive in society in the guise of news. No one was immune from Smith's jabs; colleagues, universities, and sports figures of all races could find themselves in the crosshairs if they failed to conform to Smith's vision of racial harmony. Perhaps the most intriguing example of his sarcasm was a scathing article he wrote in February 1946, criticizing the New York Sportswriters' Club for a skit it had put on as entertainment during its annual banquet. The sportswriters poked fun at Commissioner Happy Chandler by parodying him as a southern gentleman with a kind but stupid Negro butler. The butler was dressed in a Montreal Royals uniform and spoke with a stereotypical southern black drawl. Smith transcribed some of the dialogue in his column:

CHANDLER: "Robbieeee … eeee!"
BUTLER: "Yassah, Massa. Here Ah is!"

Chapter 6. "Making Democracy Practical" 135

> **CHANDLER:** "Jackie, you ole woolly-headed rascal, how long have you been in the family?"
> **BUTLER:** "Long time Kun'l. Marty long time. Evver since Massa Rickey done bo't me from de Kansas City Monarchs!"

Smith fired back with some of his most scathing copy ever.

> It is clearly obvious that they were taking well-aimed pot shots at both Rickey and Robinson. They are not all for equality in sports and they gave vent to their feelings in this vicious manner. They weren't courageous or brave enough to express their feelings in their respective newspapers ... so they put on this dastardly act behind closed doors. The parts were played well by known writers of the New York chapter of the association, but their names were not made public for fear of being reprimanded. Therefore, the entire blame for that "Nazi Opera" must be heaped upon the entire body.[63]

Such a skit may have seemed funny to the white audience but by putting the dialog in newsprint, Smith revealed it for what it truly was, offensive racial stereotyping. This tactic was one of the best weapons in Wendell Smith's journalistic arsenal. His genius was the ability to reveal the inherent small-mindedness of prejudice by using the very words of those he accused.

Another example of Smith's attempts to put pressure on a perceived injustice are his articles attacking Ed Gottlieb, the famous Philadelphia sports promoter. Today, Gottlieb is best remembered as one of the founding fathers of the National Basketball Association (NBA) and the league's Rookie of the Year trophy bears his name. Before getting more involved in basketball, however, Gottlieb owned the Philadelphia Stars Baseball Club in the Negro National League. As an owner and promoter, he made a considerable amount of money fielding Negro league games at Shibe park, usually on Monday nights when the Phillies and Athletics were not at home.[64]

At one time, perhaps, Smith may have considered Gottlieb an ally in the fight for racial equality in sports. He had generously allowed Smith to take Marvin Williams, the Stars' infielder, to Boston for the ill-fated Red Sox tryout back in 1945. But one year later, Gottlieb was in Smith's sights for not including any blacks on the newly formed Philadelphia Warriors basketball team, where Gottlieb was coach and general manager. Smith's initial exposé of November 23, 1946, published shortly after the Warrior's first game, describes Gottlieb in the most unflattering of terms.

> For the sake of identification, we'd like to point out that "Brother Eddie" is a Jewish gentleman who picks up and salts away thousands each year promoting Negro baseball. At one time, he didn't have a pot to cook in, but he mooched his way into the picture, and then virtually took over the operations of the Negro National League.... The money he salts away comes from the black hands of Negro fans who dish it out in "Brother Eddie's" parks to see his Philly Stars and the other teams he controls chase a batted ball.[65]

Smith then goes on to list the "sports questions of the week" which intimated, through a questioning format, that Gottlieb might be prejudiced and exploitative of black talent for his own personal gain. The scathing article ends with a final parting shot. Smith quizzed the readership but intoned, "For each correct answer, we're going to do for you just like 'Brother Eddie' would do—give you absolutely nothing."[66]

Two months later, Smith leveled Gottlieb in print again. "He refuses to hire a Negro player on his basketball team solely because, he says, 'It wouldn't work out.' In the summertime however, he operates a Negro baseball team and makes thousands of dollars off the Negro public. In other words, 'Brother Eddie' Gottlieb finds it convenient to discriminate in the wintertime."[67] Each new article provided another opportunity to suggest retaliatory measures. "Negroes in Philadelphia and vicinity are supposed to be highly racial conscious people. Wonder if they're going to take the stuff 'Brother Eddie' is dishing out to them now?"[68] Jackie Robinson's first year with Brooklyn took much of Smith's attention away from "Brother Eddie," but he was still taking potshots at him in 1948. Once Wendell Smith took on an injustice, he was not one to let it go quickly.[69]

In his spare time, Smith applied his skills as a ghostwriter to the autobiographies of Joe Louis, Roy Campanella, and Ernie Banks. He eventually finished his career as a columnist for the *Chicago Sun-Times* and served as sports anchor for WGN television in Chicago. His many accolades included a sports writing award from the Hearst organization and he was elected president of the Chicago Press Club. Wendell Smith was in that post in 1972 when cancer claimed him at the age of 58. Ironically, his death came only four weeks after Jackie Robinson's. In 1993, the man who had to fight to get into the Baseball Writers' Association was posthumously awarded the J.G. Taylor Spink Award for excellence in baseball journalism. As part of the

Wendell Smith (courtesy National Baseball Hall of Fame Library, 1254.94 HS NBL).

honor, his photograph occupies an honored place in the writers' wing at the National Baseball Hall of Fame, not far from the players' wing where the plaque honoring Jackie Robinson is mounted.

Why does the public know so little about this man, who was the catalyst behind one of the most important events in twentieth-century American society? Jackie Robinson's achievements on the field and off, as well as Branch Rickey's courage in bringing Robinson to the Dodgers, have overshadowed Smith's equally critical role. To most white baseball players, managers, and league officials, Smith was little more than a gadfly, tormenting the sport with his repeated jabs at racial injustice. But to the millions of African Americans who experienced segregation and prejudice on a daily basis, Smith was a heroic figure. With his *Courier* articles, he became a voice out of the darkness, bringing the ugliness of segregation to light and exposing the personal suffering of American blacks into public view.

In truth, the *Courier* had been doing that before Wendell Smith arrived on the scene. What made Smith's contribution so central was his talent to expose injustice in ways that all people, not just blacks, could understand. Thanks to his efforts, segregation in sports, a topic once treated mostly with silence, became a legitimate subject for discussion and debate. His articles exposed the dramatic truth that there was no reason blacks should be excluded from Major League teams. Suddenly, the segregationist practices most people accepted as "reality" were revealed for the expressions of hatred and ignorance that they truly were.

Within the iconography of Jackie Robinson's "mystique" are the legendary stories of his demeanor—how he stood bravely by, steadfastly and unemotionally, while facing a hostile world determined to see him fail. Smith knew that this image was mostly hype. "I knew he was belligerent. To survive, he had to be. He couldn't be a Mickey Mouse," Smith explained in a later interview.[70] To ensure the success of the project, Smith's columns frequently "sanitized" Robinson's behavior. That task began almost immediately after Rickey showed an interest in Robinson during those first discussions in 1945. For example, during the off-season months of 1946–47, Robinson returned to California and got some negative exposure in the local newspapers for arguing with umpires during an exhibition game. The incident was rather minor and would not have attracted any attention at all had it been a white ballplayer. However, Rickey caught wind of it and was understandably concerned that negative publicity might ruin his "experiment."

Smith stepped in as Robinson's champion. In a letter to Rickey, he claimed that his own sources on the West Coast reported that "[Robinson] conducted himself remarkably well under the circumstances," and that he was "aggressive in a dignified sort of way."[71] Looking back later, Smith suggested that this was the start of his role in creating the Robinson image. "I didn't want to tell Mr. Rickey 'Yes, he's tough to get along with.' A lot of us knew that. When he was aroused, Jackie had a sizeable temper." Smith's efforts to keep Robinson's volatility in check while keeping the less desirable aspects of his personality from public view may be Smith's most important contribution to the Jackie Robinson legacy. It is no exaggeration to conclude that the image of Jackie Robinson as a role model of tolerance is only part truth; much of it is a product of Wendell Smith's pen.

Smith also was something of a psychological bulwark for Robinson, who was known to have occasional bouts of self-doubt. Recounting a racial incident he experienced on the bus to spring training, Robinson remembered that he nearly decided right then and there to turn around and go home. Wendell Smith convinced him not to. Again in 1947, on the eve of spring training in Cuba, Robinson was unsure about going.[72] The Dodgers were slated to play exhibition games against the Royals in Panama and the possibility of playing in that racially charged country troubled him. Although direct evidence is lacking, one can infer from existing correspondence that Robinson also had doubts about his future in the Dodgers' organization. Once again, Wendell Smith calmed Robinson down. Putting on his cheerleader cap, Smith wrote to Robinson privately, "You shouldn't worry about the plans they have for you. As I see it you are definitely going to get a chance. All you have to do is keep a cool head, play the kind of ball you are capable of playing and don't worry about anything."[73]

What motivated Smith to make such herculean efforts on behalf of Jackie Robinson and all of America's black athletes? Answering that question is not as easy as it seems. Many see Wendell Smith as a crusader far ahead of his time who envisioned a future where blacks and whites could compete on a level playing surface, not just on the ballfield but in society in general. Such an interpretation is plausible, but it mystifies his experience—much in the same way Jackie Robinson's life was mythologized—in ways that are not entirely justified. The reality is that Wendell Smith could only do so much to bring down racial barriers and he tended to suffer, as Professor Chris Lamb put it, "from too much wishful thinking."[74] Even so, one fact is undeniable. Smith possessed a single-minded devotion to the cause he considered both just and righteous. But was this devotion motivated by altruism or by the search for retribution for the wrongs he himself had suffered? That question may be moot, since the desire to help others is often borne from personal experiences of injustice. Suffice it to say that for Smith, the crusade to integrate sports was borne out of both a sense of moral obligation and a personal commitment to social and professional equality.

Chapter 6. "Making Democracy Practical"

Consequently, 1947 was indeed a pivotal year for racial equality. Jackie Robinson opened the door for blacks in baseball and by doing so he became a symbol of fair play and racial acceptance in sport. Wendell Smith had opened doors too. His articles for the *Herald American* were harbingers that the color line in the press box and in journalism in general were slowly giving way too. Appropriately enough, Smith finally did get his application to the Baseball Writers' Association of America approved, and by doing so he became its first African American member. Both Smith and Robinson spent the rest of their lives solidifying and perpetuating the gains blacks made that year so that others could also enjoy the same successes they had enjoyed. Their biographies are stories of two parallel lives—one well known, the other more obscure—that helped change America for the better. Who is to say whose contribution was greater?

CHAPTER 7

"Nervous Frustration"

Stan Kenton and the Decline of the Swing Band Era

Early one morning in mid–April 1947, a tired and visibly shaken 35-year-old man checked himself out of a Tuscaloosa, Alabama, hospital where he had gone to seek medical help for symptoms relating to exhaustion. While still in something of a confused state, he climbed into his Buick sedan and set off on a drive without informing anyone of his intentions or destination. As he crossed from Alabama through Mississippi into Arkansas, he passed a working sawmill. Intrigued by the activity, he decided to pull over and watch the sawyers work the logs and haul around the finished boards. At that moment, he thought that the lumber yard looked "like the nicest job" he could have, so on a whim he applied for work. Following a brief interview in which he revealed that he had no experience whatsoever, the yard boss turned him down on the spot.

The would-be lumber yard laborer climbed back into his sedan and continued his journey into Texas, eventually deciding to head for his home in Los Angeles, California. This rather mundane, if a bit bizarre, incident might have gone unrecorded except for the fact that the driver of that Buick was no ordinary blue-collar laborer looking for work. The unlucky applicant was none other than Stanley Newcomb Kenton—at the time, the most well-known and arguably most successful big band leader in the United States. His music could be heard on the radio, in feature films, and on phonographs, and his face adorned billboards, posters, magazine covers, and record albums everywhere, making him one of the most recognizable individuals in the country. His orchestra had been on a grueling tour across the southern tier of states, earning thousands of dollars at each gig. But suddenly, everything ground to a halt. What could have driven a nationally famous star to consider giving up fame and fortune to become a lumberjack?[1]

Kenton's experiences and the events that pushed him to consider such a drastic change of occupation are a metaphor for what was happening in popular music in postwar America. Big bands, which had dominated music for over a decade, were beginning to lose relevance as new musical styles entered into the public consciousness. Swing dances, the most popular form of live entertainment in both America and Europe in the 1930s and early 1940s, declined steadily over the next decade and gradually disappeared completely. Were these transformations simply the result of changing tastes in the listening public, or were more complex factors involved? This chapter will argue that the arc of swing music's popularity peaked in 1947, as postwar economic trends and new social realities outside the performers' control conspired to dethrone big bands. However, external forces only tell part of the story. The decline can also be traced to creative urges within the musicians themselves, as they sought to express themselves in new ways after the war. In order to make these cases, it is important to understand first how big band jazz evolved during the Great Depression and wartime years.

* * *

The historical origins of Big Band and Swing music are, like most cultural and artistic movements, difficult to track down with precision. Most scholars agree that the big band genre emerged out of the Dixieland and Ragtime traditions of the early twentieth century, evolving alongside "the Blues." All of these styles owe their existence to African American rhythms, themes, and traditions. It is therefore no accident that the earliest manifestations of Swing can be traced to the so-called "negro" bands of the 1920s like the one led by Fletcher Henderson that featured such greats as Louis Armstrong, Bessie Smith, and Coleman Hawkins. Urban areas were incubators of the swing style, with New York City (and particularly Harlem) leading the way. The genre failed to attract a wider audience until band leaders like Benny Goodman and Paul Whiteman recorded and marketed their own renditions of the earlier compositions, giving what had once been degraded as "negro" music respectability with white audiences.

It is equally daunting to find precise definitions of this musical idiom. The term "swing" defies attempts to be "nailed down" with words. As the great percussionist, Jo Jones, once said, "It's a real simple thing but there are some things you can't describe."[2] As opposed to playing "straight," where musical notes conform to standard rhythms and are given equal duration ("du-du-du-du"), swing emphasizes asymmetrical patterns that give unequal duration to notes that otherwise should be equal ("doo-wa, doo-wa" is one example). But to distill swing down to syncopation and beat displacement neglects the fact that "swing" is more a feeling than a rhythmic pattern. In that sense, "swing" resides in emotion and its interpretation varies from performer to performer.

In contrast, the term "big band" refers more to the composition and organization of the ensemble performing the music. As the term implies, "big bands" usually carry an instrumentation of more than 12 or 13 musicians.[3] What makes things confusing is that both "big band" and "swing" can be used interchangeably to describe the same types of music.[4] No matter which word one uses, swing music (and jazz in general) is more "spontaneous" than symphonic or operatic music, because it gives the performer freedom to improvise on the melody using only the underlying chord structures. Consequently, the individuality and personalities of the performers in the band are just as important, if not more so, than the ensemble as a whole. It is perhaps this emphasis on individuality and the freedom to express oneself that made big band jazz music so popular with young people and especially with dancers. It gave them license to abandon the strictures of patterned dances (like the fox trot or waltz) that their parents enjoyed and express their youthful identity on the dance floor in new (and often wild) ways.[5]

Swing was the "pop music" of the 1930s and 1940s, and it could be heard in hotels, theaters, bars, restaurants, feature films, and private homes in both Europe and America. Just about everyone knew the names of their favorite band leaders and musicians. It is not an exaggeration to say that swing music was a national obsession,[6] in no small part due to the advent of radio. Bands that got "airtime" discovered that radio could unlock fame and stardom. If a national network picked up a local broadcast, it could potentially reach forty million people.[7] Another reason big band jazz attracted large audiences is that it is exciting in live performance. Hotels regularly booked bands to attract crowds and entertain guests, and the more prestigious establishments featured nationally famous bands like Count Basie, Benny Goodman, Artie Shaw, and Duke Ellington. Consequently, larger cities including Chicago, New York, Kansas City, and Los Angeles all gained reputations as meccas for big band jazz. For those who could not afford to attend live shows or purchase recordings, radio broadcasts from hotels brought free entertainment right into one's home.

For many, however, swing music was more about dancing than listening. Younger generations especially took to big band music because it gave them an acceptable way to socialize. Dance halls provided a central location for friends to gather, party, and "cut a rug" to their favorite songs. Practically every community had one and, as Big Band jazz gained popularity, even smaller communities devoted space (sometimes in firehouses, local Veterans of Foreign Wars auditoriums, or Grange halls) where big bands could stage music. At one time there may have been as many as 800 ballrooms and amusement parks across the United States that featured big band performances.[8] Swing music and the dancing it promoted were truly the backbone of the entertainment industry.

The big band phenomenon was also the lifeblood of musicians struggling to find work during the Great Depression. Dance bookings earned local musicians some hard cash, and the more gigs a band could book, the more money they could make. But, as even modern musicians will confirm, earning a decent living based only on income from local gigs can be difficult if not impossible. Consequently, bands went on tour, and it was not unusual for the more popular bands to log thousands of miles crisscrossing the country playing dances and concerts. The most coveted gigs were at hotels and dance halls in big cities since promoters would often hire bands for weeks at a time, allowing the musicians to settle into a routine. But while travelling between cities, bands made frequent stops en route, often for one show only (a "one-night stand") in order to earn extra income and break up the journey. Consequently, even smaller cities and towns could field nationally famous orchestras, provided they had a venue and sufficient public interest to support a visit.

The Second World War had both positive and negative impacts on big band jazz. On the one hand, it stimulated the music industry by increasing the demand for entertainment, especially the kind that both sexes could enjoy together. For soldiers, dances provided a way to set aside their loneliness and worries about facing an uncertain future, at least for a few hours. Soldiers stationed stateside frequented dances on military bases and in the towns nearby; for those deployed overseas, military unit bands played decent jazz, and the occasional USO show[9] brought quality musicians directly to them. For civilians on the home front, music proved an excellent palliative to the stress and agitation of everyday life.

Unfortunately, the wartime economy also worked against the music scene. Transportation proved a chronic problem. Touring bands had to contend with gas rationing, making any long-distance travel problematic. The best bands sometimes managed to get preferential treatment in the form of commercial gas stickers, but then they had to contend with shortages of raw materials such as rubber or glass reserved for military use.[10] Rail travel was a viable alternative to roads, but trains were often crowded with soldiers with travel orders, and smaller communities were often unreachable by rail. The biggest threat to big band music, however, was conscription. As more and more musicians received draft notices, bands found it difficult to find players. With their services now in high demand, musicians with deferments gravitated toward jobs that paid them the most. As the pool of talent dried up, smaller orchestras could not compete with larger ones and many disbanded. Others hired musicians wherever they could find them, and women stepped in to fill the gaps in big band jazz orchestras. Hundreds of all-girl bands kept the swing music alive while their male counterparts went to war.[11]

Stanley Newcomb Kenton's career was very much a product of the Depression and the wartime milieu.[12] He was born in Wichita, Kansas, on December 15, 1911,[13] the son of an auto mechanic and a piano teacher. The man who would someday log hundreds of thousands of travel miles with his big band spent much of his first years moving from one home to another. In a search for permanent employment, his father relocated the family first to Colorado then to California, where they again moved repeatedly in and around the suburbs of Los Angeles, finally settling in the town of Bell. As a child, Stanley professed more of an interest in baseball than music, but after his cousins introduced him to jazz, he turned to the piano as his primary passion. A tutor remarked that young Stanley always seemed one practice away of quitting—not for the lack of talent, but because he often got angry with himself when he struggled to master a difficult musical passage. As his enthusiasm grew, Stan landed small paying performances at local restaurants and school functions.

In 1934, Kenton got a job with Everett Hoagland's band playing piano and arranging music. This was the height of the Great Depression, and as a struggling Hoagland reorganized the band to play commercial (or "sweet") music, Kenton balked. By 1937, he had left Hoagland's band and devoted most of his time to studying or playing session music for movie studios. In his free time, he dabbled in writing experimental jazz charts based on the classical music he adored as a young man. Armed with a cache of original compositions and the drive to succeed, Kenton committed himself to his music and formed his own big band in 1940. The musicians who auditioned liked his charts, and by October the full band had recorded demo records.[14] A fledgling Stan Kenton Orchestra was born.

Kenton's big break came on Memorial Day, 1941, when his band was booked to play at the Rendezvous Ballroom on the Balboa Peninsula in California, after another band had cancelled. The show was broadcast on local Los Angeles radio station KHJ (thanks in part to Kenton's persuasion), and it drew a large enough listenership to get Kenton noticed in and around Los Angeles. By the end of the summer his orchestra was on the road, travelling to Oakland, Glendale, and other communities within driving distance. In September, they made their first commercial recordings.[15] Kenton's notoriety spread quickly around Los Angeles and among booking agents in New York who, always looking for new talent, invited him to take the band on the road to the Big Apple. But as fate would have it, a job opened up at the recently opened Palladium theater in Hollywood.

For a West Coast band, the Palladium was the gold standard of gigs. First of all, the theater booked bands for weeks at a time (provided they drew crowds), making it far preferable to doing one-nighters on the road. More importantly, the Palladium was a huge, glitzy venue located on

Sunset Boulevard in the epicenter of the entertainment industry. Consequently, shows there garnered a lot of national attention and were broadcast coast-to-coast on radio.[16] The Palladium booked Kenton to play for five weeks straight through New Year's Eve,[17] so they postponed the New York trip and opened there on November 25. Two weeks later, the United States was at war. In the aftermath of the attack on Pearl Harbor, radio stations remained on the air continuously to broadcast news updates. To fill in time between news bulletins, they played dance band music. The Palladium happened to be open late, and so the music originating there was picked up and broadcast to a captive audience all across the country. It was a fortunate happenstance for the band. As he recounted in an interview years later, "What they got was Stan Kenton whether they liked it or not. We went on coast-to-coast three times a night."[18]

Kenton's early success can be attributed to the energy of his live performances but also to the originality of many of his songs. One of his first successful tunes, "Artistry in Rhythm," became the Kenton Orchestra's theme song and the foundation of its identity for the next thirty years. Also, his music was different from what most people expected from a "dance" band. In general, Kenton liked his music played loud with forceful staccato attacks. That approach did not work well with ballads and popular dance numbers and stood in sharp contrast to the more melodious tunes played by other contemporary bands like Glenn Miller, Artie Shaw, or Benny Goodman. Many critics disliked it as well. Barry Ulanov, co-editor and critic at *The Metronome*, said that Kenton's music sounded "like a moving-man grunting under the weight of a concert grand."[19]

Critics also found it difficult to relate to Kenton's penchant for incorporating themes from classical music into his own compositions. Ticket holders were not always enamored with it either, especially those who came to dance. Despite his deep creative urges, Kenton quickly discovered that he needed to balance "his" music with the paying public's demand for danceable ("sweet") music. Accordingly, his shows featured a mixture of "pop" tunes done in styles familiar to dancing audiences and his own more *avant-garde* music inspired by classical compositions and featuring unusual rhythm patterns. This *modus operandi* served Kenton well over the years, making his band popular with both the casual listener and those who enjoyed new and innovative music. It was a compromise that would repeatedly be put to the test, however.

The jitterbugging West Coast crowds made Kenton's orchestra a success, but it still had to prove itself in The Big Apple before it could achieve national fame. So, in January of 1942, the band packed up for the arduous cross-country trip to play the Roseland Ballroom on Broadway in the heart of New York City. The band took advantage of any venue along the way that would book them (including fraternity houses on local college campuses) and did one-nighters all along the route.[20] They finally arrived in New York in early February to kick-off what was supposed to be an eight-week stay but after a few performances, both the audiences and the band realized that the booking had been a mistake. The Roseland prided itself as a venue for more "refined" dancing like rhumbas or tangos and quieter music that would not interfere with polite conversation. Almost immediately, the crowd complained that Kenton's "west coast style" was too loud and too difficult to dance to. Lots of criticism came pouring in. Turn down the volume. Stop doing so many original tunes. Add more danceable numbers. Everyone had an idea what they thought would "improve" the band. The Roseland gig lasted less than three weeks.[21]

Although the 1942 East Coast trip got off to a bad start, it was not a total loss. The shows from Roseland were broadcast on radio, helping the Kenton orchestra gain much needed East Coast exposure. Coming to New York also introduced the band to new venues, including the Meadowbrook Ballroom in Cedar Grove, New Jersey, one of the biggest and most famous big band locales anywhere. Sites in Philadelphia, Boston, and Baltimore all opened their doors to him as the band toured the East Coast that spring and summer. As might be expected, theater engagements generally did better than dance gigs. But the critics continued to be less than charitable. Writing for *The Metronome* magazine, George Simon reviewed the Kenton phenomenon that August: "The intense driving is the Kenton band's chief characteristic. It's also one of its chief drawbacks. For though it may be somewhat ingenious, and though it does serve as an identification tag, it produced a tenseness that makes both relaxed listening and dancing pretty much impossible."[22]

Another critic called the Kenton style "machine gun music." Despite the panning in the press, Kenton's band kept getting hired. It took many more months of successful shows, but eventually the critics grew to tolerate, if not enjoy, the music.[23]

Kenton's East Coast tour and the relative lack of success he experienced at the Roseland proved to be a formative period in his evolution as both a composer and performer. Kenton had always been somewhat flamboyant as a band leader, but now he began to incorporate even more "shtick" and humorous dialogue into his performances. One favorite tactic was to put "plants" in the audience who would disrupt the show, thereby providing him an opportunity to crack jokes or fool around with his band. This tendency to use gags and poke fun (even at himself) stayed with him and served him well throughout his entire career.

Although the membership of the band changed continually, Kenton's personality and showmanship provided the continuity audiences

Chapter 7. "Nervous Frustration"   147

associated with the band for years to come. More importantly, those months witnessed Kenton's maturation as a businessman. The musician in him had always admired the innovative music of other jazz greats like Duke Ellington and Woody Herman, and late in 1942 he felt ready enough to branch out in his own creative directions by incorporating even more themes of classical composers like Stravinsky and Milhaud into his jazz compositions.[24]

But the businessman in Kenton realized that there were limits to such innovation. Dance gigs were still a jazz band's bread and butter; they brought in the cash and cash paid the bills. Consequently, Kenton had to balance his creative urges against the need to earn money, at least for the time being. But that did not mean he had to like doing it. In February 1943, Kenton revealed his commitment to innovative music to *Down Beat* magazine. "I'll go back to playing redlight piano in a saloon if my style of music isn't accepted by the public," he quipped. "You can lay this on board—we are going ahead doing what we think is right."[25] However, in July of 1943, Kenton had to admit that he had scaled back on his creativity and added more popular tunes to his orchestra's repertoire out of necessity. "Sure, I've made concessions ... it was either that or completely giving up a musical idea that I still think is right. But don't think that I've said so long to my original ideas.... I still think the kind of music we used to play exclusively was the best kind."[26]

Apparently, a war-weary population was interested more in popular tunes and danceable music than in innovative experimentation. As a concession to public tastes, his dance gigs featured three popular songs for every original tune, simply to keep the crowds happy and buying tickets. Nevertheless, through it all Kenton still clung to his vision of a new kind of jazz music. It was not yet the right time to realize it.

The early 1940s were halcyon years for big bands. The war caused a spike in the demand for entertainment and gigs were plentiful. As Kenton's band headed back to the West Coast by way of Chicago, it had lots of work, stopping at scores of military bases and civilian venues all along its route. Steady employment continued once back in California as the band regularly played the Hollywood Canteen and returned to the Palladium. Then, Kenton got the break of a lifetime when he received an offer to be the stage band behind Bob Hope's radio broadcasts. It was too good an opportunity to pass up. The gig provided his orchestra with 39 weeks of stable, regular employment that would not require any travel. Furthermore, Bob Hope was a national celebrity. Any tie to him and his nationwide broadcasts could only add more prestige to Kenton's already growing public persona.

On the downside, the gig afforded the orchestra members few opportunities to display their individual talents, since their main requirement was to play background music or cues rather than complete numbers.[27] It also meant that Kenton would have to give up playing at the Palladium and other local spots, as the contract with Hope forbade any public performances longer than one night within a 100-mile radius of Los Angeles.[28] Although the gig did not pay a great deal, Kenton accepted. Working for the show gave his home life stability and his personal connection with Hope got him the much-coveted commercial gasoline sticker, allowing his band to venture outside of the Los Angeles confines for a one-nighter when it had the chance.

The contract lasted into 1944[29] and once freed of the obligation, Kenton embarked on another string of public performances. By then, the orchestra could claim a string of hits. In addition to covers of tunes like "St. James Infirmary" (1942) and "Peanut Vendor" (1944), Kenton had become famous for his original charts, particularly the songs that became his signature pieces, "Artistry in Rhythm" and "Eager Beaver," both recorded in 1943.[30] With the addition of singers Anita O'Day and later June Christy, Kenton's orchestra scored more commercial hits with "And Her Tears Flowed Like Wine" (1944) and "Tampico" (1945).

At the war's end, the band was again crisscrossing the United States. Early August found it back in New York City working at the Hotel Pennsylvania's Café Rouge and broadcasting on NBC radio. By November they were back at the Palladium in Los Angeles, and when not performing they were doing recording sessions for record companies and film soundtracks, including one feature length film ("Talk About a Lady").[31] But for the music industry in general, the end of the war precipitated major changes. Demobilization meant the return of many seasoned musicians to civilian life, and bands all across America saw an influx of talented sidemen ready to get their chops back in shape and find work. Smaller orchestras re-formed to meet the demand and suddenly swing music became even more accessible to the public. Kenton's orchestra also benefited from demobilization as some of the best musicians of their era signed on, including Eddie Safranski on string bass, Kai Winding on trombone, and Shelley Manne on drums.

One new addition to Kenton's staff, a former army private who also happened to write music, would change Kenton's musical life forever.Pete Rugolo was born to an Italian family that emigrated to the United States when he was only five years old. As he matured, he studied music with Darius Milhaud at Mills College where he came to love contemporary classical composers like Maurice Ravel and Aaron Copland. His favorite, however, was Igor Stravinsky. "His colorings, rhythms and harmonic structures have showed us new possibilities in music," Rugolo opined. "If more orchestra leaders listen[ed] to him and the other classicists, dance music would sound less dated and hackneyed."[32]

Chapter 7. "Nervous Frustration" 149

June Christy fronting the Stan Kenton Orchestra at the Hollywood Palladium, date unknown (courtesy Stan Kenton Collection, University of North Texas Digital Library, sk_0356, metadata 11258).

During the war, Rugolo directed the Army band at Fort Scott in San Francisco and having heard Kenton's music, began to write charts for him. After Rugolo submitted a few arrangements that he had penned during the war, Kenton was impressed enough to offer him a job once he got out of the Army. The day he was discharged, Rugolo joined the band as composer and arranger.[33] In Rugolo, Kenton had found his musical soul mate. Not only did the two men idolize the same classical composers, but their personalities were also perfectly complementary—Kenton, the outgoing extrovert perfectly comfortable fronting the orchestra in large crowds, counterbalanced by Rugolo, the shy, behind-the-scenes introvert.

Kenton trusted Rugolo to run with their ideas and produce progressive charts featuring symphonic voicings and classical themes. Most of them were never meant to "swing," and consequently some of the arrangements shocked older band members who had cut their teeth on more traditional music.[34] Rugolo's arranging, combined with Kenton's flair for publicity, took the orchestra to dizzying new heights of popularity. The collaboration between the two men became the battery powering the Kenton phenomenon.

The year 1946 was a heady one for Kenton and his band. *Look* magazine named the orchestra "Band of the Year," predicting that it was the one most likely to hit the top of the charts. Even though he enjoyed a string of successes, Kenton still suffered from self-doubt. He was still under a good deal of pressure to conform to the public tastes, and for a time he considered fielding a mostly commercial band. But after an overnight stay in Boston, he made the decision that going completely sweet was not the answer. He needed to create what he called "a jazz mood";[35] i.e., his own distinctive sound. The end product was Kenton's most famous album, *Artistry in Rhythm*. The recording broke new ground, in that it was Kenton's first major attempt to put his musical agenda—what he was now referring to as "progressive jazz"—on vinyl. Many of the cuts on the album were written to be heard and not danced to. Two in particular, "Artistry in Bolero" and "Opus in Pastels" reflected Kenton's vision and his admiration for the classics. Interspersed were commercial tunes designed to keep those audiences happy as well.

Artistry in Rhythm was the opening salvo in Stan Kenton's personal war between artistic and commercial music. Its success spawned a series of songs and albums all based around the "artistry" concept and soon became Kenton's indelible mark on the jazz music world. It was something of a commercial gamble, however, but judging by the number of gigs they did that year, the new music was well received. "Band boy" Ed Gabel claimed that Kenton and his musicians hit all 48 states that year, in the process logging upwards of 100,000 miles.[36] Additionally, the orchestra appeared on an estimated 450 radio shows in conjunction with the on-site gigs. June Christy recalled that the public's response to them was varied.

> The audience reaction to that band was usually great but it depended upon where we played. If we played for an audience who expected to listen to the band and not dance, they were avid fans, and they wouldn't budge a muscle. They'd just listen with their eyes wide open and their ears wide open, but as we often did, sometimes we'd be booked into a dance palace, and people looked at us as if we were freaks because there was nothing to dance to and the band was always loud.[37]

After five years of very hard work, Stan Kenton and his Orchestra were finally a national sensation. Fan clubs sprang up all across America.[38] There was a high demand for live performances and shows sold out almost everywhere they went. Success had a downside, however. Life on the road as part of a touring jazz orchestra was less than glamorous. The constant travelling from one-nighter to one-nighter took both a physical and mental toll on the performers. "We never seemed to get off the bus," June Christy remembered. "There were a lot of times we didn't have the time to check into a hotel and we'd have to do the gig and then get back to the bus and go to the next job. And particularly for a girl it was not too much fun because I think a woman has a little more to worry about to look good."³⁹

Saxophonist Bob Cooper, who eventually married Christy, agreed with her assessment. "The itineraries, they just went month after month, sometimes with no days, no nights off. And if we did get a night off, it might be travelling on the bus all night long. After a few years it got very tiring."⁴⁰ But as difficult as that life may have been for the musicians, it was doubly taxing for the band leader. Kenton always drove ahead of the bus in his own car to do advance publicity in the next town on the itinerary. Often, that meant doing live radio interviews or meeting with disk jockeys in order to drum up support and encourage attendance at live shows.

To combat the stress of incessant travel, Kenton frequently booked longer engagements at theaters or hotels, but those gigs produced their own variety of stress. The band normally did three or four shows daily, so a typical workday might begin at 10:00 a.m. and not end until midnight. Hence, band members had precious little time to rest or leave the premises. Musicians spent what free time they had between gigs grabbing a quick bite to eat or catching a brief snooze. Some succumbed to the lure of

The Stan Kenton Orchestra posing with tour bus, ca. 1947 or 1948 (William P. Gottlieb Collection, Library of Congress, LC-GLB23-0516).

alcohol as an escape from the physical and emotional grind of daily performance. Despite the hardships and inevitable squabbles between the musicians, the force of Stan Kenton's personality kept the band together. Bob Cooper said that "he was like a father to us. He worried about people's problems and tried to resolve them when he could."[41] Drummer Shelley Manne considered him to be a "father confessor."[42] Most everyone agreed that he was a gentleman to all, even to audiences who were not always receptive to the music. Nevertheless, the strain slowly debilitated Kenton. His marriage was in jeopardy, and by the end of 1946, his closest associates noticed changes in his personality brought on by stress.

Kenton's success belies what was really going on in the music business at the time. The November 1946 issue of *Down Beat* magazine summed it up with the artfully phrased headline, "the music biz just ain't nowhere." Indeed, the business was in trouble. Demand for big band services had declined since the end of the war, in part because the number of bands with good musicians had increased. Postwar inflation also played a large role in the decline. As the cost of food and lodging rose, life on the road became very expensive. Many musicians complained that they had little of their salary left over at the end of the week after paying their expenses. To compensate, band managers asked ever higher booking prices and demanded a contractual minimum payment guarantee in case the gig was a bust. A good band could expect thousands of dollars in guarantees just for signing a contract and an even greater take if the contract allowed it to take a percentage of the proceeds from the gate.

Promoters, however, could not control how many people would show up for any given night since any natural catastrophe could intervene and keep the crowds from showing up. Hence, making a large guarantee was risky business; a single failure could bankrupt a promoter.[43] As if to add insult to the injury, the so-called "cabaret tax,"[44] the 20 percent wartime tax on entertainment venues, was still in effect. Ticket prices and cover charges began to rise[45] and consumers, faced with the choice of spending money for a live performance or staying at home and listening on the radio for free, often chose the latter. Hotel show attendances declined concomitantly, sometimes by as much as 40 percent. To an extent, big bands were also victims of their own success. During the war when gigs were plentiful but good sidemen hard to come by, the best musicians could not only find plenty of work, but they were also well paid. With a steady stream of money coming in, band leaders took on more musicians, and larger orchestras meant larger weekly payrolls. All of these factors proved a drag on the big band industry, and some musicians began looking for alternatives.

As the big bands struggled with the harsh economic climate, a new jazz genre was starting to attract more and more attention from jazz listeners. "Bebop," as this style is known, is the antithesis of big band music in that it de-emphasizes melody and focuses even more on solo improvisation based on the underlying chord patterns. As a result, the technical proficiencies of the performing artists became more important than the tune itself. The style originated in the late 1930s and early 1940s and grew in strength among young musicians during the war as a form of rebellion against the "formulaic" nature of big band jazz. For some, it was an attempt to take jazz back closer to its roots in Dixieland and Ragtime. For others, bebop was a form of social rebellion. It grew out of the hopes among African Americans that the war would bring changes to the racially divided society in which they lived. At the very least, it was a new music that attacked norms and questioned the status quo.

Bebop combos had several advantages over big bands. First of all, they were smaller (typically four or five musicians) and hence the lower payrolls and decreased travel costs made their asking prices much more attractive to booking agents. Moreover, the new genre allowed performers the freedom to improvise, so the audience experience could (and did) change substantially from one night to the next. Consequently, there was no need for arrangers to write complex musical scores. The most attractive feature of bebop was that the music was never intended for dances; in fact, dancing to bebop was virtually impossible because it was often played at a frenetic pace with frequent and sudden tempo changes. Because there was no dancing involved, the cabaret tax did not apply. As the genre caught on with the general listening public, bebop artists garnered more and more publicity. Names like Dizzy Gillespie, Coleman Hawkins, and Charlie Parker started to appear in the *Down Beat* polls among the best musicians and band leaders. Jazz aficionados had a new and vibrant alternative to traditional big band music.

By the end of 1946, the slumping demand for big band music and the threat posed by bebop forced orchestras to consider drastic changes. One option was to add either progressive or bebop arrangements into the mix in order to sound more "fresh." Woody Herman and Boyd Raeburn, among others, tried that with varying degrees of success. Going more "bebop" was not an attractive option for the more established big band leaders; most refused to mess with the identities that had gotten them their fame in the first place. As Buddy Rich, one of the greatest big band drummers of all time, once said, "people are too accustomed in big bands on the stand—they feel cheated with anything less."[46] Another option was to surrender to the marketplace and retool set lists to provide more popular music. Some bands caved in and went completely "sweet." But for those leaders who detested commercial music, Kenton included, such surrender was unthinkable.

A final option was to downsize payrolls by dropping musicians, but that would involve restructuring sections and reworking arrangements. Nevertheless, many bands took this option. One by one, some the greatest of the musical acts of the day disbanded, at least temporarily, until they could "retool" their music. The list of orchestras that threw in the towel toward the end of 1946 reads like a Who's Who of jazz. Harry James put his band on a two-month hiatus at the end of November. Les Brown announced that he would break up his band entirely. Tommy Dorsey, Benny Goodman, Woody Herman, Jack Teagarden, Billy Eckstein, and others all called it quits to reorganize.[47] The wartime bubble of demand for big bands had burst.

Stan Kenton's progressive jazz helped him manage these pressures, but it did not insulate him from them. In an attempt to stay relevant as a musical innovator, Kenton experimented by adding Latin rhythms into his music. The addition of Brazilian guitarist Laurindo Almeida and bongo player Jack Costanzo to the rhythm section gave his music a new and exciting feel without sacrificing his progressive jazz vision. Besides, he was still pulling in crowds with his own music so drastic changes seemed unwarranted. Despite his continuing success, Kenton's mental and physical state deteriorated as did his marriage to his wife, Violet. Taking note of the steady stream of band leaders who had hung it up, he told friends confidentially in early January 1947 that he too was considering breaking up his band.[48] But being the consummate businessman, Kenton wanted to honor contracts that had been already signed—bookings that stood to earn the band a great deal of money. So, against the advice of physicians, Kenton forged ahead, thinking that a reduced workload would alleviate enough stress to allow him to continue functioning. But that reduction in work never happened, in part because Kenton decided to lower his "guarantee" to $1,750 per show against 60 percent of the box office take, simply to make his band more attractive during the difficult economic climate.[49] As more bookings started to come in, Kenton worked more feverishly than ever. His devotion to the band and his work ethic even attracted the admiration of his competitors. "I've never seen anything like it in all the years I've been in this business," one agent for another band remarked, "I have never seen a leader work so many hours or cooperate so readily on all kind of promotion."[50]

As 1947 began, Stan Kenton and his Orchestra could boast that it was the only profitable big band left on the road. They kicked off their schedule by touring across New England doing gigs and one-nighters, leading up to New York for a recording session at Capitol Records. Staying true to the formula that got him this far, Kenton got Capitol to agree to make records with one side "a sort of straight jazz side" featuring "an unorthodox, progressive arrangement." The other side would contain what Kenton called a "juke box special" (a commercial ballad or popular vocal).[51] That way, his band could continue to provide sweet music for the dancing public while at the same time promoting its progressive jazz agenda.

He might have stayed on the East Coast longer, had it not been for a mix-up between his agents and the owners of a ballroom in Los Angeles. Nine months earlier, the owners of the recently opened Avodon ballroom had booked the Kenton orchestra for a four-week gig slated to begin on February 4. When the business turned sour in December of the previous year, Kenton's manager, Carlos Gastel, and the Avodon executives discussed voiding the contract. Gastel believed that they had reached an agreement to do so. But following a long, successful stint by the Count Basie orchestra, the Avodon owners denied that any such agreement existed and decided to enforce the deal; a decision made in part because the negotiated price was favorable to the ballroom.[52]

With no way out of the contract, Kenton and his promoters shelved plans for a long East Coast tour.[53] But before loading up the band, Kenton staged an unpublicized concert at the Lyric theater in Baltimore on January 24. What makes the Lyric gig so important is that it was an experiment in a pure concert setting. Despite having little or no dance music in the program, the concert drew 2,600 people paying ticket prices ranging from $1.50 to $4.40.[54] Kenton interpreted his success there as evidence that progressive jazz could work in a concert venue without the need for a ballroom or dance hall. That Baltimore concert was a harbinger of things to come.

Kenton headed back to Los Angeles to fulfill the Avodon contract. The four-week gig went by with relative ease, even if the expected crowds failed to show up.[55] With the band again free to go on the road, Kenton planned a loop through California, Oregon, and Washington to hit at least 21 different venues in the span of 26 days. Out of the 21 gigs, 18 of them paid the band percentage money. Operators up and down the coast had not seen that kind of attendance in over three years, and the huge crowds stoked their hopes that business would pick up during the summer season.[56]

At the conclusion of those first three weeks, the band got a three-day respite from the rest of the tour to record for Capitol Records in Hollywood. The sessions produced "Concerto to End All Concertos," and was one of Kenton's most ambitious recordings to date. A review in *Swing* magazine said that it "marked a new era for Stan Kenton fans." It went on to describe the music as "weird and excitingly different ... a masterpiece of melody, harmony, and rhythm. It's the most unusual jazz platter at this time."[57]

Kenton was already showing signs of fatigue and exhaustion and his doctors advised him to start taking it easy lest he suffer a complete collapse. His band was worn out too, so during the recording session (on

April 1) Kenton surprised the music world by announcing that he would disband the orchestra and take a three-month vacation beginning in May. Unfortunately, the band was committed to another extended road tour—this time an eastward trek across Texas, Louisiana, and Alabama and onward into Tennessee, Virginia, the District of Columbia, and Pennsylvania before ending up at the Meadowbrook in New Jersey—all within the span of four weeks.[58] Disbanding would cost Kenton $150,000 in forfeited contracts, so his booking agency, General Artists Corporation (GAC), asked Stan to postpone his vacation until after the completion of the tour. After considering for a day or two, he relented.[59]

Kenton tried to put a good spin on things, telling his friends "I'm not in quite as bad shape as my doc thinks. Breaking up my band, even temporarily, would hurt me more than a physical breakdown. It's all I live for."[60] Against medical advice, Kenton continued the extended road trip. A steady pace of gigs followed. In Texas, the band performed at the Lake Worth Casino in Fort Worth (Easter weekend, April 4 and 5), the Plantation Club in Dallas (April 9) and the Pleasure Pier Ballroom in Port Arthur (April 10). Two college dates followed, first at the University of Texas in Austin (April 11) and then at Texas A&M (April 12). The next day had the band booked at the Cedar Lane Club in Opelousas, Louisiana.

By the time they got through the Lone Star State, Stan's orchestra was showing signs of outright exhaustion. June Christy got through the performance at Cedar Lane but lost her voice thanks to a bad case of the flu and left the band to recuperate. Kenton, who had maxed out his schedule by doing personal appearances and record signings during the afternoons in addition to the performances at night, was now showing signs of severe stress. Even the trade presses reported that he was on the verge of a nervous breakdown.[61]

The bottom finally fell out on Wednesday April 16 as the orchestra headed to Tuscaloosa to play the Junior prom at the University of Alabama. Kenton later recalled that he took sick en route and, after vomiting blood, decided that this would be the last gig for a while. The schedule featured the usual concert from 4:00 p.m. to 6:00 p.m., followed by a four-hour dance gig from 8:00 p.m. to midnight. Although the afternoon concert went well (despite playing to only a half-filled auditorium), the overworked and exhausted band leader broke down[62] after the packed evening performance and admitted to the band that he could not continue the tour. At the end of the day, the band gathered back at the hotel where Kenton gave each musician an extra month's salary and a ticket to wherever they wished to go. A terse telegram to his booking agents in New York, sent on the 17th, told the tale. "Had to break up tonight. Couldn't go further. Am terribly sick. Please notify everyone in the office."[63]

Chapter 7. "Nervous Frustration"

Kenton's exhaustion caught no one by surprise, but the suddenness of the announcement rattled the band members. Most of them had no contingency plan for what to do if the gigs stopped. Some went to their homes, others traveled to New York or Hollywood in the hopes of landing other employment. The breakup occurred at the height of the band's earning power, underscoring the irony that the Kenton orchestra—the last one to hold on to their swing/progressive identity—was the only major band to quit because of the health of the leader and not because of economic difficulties. Reflecting on the experience several months later, Stan said "I got through Texas all right and I really felt I could get well by continuing on the road and taking things a bit easier. But that night in Tuscaloosa the walls caved in. I should have taken the doc's advice in the first place."[64]

Apparently fearful for his health after the vomiting scare, Stan presented himself to the local hospital for a check-up. His decision to drive home and the incident at the Arkansas sawmill, recounted earlier, have become part of Kenton folklore. Stan later admitted that he was a bit "out of [his] head" when he decided to apply for work there. But there was nothing insane about the network of promoters and fans supporting him. Most everyone associated with the band expected Kenton would not be out of circulation for very long and they wanted to be prepared to reform the band when he was ready. While Stan recuperated on a ranch outside of Hollywood, his manager stayed connected with the band members, asking them to take only temporary jobs so that they could rejoin Kenton sometime in September. Capitol kept releasing records that had been pressed earlier, and his publicity agents continued to dog disc jockeys to play them in their broadcasts. Kenton, the man, was temporarily out of circulation but his music and the money-making machinery underpinning him continued unabated.

Kenton spent the summer of 1947 recuperating in California. Most of the time, he isolated himself from even his closest friends and associates, preferring instead to go to the beach on weekends, get a tan, and relax. But by August, the band leader in him was once again itching to "get back into the whirl."[65] He set September 27 as a target date for his return to public performance, and messages went out to all the previous band members, inviting them back. Kenton boldly predicted that "the band will be a better one than we had last spring,"[66] but getting his musicians to return was not a given. Several had combined with saxophonist Vido Musso to form "Stan Kenton's All-Stars" and had landed an eight-week gig at the Sherman Hotel in Chicago.[67] June Christy took the time to record a couple of solo records and sing in clubs as a single.

In the end, however, June and most of the sidemen did come back to the band.[68] The last thing Kenton wanted, however, was a return to the status quo. His illness and hiatus from performing proved that he could not continue his past work schedule and lifestyle. So, Kenton decided that from then on his music would be geared toward concert venues and not dance halls. Concerts would lessen the stress of touring and reduce the number of days he needed to be on the road. Also, eschewing dances would allow him the freedom to satisfy his creative urges better. It was a fateful decision, but was it an economically viable one?

The new progressive jazz orchestra kicked off on September 27 as planned, appropriately enough at the Rendezvous Ballroom on Balboa Beach, California, where his career had begun six years earlier. To say the shows were a success would be a gross understatement. A total of 9,000 fans showed up over the two days. One day's draw of 5,170 broke a four-year-old record held by Tommy Dorsey.[69] The band then headed up the Pacific coast again for what Kenton called a "shakedown" tour. "The idea behind the tour is to add another showcase to the music we feature not styled for dancing. We've done it on records and now I'm going to give people a chance to see how it's done," Stan explained to *Down Beat*.[70] Nevertheless, at the gig at San Francisco's Edgewater Beach ballroom, Kenton relented and played a couple of dances as well as a main concert. Kenton was back, and evidently as much the promoter as he had been before he took sick.

One anecdotal story explains just how fired up the rejuvenated Kenton was. At one gig on the tour, Kenton found out that the promoter had actually lost a little money on that night's performance, so Kenton promised that if the next night's take did not recoup those losses, he (Kenton) would reimburse the difference out of his own pocket. As it turned out the promoter did draw even with the profits from the next show.[71]

At the end of the shakedown tour, the band returned to California to record tracks for a new album entitled *Concert in Progressive Jazz* at Capitol Records. Despite Kenton's hope that the travel demands would lessen, the calendar for November and December featured another grueling schedule of one-nighters across the Midwest reminiscent of the previous years' tour. November alone had the band making 17 appearances in 22 days ending up with a major concert appearance in Chicago's Civic Auditorium. At least there would be a respite in December, with a long-term engagement at the Commodore Hotel in New York City.

In describing his intentions for the new band, Kenton was brutally blunt and direct. "Public likes and dislikes have nothing to do with the progress of modern music. Bands with guts will play what they like," Stan opined.[72] Doubling down, he predicted that there was "no hope for the so-called sweet bands. Two years will tell the tale. People are tired of the old 'drone' chords. Dissonances are required. I think the greatest contemporary composer is Stravinsky, with Milhaud a close second. The generation that makes my band known will make Stravinsky's music as popular as Beethoven's."[73] Kenton was predicting that modern jazz would be moving in a new direction, and he was not-so-subtly explaining that he intended to be at the vanguard of that movement. "I am not, however, influenced by Stravinsky, nor by Dizzy.... I like to feel that the band isn't influenced by anybody or anything except perhaps sound. My music is typed to sounds ... not necessarily to emotion."[74]

And Kenton was willing to back up his beliefs with actual practice. To play the dissonances and extended chord structures his music demanded, Kenton had to carry more musicians than most "sweet" bands playing standard music. When confronted with the usual criticisms that his music was too loud and discordant, Kenton lashed back, saying that those critics "should see the faces of kids who have driven a hundred miles, through the snow to see the band ... to stand in front of the stand in an ecstasy all their own."[75]

Such comments may seem overly self-confident or even egotistical, but the box office receipts confirmed the truth in his contentions. On October 21, a Los Angeles disc jockey arranged a "Just Jazz" concert in Pasadena billed as the "Artistry in Rhythm Concert," and it drew huge crowds. The Chicago Opera House concert was also a success; over 4,000 people attended and despite added seating, an estimated 1,500 more had to be turned away.[76] The reviews of his stay at the Commodore in New York gushed. "Not in some years has a hotel crowd stood around a band-stand, watched avidly, cheered, applauded and yelled at everything the band did," wrote Michael Levin for *Down Beat*. Even "the unhippest in the room stood around to watch and marvel."[77] Bernie Woods, the music scene reporter for *Variety*, had a similar reaction:

> Kenton is doing things that many thought no longer possible in the band field: (1) He's playing to heavy crowds exclusively made up of kids who (2) rush to surround the band stand the second the first musician puts foot on the stand to start a set and (3) then stand around open mouthed, drinking in his surrealism in music like they knew what it was all about. In short, some dance, but the majority listen. There's only one answer to the newly-found success of Kenton in New York. His band plays the most exciting music to be heard anywhere.[78]

Woods admitted that although he personally thought much of the music was "aimless and often just plain uncomfortable noise,"[79] he acknowledged that at least it was not the same tired old music. And he was further impressed that the new compositions seemed to connect with young people. Kenton noticed that connection as well. In an interview in 1948, Kenton said:

We are placing our hopes in the youth of the world. It's not that the older generation is anti-progressive. Two wars, depressions, unreal prosperity and other uncertainties have been too much of a strain on their emotions. It's the youngsters that will be making the greatest contributions to the art forms. They're more honest with their emotional selves. They're searching for new colors, new tones, new tempos, new everything.[80]

Kenton had evidently tapped into the pulse of a new generation.

The audience response was truly amazing, given the in-your-face sarcasm that Kenton brought to his public performances. "This is our music. If you don't like it, don't come," he implored from the stand. Before concerts even started, Kenton warned crowds not to dance because of the "vicious tempo changes … somebody's liable to break a leg."[81] In New York, he cut the number of radio performances in half and refused to play popular songs during the broadcasts. He was often heard to tell his audiences, "Don't dance, just listen." Kenton was equally straightforward with his response to the critics of the progressive jazz style: "When people tell me they don't understand our music, it sort of makes me a little impatient. Understand it? You don't have to understand it to like it—you have to feel it. Music is for the emotions! You can't always dance to our arrangements because music—we believe—ought to be written and played more for the ears than it is for the feet."[82]

Still, Kenton could not divorce the band from sweet, danceable music entirely. Although his emphasis was still on booking concerts, he conceded that if there was not enough income from them to sustain the tour, he would reluctantly agree to do one-night dance gigs.[83]

As the year drew to a close, Kenton's crew retreated to the recording studio (as did most bands) to lay down as many recordings as possible before the second Petrillo recording ban was to go in effect on January 1.[84] He and his Progressive Jazz Orchestra closed out 1947 on top of the heap. When judged solely by the box office take, the new band was even more successful than the 1946 band that had won him accolades and international fame. An adoring public rewarded him with top band honors in *Down Beat's* annual poll, beating out the perennial favorite Duke Ellington by a wide margin of votes. June Christy won for best band singer, Pete Rugolo took home the best arranger honors, and two of his sidemen (Safranski on bass, Manne on drums) walked away with first chair honors as well. But the results indicated that there was a different wind blowing as well. For the first time ever, *Down Beat* changed its rules to allow individual performers who were also small combo leaders to compete in the poll. When the final list of winners appeared, Charlie Parker won alto sax honors and Dizzy Gillespie's combo came in fourth overall in the favorite bands category.

Reflecting on all that had happened in the previous year, Kenton

Chapter 7. "Nervous Frustration" 161

waxed philosophical during an interview with *Down Beat* following his first-place victory. When asked about what progressive jazz meant for music, he was again blunt and deliberate. "Swing is dead, gone, finished. It was useful as a transitory form, but what we are doing now not only out-dates it but makes it sound playfully elementary."[85] When asked whether his band was good for dancing, Kenton replied "definitely not." Interestingly, when the subject turned to bebop, Kenton gushed with praise. "It's doing more for music than anything else. It's educating the people to new intervals and sounds ... the trouble with it is that it lacks emotion.... It's not the new jazz, but it's the hot-foot on the way."[86]

And when asked about his band's future, Kenton was equally direct. "From now on as much as possible, we are through with dances, [we] will play only concerts. The music must broaden in color, dynamics, harmonics and emotion. The extent in which we are successful will determine our future. Our jazz is dissonant and often strident. So is the age in which we live and the people to whom we play. Neurotic? Yes—aren't most of us today, to one extent or another?"

In 1948, Kenton's "progressive jazz" concert tour travelled all over the United States. In February, the orchestra played to a packed Carnegie Hall, where the audience went wild when they played "Prologue Suite" and "Concerto to End All Concertos." Another concert at Chicago's Civic Opera House saw all 4,200 seats plus standing room tickets sold out two weeks before.[87] Boston's Symphony Hall, and various theaters in Baltimore, Washington, D.C., and Newark, New Jersey, all fielded performances. In June, a concert at the Hollywood Bowl brought in 15,000 adoring fans. Success on the road meant that the band could continue its experimentation with discordant sounds and rhythms, and Kenton's music became more and more like that of the classical composers he admired.

The culmination of this musical transformation may have been the addition of Bob Graettinger as arranger, a man some considered "eccentric"[88] who loved to work with discordant sounds and time signatures. His most notorious work, entitled "City of Glass" was a composition with no discernible melodies or harmonies, featuring instead musical "tensions" between sections and individual performers. Kenton lauded the chart publicly, claiming that it was "an example of the kind of music jazz is going to become. The modernists deserve the credit for proving that jazz doesn't have to be danced to."[89] The musicians who first practiced it had other reactions. Some remarked that they were so lost trying to follow the score that they never knew if they were at the right place at any given time. At its debut at the Chicago Opera House in April 1948, the mystified audience failed to recognize the conclusion of the piece; they just sat quietly until Kenton goaded them to applaud.[90]

But as popular as his progressive jazz concerts were, the public's

The Stan Kenton Orchestra running through some charts, place and date uncertain (possibly Richmond, Virginia, 1948). Foreground, from left: Shelley Manne (on drums), Stan Kenton (seated at piano), Eddie Safranski (on acoustic bass), and Laurindo Almeida (seated, on electric guitar (William P. Gottlieb Collection, Library of Congress, LC-GLB13-0515 DLC).

desire for danceable music persisted. Progressive music played well in the big cities, but the fans at smaller venues still tended to want more "sweet" music. Fans remembered tunes like "Peanut Vendor" and "Eager Beaver" and wanted to hear (and dance to) them, so the Kenton orchestra did its best to accommodate them. Sometimes, audiences split between the two styles, and unless advance publicity was crystal clear about what was to come, patrons were never quite sure what they would get for their money.[91] Even those working closely with Kenton sometimes disagreed with him. Carlos Gastel, the band's manager, quit over Kenton's decision to forego dance gigs. Many of the band members also disliked the new music and departed to pursue other opportunities. The Progressive Jazz tour ended in December with Kenton just as emotionally and physically exhausted as he was in April the year before. He left the music business again in 1949, this time contemplating enrolling in a university to study psychiatry.

Despite two emotional and physical collapses, Stan Kenton remained undefeated. Like the proverbial phoenix, he rose yet again from the ashes in 1950 to field another tour band based on a concept he titled, "Innovations in Modern Music." His intention was (again) to lessen the stress and travel and focus on his progressive ideas. But to accomplish it, he doubled the size of his orchestra, making transportation difficult and the size of the payroll explode. From that point on, Kenton experimented with unusual time signatures and even stronger dynamics than he normally played. Graettinger was still producing more and more arrangements for the band and Kenton eventually honored his efforts by devoting an entire album to his charts (*City of Glass*, 1951).

But as fewer and fewer vocals, ballads, and dance tunes found their way into his concert set lists, his popularity with young listeners waned. Both his Innovations tours lost money. Concert tickets went unsold, and sales of his records slackened. Feeling the financial pinch on his bank account and in trouble with the Internal Revenue Service,[92] Kenton succumbed and stopped doing concerts entirely for a while, simply to bring in more cash to pay the bills. The balance he longed for between his musical vision and the demands of the business never really materialized. He and Violet divorced that same year.

As the years passed, small combo music and vocal artists gradually eclipsed big band jazz in popularity. The big band style continued on as backing for popular singers like Frank Sinatra and Ray Charles, but henceforth it was the vocalist who was the attraction, not the band. Rock and Roll captured the imagination of a new generation and in a world dominated by electric guitars and basses, huge brass and saxophone sections were unnecessary. Undaunted, Stan Kenton continued to push forward with his vision. Over the next three decades, the Kenton orchestra toured and recorded, still trying to strike a balance among commercial, innovative, and progressive genres. Under his direction, the orchestra released scores of new albums and re-released old ones, assembled compilations, and pressed new singles. The travelling orchestra played shows well into the 1970s, many in the form of clinics at colleges and universities, as he took on a mission to educate young musicians in the art of jazz performance.

Kenton still prided himself on playing "progressive" jazz, featuring new arrangements in unusual time signatures, like the songs "Time for a Change" and "Chiapas" written in the 1970s by composer Hank Levy. But at the same time, he kept his finger on the pulse of popular music and peppered his shows with jazz arrangements of pop tunes like "Macarthur Park" and "Hey Jude," thereby capturing the imagination of a new generation of young musicians. It is reasonable to claim that Stan Kenton was the most influential jazz educator of his time.

* * *

For jazz music, 1947 was a transitional year as two different, yet related, genres competed for the mantle of "modern" or "progressive." Big

Band jazz music was by then over a decade old. It was struggling but still holding its own against the onslaught of small combo jazz music. Both big band and bebop were taking music in new directions, but neither direction included dancing. Jazz was gradually evolving into forms antithetical to the gigantic ballrooms and dance halls that had once been so ubiquitous across the American social landscape. While it is true that dances and dance bands did not disappear immediately, the handwriting was on the wall. Within the next five years, many venues shut their doors—victims of rising ticket prices and municipal entertainment taxation policies as much as changing tastes in music.

Once music became more available in record stores, on radio, and on television, dance halls became expensive anachronisms. Some were repurposed into social halls for weddings and record hops, other buildings simply locked their doors and languished. The Rendezvous Ballroom, where Kenton was discovered in 1941, burned down in 1966 and was replaced by condominiums. Today, there is nothing there to remind those residents of the great music that once emanated from that place except a small plaque near the parking lot. The dance halls may be gone but the sound lives on in various forms today, including the music of Michael Bublé, Harry Connick, Jr., and Brian Setzer, and it shows no sign of dying out. It is still popular in high schools and colleges where it is taught to new generations of young musicians. But the crowds, the dances, and the halls now belong to history.

Stanley Newcomb Kenton died in 1979, but his music lives on in the albums and recordings he made over the four decades of his career. His impact on contemporary music is undeniable, but how does progressive jazz "fit" in the overall context of mid-century history? One way to interpret the Kenton legacy is to see it as another example of social experimentalism following the Second World War. The wartime era and the immediate postwar years produced many individuals who, when faced with the inhumanities of war and postwar deprivations, questioned what "normal" was. The composer John Cage sought to redefine symphonic music by questioning the whole idea of music.[93] Jean-Paul Sartre, Albert Camus, and other existentialists reconstructed philosophy and challenged the boundaries of traditional literature with their themes of alienation and the absurdity of existence. Tennessee Williams' *Streetcar Named Desire* shattered existing norms about the theater.

Just like these other experimentalists, Kenton understood that music also had to respond to the forces of modernity and move beyond the past. In describing the intersection of his music with contemporary society, he opined that "the human race today may be going through things it never experienced before, types of nervous frustration and thwarted emotional development which traditional music is entirely incapable of not only satisfying but representing."[94] In just a few sentences he had not only described his own personal travails, he summed up the collective angst of a society struggling to cast off the past and create a better, more modern world.

But to paint Kenton's accomplishments with such a broad-brush stroke would be to overlook the unique impact his personality and his vision had on contemporary music. He was not the first or the last to rebel against the vicissitudes of the music business. Musicians today must still choose between playing the songs they prefer or the ones the audience wants to hear. Neither was he the only person ever to suffer from the demands of touring. Even in the twenty-first century, performers have to strike a balance between earning money on the road with the needs of a normal home life. In those respects, Kenton was no different from any other musician, past or present. Yet, Stan Kenton stands out in the history of music because he struggled mightily to remain true to his individuality in the midst of intense pressures to conform.

In his contribution to the "This I Believe Series" hosted by Edward R. Murrow, Kenton summarized this need to create. "I must help through my music to make life more rich in emotional awareness.... I am attempting to replace the conventional type of hackneyed material with a more contemporary form of music that will more nearly satisfy the needs of today."[95] One *Variety* writer summed up Kenton's legacy succinctly. "When it comes to music, Kenton's pride is that he has stuck to concepts and ideas of his own and tried to keep a step ahead of the others." That is high praise, and the fact that he remained reasonably successful over 35 years of making music is evidence that he had tapped into the imaginations of several generations of listeners. Legions of jazz aficionados still revere his music, four decades after his death. Love him or hate him, one fact is clear: he channeled his own "nervous frustrations" into a new music for a new age.

CHAPTER 8

"See Yourself!"
Irene Murphy and American Television's Coming of Age

On Tuesday, July 8, 1947, hundreds of shoppers in Grand Rapids, Michigan, took advantage of a sunny morning to line up on the sidewalks and watch a spectacle unfolding on Monroe Avenue. A police escort processed down the street, leading a circus parade with the requisite clowns, elephants, and horsemen on a half-mile route down the 100 block past the center city shops. The procession bore the trappings of any typical holiday celebration with a military honor guard, two marching bands, several jeeps carrying uniformed soldiers, and automobiles presumably carrying politicians and other dignitaries.

Today's parade, however, was unlike any other Grand Rapids had ever staged. In the lead, just behind the police motorcycle escort, lumbered a huge float advertising Herpolsheimer's Department Store, at the time one of the city's biggest retailers[1] and the parade's final destination. The float heralded the long-anticipated arrival of six brand-new Willys Overland station wagons carrying a cadre of performers, engineers, and technicians escorting audio and video equipment valued at over $100,000. Herp's (as it was called by the locals) had landed a major publicity coup by being selected to host the city's first exposure to a newfangled technology. Television had finally come to Grand Rapids.

Herpolsheimer's was the eighth stop on the itinerary of the "RCA-Allied Stores Television Caravan," a cross-country tour designed to introduce television to 22 cities that had little or no exposure to television services. At every stop, locals celebrated the caravan's arrival with spectacles and pageantry befitting the return of a war hero or the visit of a notable dignitary. Town and city governments feted the celebrities with welcoming breakfasts, honorary dinners, and receptions culminating with various official proclamations of "television day" (or "television week") and the traditional gifting of the "keys to the city." State governors cleared their schedules in order to be present, hoping to claim the honor of being their state's first political figure to appear on television. Crowds of people, lured by the advance publicity in newspapers and on radio, queued up in long lines at department stores to see the demonstrations firsthand and perhaps even become part of an actual broadcast.

The caravan's popularity proved that the public's perception of television was changing. At one time a luxury item available only to the wealthy, television was now becoming a commodity within the grasp of average consumers. Before 1947, concerns about technology, shortages in manufacturing, and a lack of consumer confidence all conspired to hold back the expansion of television service after the war. But those impediments had eased and as the availability of sets increased, television executives and retailers pondered how best to use this technology. Was television just an entertainment vehicle, or might it actually be able to influence consumer buying habits? Could television be the next big innovation in the U.S. mercantile economy? This chapter will address these and other questions, and in the process reveal television's first forays into the public's consciousness as a force for social and economic change.

* * *

The science of television was already decades old by 1947. One of the first practical demonstrations in the western hemisphere occurred in April 1927 when Herbert Hoover (then Secretary of Commerce) addressed a small crowd of Bell Telephone Laboratory employees and guests in New York City via television from Washington, D.C. Although the images were sent by wire, a separate radio transmission arrived from an experimental station in New Jersey with the audio.[2] The technology was equally well advanced in Europe, as famously demonstrated in the United Kingdom by the BBC's broadcasts in the early 1930s and the German closed-circuit broadcasts of the Olympic Games from Berlin in 1936.

Back in the United States, the unofficial "launch" of television may have been President Roosevelt's address at the opening ceremonies of the New York World's Fair on April 30, 1939, which was picked up by mobile vans and broadcast from transmitter towers high atop the Empire State Building.[3] It was a seminal moment in the history of American television but in truth one of limited impact. Only an estimated 100 to 200 receivers were in operation in the New York metropolitan area, and most of them were not in public hands; hence, that transmission reached a limited audience of perhaps 1,000 viewers.[4]

In anticipation of a rising public demand, however, Bloomingdale's and Macy's began selling new television sets the very next day[5]—but sales were lackluster as wary consumers balked at investing a lot of money in a technology that could quickly become obsolete. Other stores hesitated to stock receivers for much the same reason.[6] Although the public was not yet interested in purchasing, it was nevertheless exceedingly curious about the new technology. Manufacturers, including the Radio Corporation of America (RCA) and Farnsworth, did their best to satisfy that curiosity by staging television demonstrations in schools, stores, and at fairs all over the country.

Television's popularity grew steadily in the two years before the United States' entry into the war, and the new medium scored a number of notable "firsts." The Republican National Convention, convening in Philadelphia in 1940, was televised. A workable system for color television was demonstrated the same year. But the attack on Pearl Harbor brought the United States into war, and as telecommunications companies retooled to produce radar and other electronics equipment for the war effort, the consumer television industry all but ceased completely. Existing commercial broadcasting continued but on a limited schedule of about four hours a week per station. The fledgling networks, including the National Broadcasting Company (NBC) and the Columbia Broadcasting System (CBS), curtailed much of their broadcasting and filled their on-air time with civil defense information and air raid instruction.[7]

Once the war ended, companies rushed back into consumer television manufacturing, and as many as ten different companies competed to gain a share of the market by 1946. Most of the newly sold receivers found their way into bars and restaurants as trade stimulators. For most average home consumers, however, television remained an unaffordable luxury. One reason was the difficult economic times in the immediate postwar economy. Inflation ate up much of the public's discretionary income and most families had precious little extra cash to spend. Another reason consumers failed to respond was the lingering suspicion that new technology brought with it rapid obsolescence.

In an attempt to understand exactly why television sales still lagged, *Television Magazine* sent a reporter into the stores to conduct firsthand field research. The reporter's findings were discouraging. Many stores had no sets in stock and those that did had only a limited number. Moreover, the $350 price tag (plus an additional $50 for installation) for a basic model was enough to scare away all but the wealthiest of potential buyers.[8] Additionally, television was as new to department store employees as it was to the buying public, hence there were not enough knowledgeable salespeople to sell sets effectively. The correspondent was especially perturbed that manufacturers were not making good on delivery promises. Even a major producer like RCA, which had advertised and promoted a Christmastime sale on sets, failed to deliver enough sets to retail outlets to meet existing demand.[9]

As pernicious as these problems were, the biggest impediment to the expansion of the consumer television market was a controversy raging within the industry itself. In the prevailing milieu of black-and-white picture transmission, color images were the "holy grail." CBS took the lead in developing color reception, and as early as 1940 had already demonstrated a way to produce color images in receivers. Their method, called "sequential" imaging, required the addition of rotating colored disks between the cathode ray tube and the electron emitters. The system worked in practice and their New York station, WCBW, regularly broadcast color shows in the months before the United States entered the war.[10] After the war, RCA developed a competing technology that required no colored disks. Their system, known as "simultaneous" imaging, beamed three separate colors in varying intensities at the cathode ray tube at the same time, with the mixture of hues resulting in a multi-colored image.

In an attempt to win over the market, CBS asked the Federal Communications Commission (FCC) in 1946 to sanction its sequential imaging technology and open new channels for color broadcasts, particularly in the new UHF bands. RCA (in conjunction with DuMont, Philco, General Electric, and eight others) filed suit with the FCC to block the approval. Eventually, the competition between RCA and CBS and their different color delivery systems escalated into an all-out war.

The FCC hearings began in December 1946. Each side presented expert testimony, field testing results, experimental data, and even information on how the human eye functions[11] in an attempt to make the best argument. CBS had the advantage that their color technology could be made available to the public immediately while still being flexible enough for future improvements and enhancements. RCA countered that the immediacy of the service was not really an issue, since they projected that their system would not take much longer to perfect than CBS's system (four years for CBS, five for RCA).[12] Instead, they focused their attack on the picture quality of the CBS system, which often suffered from flicker and brightness issues.

Most crucially, the CBS sequential color transmission was incompatible with existing black-and-white transmission technologies, necessitating an entirely new system of signal broadcasting. In contrast, RCA's simultaneous method allowed both color and black-and-white transmissions to use the same carrier signal, and thus there was no need for separate facilities. Existing sets could be adapted to color with a converter or just allowed to continue functioning normally since the color signal would also be visible in monochrome.

The contentious debate had effects that rippled across the entire television industry. Adopting the CBS system would have been a nightmare for station owners. Any new television broadcast facilities would need entirely new equipment and (according to testimony at the hearings) existing stations would need a second, separate facility dedicated to color broadcasting.[13] Existing set owners also had a stake. A decision favoring CBS would have rendered all existing black-and-white receivers immediately obsolete, thereby validating (and perhaps even perpetuating) the public's distrust of new technology.

Manufacturers also shared the public's misgivings about obsolescence. Industry forecasts posited that there was enough demand for sets to warrant ramping up monochrome production in 1947 but in this climate of uncertainty, most television manufacturers were loath to begin full-scale production. The FCC faced a decision of tremendous consequence. It had to choose sides in bitter dispute between two giant corporations, with nothing less than the interests of television manufacturers, station owners, and the viewing public at stake.

The hearings concluded on February 13, 1947. In its final report issued in March, the FCC denied the CBS petition arguing that "there had not been adequate field testing ... to perceive with confidence that the system will work adequately in practice."[14] But the FCC refused to take sides in the sequential versus simultaneous debate, equivocating that it was entirely possible that "wartime developments may show that there is an entirely different method ... which is superior to both." The commission's paramount concern was affordability, and it urged both sides to find a solution that allowed for "development of the best possible system, employing the narrowest possible bandwidth, and which makes possible receivers at a reasonable price."[15]

The decision stunned CBS, whose executives had withdrawn four applications from major city markets as a way of demonstrating their confidence in their system. They had also advised many other stations that might have joined the network to postpone filing their applications until the matter was resolved. The failure of CBS's gamble cost the network valuable time and wasted millions of dollars expanding into markets they might have otherwise had for much less.[16]

The FCC's ruling was not what CBS wanted to hear, but it did at least have one positive outcome for the industry in general; manufacturers were now free to build sets without fear of obsolescence. And produce they did! *Television Magazine*[17] estimated that only a paltry 20,000 to 25,000 sets had been built during the entire 12 months of 1946 (the majority by RCA and DuMont).[18] In the first three months of 1947 alone, manufacturers produced 18,000 new units, and thereafter the monthly production figures continued to climb with regularity (see Tables 1 and 2, below). By the end of 1947, manufacturers had produced an estimated 150,000 units, falling short of the glowing 360,000 prediction made earlier that year but nevertheless an impressive figure.[19] On average, manufacturers were producing as many sets every two months as were built during the entire previous year.

Table 1: Television Set Production by Month, 1947

Apr-47	May-47	Jul-47	Aug-47	Sep-47	Oct-47	Nov-47	Dec-47
no data	8,690	10,007	12,283	15,728	23,696	24,134	no data

source—Radio Manufacturer's Association

Table 2: Cumulative Set Production Figures, 1947

Total Up to March	18,329		
After 5 months	34,896	underreported	(erroneous) 37,697
After 6 months:	46,389	underreported	
After 7 months	56,396	underreported	
After 8 months	68,679	underreported	
After 9 months			
After 10 months	101,388	*	
After 11 months	125,081		

*16,991 sets constructed before September but previously unreported added here
source—Radio Manufacturer's Association

Although it was difficult to know precisely the number of sets in use in their viewing area and how rapidly their market was expanding, local stations had low-tech but effective ways of gathering viewership data. Purchasers of new sets were asked to send in a "registration card" containing their names and addresses, in return for a promise to receive programming schedules and other information by mail. The method was not foolproof, but it did help stations get a rough picture of the size of their market. (Table 3 shows the distribution of sets in the major markets during 1947.) By the end of the year, about 155,000 sets were in use with most of the sets going into homes along the northeast corridor (New York, Philadelphia, Baltimore, and Washington, D.C.).

Table 3: Estimated Numbers of Sets in Use by City and Month, 1947 (in Thousands)

Location	May	July	Aug.	Sept.	Oct.	Nov.	Dec.
New York City	25.0	35.0	40.0	45.0	65.0	70.0	94.0
Philadelphia	5.0	7.6	8.5	10.0	12.0	15.0	18.0

Location	May	July	Aug.	Sept.	Oct.	Nov.	Dec.
Chicago	n.d.	4.1	5.3	5.9	7.3	9.1	12.0
St. Louis	0.4	0.6	n.d.	1.5	2.0	2.5	3.0
Detroit	0.6	2.0	2.0	3.0	3.0	3.0	4.0
Schenectady	0.6	0.6	n.d.	0.8	0.8	1.0	1.2
Washington, D.C.	1.4	1.5	0.6*	2.5	3.0	3.3	5.5
L.A.		3.0	3.0	4.5	5.0	9.0	12.0
Baltimore					1.0	2.5	3.7
Milwaukee						0.3	0.8
Cincinnati						0.7	1.0
	33.0	54.4	58.8	73.2	99.1	116.4	155.2

*Error, likely 1.6
Source—Television *magazine from station data*

The FCC decision proved equally important for the spread of television licensing applications and the construction of new stations. At the close of 1945, nine commercial television stations were in operation. Three were located in New York City alone: WNBT, WCBS, and WABD, representing the NBC, CBS, and DuMont networks respectively. Another two stations (still carrying their experimental call letters W6XYZ and W6XAO) broadcast in Los Angeles. In several other cities, only one station dominated the airwaves despite the FCC's designation of multiple-station channel slots. In the Philadelphia market, WPTZ (Philco) was the sole player. DuMont's stations WBKB and WTTG dominated the airwaves in and around Washington, D.C.[20]

Despite industry predictions that seven new stations would get on-air in 1946, not one new station was built, in part because of the color controversy but also of a shortage of transmitters. With both problems resolved by the end of 1947, the number of operating stations doubled to 18. Among the new stations were KSD-TV St. Louis, WWJ Detroit, WNBW Washington, WMAL Washington, WMAR Baltimore, and WEWS Cleveland, and an experimental station W8XCT in Cincinnati. Fifty-six more grants were approved and awaiting construction.

KSD-TV in St. Louis holds the distinction of being America's first post-war commercial television station to go on air. Its experience is indicative of the excitement new television stations generated in their communities as they got off the ground. Five months before the opening, KSD-TV ownership started recruiting radio personnel for the specialized training required to operate video equipment. Every recruit was expected to learn all aspects of production and then only later specialize in any one given task. With transmitters located atop the St. Louis Post-Dispatch Building (the parent company),[21] KSD-TV's initial broadcast range was only about forty square miles but that proved powerful enough to cover the city and the immediate suburbs. Months before the debut, the city was awash with advertising on buses, cabs, street cars, and store windows heralding the new station.[22]

As the initial broadcast date approached, department stores stocked up on sets for display and public purchase. Evidently, all the hype worked. According to one article, "thousands" came to the department stores to see the latest devices. Crowds were so thick that "in some places throngs blocked the store entrances."[23] At first, KSD-TV only broadcast for about twenty hours a week and most shows were scheduled for the late afternoon hours (often from 3:00 p.m. to 5:00 p.m.) in order to provide a signal so that department stores all over the city could demonstrate set operation.

Programming remained simple at first, consisting mostly of remotes, interviews, films, and news. Equipped with new image orthicon cameras, KSD-TV secured its future by contracting with the Cardinals and Browns baseball teams to televise their games. Consequently, the first set installations went into bars and restaurants (as was the case in New York), in the hopes that curiosity would draw in more patrons. All the while, the station was mindful that it would play a major economic role in the city. Station officials approached the St. Louis Chamber of Commerce, parent-teacher groups, and other civic organizations to promote television as a sales tool.

As successful as television had become in the summer of 1947, it was still a long way from being the ubiquitous communications medium that it ultimately became. Despite the inauguration of broadcasting in St. Louis and Milwaukee, television was still very much concentrated New York, Philadelphia, and Los Angeles. The major networks, NBC, CBS, and DuMont had no cross-country links yet, but industry analysts forecast that a coax cable would link much of the Midwest through Cleveland, Cincinnati, and Baltimore by the end of the year. Some felt confident to say that a coast-to-coast linkage would be available by late 1948.

Judging by all the applications for station permits filed with the FCC in 1947, American entrepreneurs shared that optimism. It was in many ways a leap of faith, because for most of the general public television was still an abstraction. Millions of people had never seen a television set outside of pictures in magazines, let alone watched an actual program. Despite the technological progress, vast swaths of the United States still had no access to a television signal, let alone a local station in operation. Television was still too concentrated in larger population centers to be considered a nationwide phenomenon.

***

At the same time that television was enjoying an explosion as a communications and entertainment medium, there was a growing debate over the role of television in the marketplace. Television had already demonstrated its value as a way to attract patrons to bars and restaurants, but more enterprising individuals felt that it could have an even larger role to play. Might television actually be used to influence consumers' buying habits and drive consumption? The idea to use television as a marketing tool had roots in the 1930s; indeed, department stores that had previously relied on radio and newspaper for advertising were keen on finding ways to use the new technology well before the war began.

Stations also found the cooperation with retailers advantageous, since department stores were typically good sources of sponsorship money. The partnership between department stores and television reemerged late in the war as broadcasters, searching for inexpensive programming that would attract a viewership, fielded shopping shows. For example, WABD (New York's DuMont station) sold airtime to Macy's in 1944 to televise a brief spot called *Teleshopping with Martha Manning*, which was essentially a glorified showcase for Macy's goods. In the lean wartime years, such shows became a staple of programming on the major networks. The cooperation between station and store even extended to the sharing of physical space. In the autumn of 1945, WABD struck a deal with New York's Wanamaker's Department Store to construct studios in the store's second floor auditorium, making Wanamaker's the first department store in the United States to have in-house television broadcasting facilities.[24]

Some bold retailers and television executives felt this arrangement could go even further. Could television be utilized within department stores to highlight products and drive consumer spending? This too was not a new idea. Many pundits had noticed that televisions were in some ways like department store windows; each was an effective way to display and demonstrate wares, attract the buyer's attention, and stimulate sales. The idea was already on the minds of personnel staging the RCA and Farnsworth television tours of 1939, and so they deliberately used department stores as broadcast sites and staged "commercials" of available goods in their demonstrations. One writer, commenting on department store television in 1944, opined that the "customer of the future ... will find herself looking into active moving exhibits of merchandise" once television gets into the business of selling.[25]

There was therefore a long standing but relatively untested belief that strategically placed television monitors in department stores could entice consumers and thereby drive sales.[26] A poll taken by *Television Magazine* in January 1945 revealed that 51 percent of all the department store executives queried planned to use television in one way or another once the war ended; 35 percent answered that they already believed intra-store television would become valuable as a sales tool.[27] Many major retailers had already applied to the FCC for a broadcast license.[28]

In October that year, Gimbels Department Store in Philadelphia became the first of several department stores to experiment with intra-store television. Over three weeks that autumn, an estimated quarter of a million store visitors viewed ten-minute spots highlighting store goods and entertainment over twenty receivers placed throughout the store. The response was so positive that the store contracted with WPTZ to broadcast 13 weeks of prime-time programming featuring Gimbels' products and services.[29]

The results revealed widespread consumer enthusiasm for merchandise seen on store television.[30] In March 1946, the Gertz Department Store in Jamaica, New York, tried the same experiment,[31] and in June, Kaufmann's in Pittsburgh (where there still was no established station on-air) followed suit.[32] Clearly, the East Coast was taking to the idea of intra-store television, but would the rest of America, where there was still little or no exposure to broadcast television, think the same?

That question ruminated in the mind of Sam Cuff, WABD's general manager. Born in Jerusalem in 1902 to British parents, Cuff's "business voice" still evinced a slight accent when he spoke. At first glance, his appearance was not what one would expect from a television personality. Cuff's receding hairline made him appear much older than he was, but he compensated with a sporty Clark Gable–like mustache that gave him a distinguished look. He first achieved television exposure in 1939–40 as the host of a show called *The Face of the War* that aired on WNBT.

The attack on Pearl Harbor propelled him into the limelight,[33] and his use of maps and pointers to describe the geography of Hawaii became a trademark of his public persona. After making a jump to WABD in 1943, he went on-air as a news analyst and war commentator. As a published author and frequent contributor to trade magazines, Cuff gained a national reputation as a knowledgeable television technician and businessman. As a station executive, he was known as an extremely good administrator and an excellent boss among those who worked for him.

The WABD relationship with Wanamaker's gave Cuff the opportunity to enter the debate on the use of television in department store settings. In an article he wrote for *Televiser* in the winter of 1945, he postulated that strategically placed television monitors in department stores could "place impulse purchases before customers without requiring that they pass the items" and thereby "expose consumers to temptation."[34] As interest in intra-store television reemerged in the stagnant postwar economy,

Cuff conceived an idea to evaluate the concept. He proposed to send an entire crew of technicians and performers on a six-month trek across the United States with all the television equipment needed to field remote broadcasts.[35]

In a manner similar to the Gimbels and Gertz experiments, the entourage would set up makeshift studios in department stores and demonstrate television to patrons by staging informative "commercials" broadcast to monitors placed throughout the store. In order to take this effort beyond what had been done in the past, however, Cuff wanted a "scientific" way to assess intra-store television by collecting consumer responses with on-site direct polling. Patron reactions could then be assembled and analyzed with quantitative data. Such a tour, if it came to fruition, would introduce hundreds of thousands (if not millions) of people to television, further accelerating the public's demand for broadcasting services at a time when station building and applications for licenses were beginning to take off.

Cuff's plan was a novel idea, but there were many obstacles to pulling off such a stunt successfully. First and foremost among them was the cost. A cross-country tour would necessitate paying wages for a cast and crew, not to mention food and lodging expenses, for a full six months. Second, television cameras of the day were notoriously fickle instruments; getting them across the country on some marginal stretches of road was an errand fraught with danger. Any unforeseen hazard could easily jostle the equipment and cause irreparable damage to the imaging tubes or other components.

For most people, these problems would have posed a logistical and organizational nightmare, but not for Sam Cuff. He surmised that the funding problem could be solved by lining up sponsors, and his hunch proved correct as a variety of corporations, including such familiar brand names as Hoover vacuums, Westinghouse appliances, Sherwin-Williams paint, B.V.D. clothing, and several others agreed to take part.[36] Three magazines joined the tour (*Charm*, *Pic*, and *House Beautiful*), and the Gulf Oil Corporation agreed to underwrite the gasoline and oil expenses.

For the corporate sponsors, the investment proved worthwhile since they received not just valuable publicity, they also got a quick primer on how to present their products on television with the greatest effect. Equipping the tour was still a concern, but RCA agreed to loan all the field equipment necessary to put on remote telecasts. In addition, RCA provided two older but functional iconoscope cameras rather than the newer Image Orthicon ones that were coming into more general use.[37] Protecting their investment on such an arduous trip took some ingenuity, however. The United States Rubber Company agreed to provide special pads made with cellular foam rubber filled with nitrogen gas to sheath the cameras from roadway perils. U.S. Rubber was so confident of the protective qualities of the rubber sheets that it boasted a raw egg could be dropped on one without breaking the shell—a claim that would be put to the test repeatedly on the tour.

Two final tasks remained. The tour needed both a manageable itinerary and an academically sound research methodology. The first was resolved when Allied Stores Corporation, a conglomerate of department stores that included some historically famous names in local retailing including The Bon Marché in Seattle, Jordan Marsh in Boston, Joske Brothers in San Antonio, and Maas Brothers in Tampa,[38] volunteered 22 stores as demonstration sites. To find a sound experimental methodology, Cuff approached the Bureau of Retail Research in New York University's School of Retailing. The experiment was tailor-made for a marketing research project, so a team of academics agreed to design study parameters. Ms. Hilda Jonas, a graduate of Adelphi College and a research associate at New York University got the honor of traveling with the tour to sample crowd reactions and conduct the research. Her efforts would prove invaluable in reaching conclusions about the effectiveness of intra-store television as a retail sales stimulator.

Cuff's efforts proved timely, as staffing cutbacks at WABD in March of 1947 cost him his job. Freed of his television responsibilities, Cuff needed only to find the right personnel to make the tour a success. Luckily, Cuff could draw on a pool of talented individuals he knew from his days as manager of WABD. He could not have found a better director and road manager than Louis A. Sposa. Sposa was a young 36-year-old with an appearance that some of his coworkers compared to Douglas Fairbanks. His relative youth notwithstanding, Sposa had all the technical experience and personal qualifications for the job. During the war, he worked for DuMont Laboratories helping to build electrical equipment. That job evolved into part-time employment for DuMont television doing every conceivable task from transmitter operator and production assistant to camera operator and director. The knowledge he gained from years of experience in television production allowed him to write many magazine articles, publish a widely respected book on the subject,[39] and teach college courses on television production at City College and New York University. One contemporary newspaper rightly dubbed him "one of the busiest men in television today."[40]

In January of 1947, Sposa became Director of Commercial Operations at WABD and a few months later, Manager of Program Services, and thus in charge of station personnel. He too had lost his job at the same time as Cuff, so he was well prepared to assemble and lead a team for the cross-country project. For his chief engineer he chose Bernard A. Brink, a

Lou Sposa (left) discussing the RCA-Caravan itinerary with Sam Cuff (courtesy Irene Murphy McInerney).

technician from Kansas who friends described as an "engineering genius." Brink translated his ardent passion for electronic equipment and cable hookups into a career in television that lasted decades. Brink's two assistants were Minneapolis native Ralph "Red" Johnston and Paul Adams from Arkansas. Benjamin T. Hill, Jr., a tall, handsome man who had formerly been a model in New York City, was hired as a camera operator and general assistant. Joseph Tery did the advance publicity, and Jim Hoskinson, an editor with *PIC* magazine, travelled with the group to promote the magazine sponsors.

As skilled as all of these men were, it was the three young and talented women accompanying them who were the public faces of the caravan tour. Lygia Jarantow was a model cum actress who hailed from Fair Lawn, New Jersey. She had worked for several years in the television industry as a model and announcer and was picked to go on the tour as an on-air actress and presenter. Her poise and sense for fashion projected a sophistication that translated well in photographs and on the television screen. One might expect that a glamorous on-air personality like Lygia would draw the most public attention, but as it turned out, she had to share the limelight with two other women on the tour. One was camera operator

Chapter 8. "See Yourself!" 179

Irine Petroff. "Petey," as she was affectionately called, grew up in Benton, Illinois. After high school, she attended Northwestern University where she served on the editorial board and wrote for the *Daily Northwestern*, the school's newspaper, graduating in 1945.[41]

In search of work and perhaps some excitement, Petroff relocated to New York City with several fellow Northwestern alumnae, one of whom was a young and still undiscovered actress named Patricia Neal. Life in a small New York apartment at the end of the war was apparently both stressful and exhilarating as the struggling women had to pool their resources in order to pay the bills.[42] Following an ill-advised keg party one night, the group was evicted and Petroff went to share an apartment with another fellow Northwestern alumna. Although she had studied radio and theater production, she kept an open mind about her job options. "There were too many obstacles for women in radio," she explained in an interview. "I decided I could do better in television."[43] Despite being told that television "isn't a job for a woman," Petroff persisted. WABD was the second station she visited, and landing a job there proved to be her big break.

Petroff's career path as a broadcast pioneer is an intriguing case study of television's impact on women in the workforce. From the very beginning, she got resistance from her male coworkers. "My boss told me after I got the job that I had a man's name, I dressed like a man, and did a man's job," she recounted for a newspaper interview. "And he added that I would be treated like a man."[44] She started out as an engineer's assistant charged with lugging around cables and microphones but soon expanded her work as a microphone boom operator. Eventually she was promoted to camera operator, becoming one of the industry's first females to hold that job.[45]

Many considered such jobs unbecoming for a woman, in part because she wore a company technician's uniform consisting of drab overalls. She once admitted that the attire was "not very lady-like,"[46] but she found wearing slacks and blouses while on the job preferable and appropriate. As she set about her work, Petroff attracted a great deal of attention from onlookers. The incongruity of seeing a woman taking direction through headphones and dollying cameras that weighed as much as she did was ample reason, but it also helped that she was a blonde with a broad, beaming smile. Photographers gravitated to her and newspapermen stumbled over themselves to meet and interview her.

Given the novelty of finding an attractive woman working in what many perceived to be a "man's occupation," writers felt it necessary to describe her with adjectives like "comely," "petite," or "a wisp of a girl," while downplaying or ignoring her substantial technical qualifications as a camera operator. One Tampa newspaper published a photograph of her under the caption "Blonde Vision Shoots Television."[47] Indeed, Petroff was attractive enough to be a performer, but she repeatedly shunned such suggestions in deference to her job behind the camera. She was, perhaps for all the wrong reasons, one of the big stars of the tour.

The most experienced and talented performer of the tour was the mistress of ceremonies, Irene Murphy.[48] She was born in the Bronx and attended school first at Villa Maria Academy and then the College of New Rochelle where she majored in Speech and English. After a brief stint as a flight attendant and then later as a substitute teacher (a job she found deplorable), Murphy set out to find a career in radio. But, like Petroff, she eventually decided to turn to television.

On a whim, she showed up in person at the Charles Stark production company offices to apply for a job. As she left the interview, she overheard the interviewer describe her as "just another Irish kid trying to break into the business." Incensed, she decided to confront him. Marching back into his office, she explained that she was only half Irish; she was also part Czechoslovakian. As it happened, the interviewer (Charles Stark himself) admitted that he too was part Czech. Their ensuing discussion, and no doubt her assertiveness, landed her a job with the agency.

Murphy's first foray into television was on the game show *Cash and Carry* as the assistant to the host, Dennis James.[49] The show's format can best be described as "slapstick audience participation" where contestants had to perform stunts to win prizes. Murphy introduced the show and assisted in many of the on-air stunts. For her, working in television was an exciting experience, in part because most of the people in the business were young and idealistic. As soldiers returned from the war expecting to get their old jobs again, television proved fertile ground for younger people willing to try something new. It was not without its dangers, however.

One day, an electrical short in a telephone line on the set caused a malfunction in the receiver Irene was using, injuring the nerves in her inner ear and leading to permanent hearing loss.[50] Undaunted, she continued to work for *Cash and Carry* until she got a phone call one day asking her to be the Mistress of Ceremonies for the television tour. When asked years later what she thought of the offer, Murphy recalled, "The appeal? To tour the country, for free?"[51] With little hesitation, she left *Cash and Carry* and joined the cast and crew of Sam Cuff's caravan.

The tour kicked off on May 12, inauspiciously enough from a garage on 64th street in the heart of New York City, where the team's brand-new Willys Overland station wagons had been parked. Each traveler was allowed only two suitcases since the Jeeps (as they called them) would eventually be loaded down with television cameras and audio equipment. They drove down Fifth Avenue to a windy Rockefeller Plaza, where police had roped off the street for publicity photos. After a brief private exchange

Chapter 8. "See Yourself!"

of goodbyes with RCA and Allied Stores officials, they drew the attention of a crowd of New Yorkers, providing a foretaste of the fame and notoriety that awaited them on their tour.

From Rockefeller Center, the entourage stopped at U.S. Rubber Company to exchange another round of platitudes and well wishes. Wending its way through the crowded New York streets to the George Washington Bridge, the tour got another brief introduction to what the rest of the trip might be like. One of the Jeeps had taken a separate route to pick up klieg lights but was now overdue for the rendezvous, so the rest of the team had to sit and wait. The wayward Jeep finally caught up with the others, but it was clear that there had been a miscommunication as to the location of the meeting point. The next stop was Passaic, New Jersey, to pick up the special rubber protective pads.

From there the tour drove to a Gulf station near Newark to pick up credit cards, refuel, and submit to another round of promotional photos. At least now they had a police escort so the driving was not as difficult as it might have been. From Passaic, the caravan motored on to the RCA manufacturing plant on the Delaware River in Camden, New Jersey.

The RCA-Allied Stores Television Caravan parked at Rockefeller Plaza, getting ready to leave on its cross-country trip. From left: Lygia Jarantow, Irene Murphy, Irine Petroff (courtesy Irene Murphy McInerney).

Unfortunately, the delay at the bridge in New York and all the publicity at Gulf put the caravan behind schedule, so they failed to get there before closing time. An unanticipated search for hotel rooms capped off a day filled with highway headaches.

After loading the cameras the next morning, the caravan left Camden for its first performance location, Pomeroy's Department Store in Reading, Pennsylvania. Sam Cuff had wisely set aside two weeks for the Reading stay so that the crew members could get acclimated to their new jobs. No one knew exactly what to expect, so they spent most of their time rehearsing, revising scripts, and testing equipment setup strategies. With practice, the group perfected both the technical and presentational aspects of the show. Irene Murphy remembered her stay in Reading fondly. Setting up shows was hard work, but at least the tempo was leisurely. The hurried pace that characterized the latter parts of the tour was absent here. In the off hours, the crew could relax and enjoy the hospitality of Pomeroy's administration, spend time playing poker, tour the Pennsylvania Dutch countryside, and party.

The stay at Pomeroy's gave the troupe the opportunity to perfect a production format that was to be duplicated at every caravan tour stop. Each host department store set aside a floor (or part of a floor) to serve as a makeshift television studio. Before the caravan arrived, advance agents recruited local college students and other volunteers to help the crew set up the cameras, audio, lighting, and director's control station. In some locales, store personnel assisted in the set up. Once the equipment was ready, the crew divided the remaining space into smaller sound stages, one for each of the products to be advertised during the televised sessions. Cameras and microphones could then be dollied from stage to stage, depending on which segment was being aired.

Monitors, strategically placed throughout the department store and linked by coax cable to the control console, carried the shows to the shoppers. In general, the crew fielded three shows daily.[52] At the start of every show, Irene Murphy took time to explain the mechanics of television to the audience. Then began a schedule of entertainment features provided by local musicians, singers, or radio personalities, or an audience participation show called *Telefun* featuring Murphy as emcee with Jim Hoskinson as her assistant. Both Murphy and Jarantow filled the intervals between features with commercial segments, skits about featured products, and interviews.

The Reading shows ended on May 24 and the crew packed up for their next destination, Laubach's Department Store in Easton, Pennsylvania. Thus began a trek that lasted five more months and took them to a total of 22 cities. The itinerary took the caravan on a circuitous route dictated by an appearance schedule structured to accommodate department store calendars, not geography. For example, the caravan stopped in St. Paul, Minnesota, for shows from September 2 through 5, but because of intervening scheduled appearances in Idaho and Washington, it returned to Minneapolis only a month later! The longest distance between shows was the trip from St. Paul to Boise, a drive of close to 1,500 miles.[53]

The most harrowing journey may have been one of the shortest. In an attempt to get from Long Island to Boston, the Jeeps failed to make a planned rendezvous and then lost contact with each other in a rainstorm. The most arduous stay may have been in Lake Charles, Louisiana, which was experiencing a record-breaking heat wave with temperatures reaching 102°F.

As one might expect, the crowded itinerary left little time for sightseeing. The schedule had built-in travel days, but arrival and departure dates had been set well in advance and could not be changed. Any delay could throw the entire schedule into chaos. Murphy later recalled the "hectic" pace of the travel, driving at or beyond the speed limit in an attempt to make it to the next locale on time. If the group wanted a day off,

Irene Murphy (right) taking a break from the tour with cameraperson Irine (Petey) Petroff (courtesy Irene Murphy McInerney).

they had to drive even faster to get to a locale well ahead of schedule. Such days were rare and highly coveted.

The cordial receptions the caravan received made the frenzied pace of traveling worthwhile. No matter where they went, the Jeeps were greeted with police escorts, parades, public celebrations, and jubilant crowds thanks to the extensive publicity done in advance of each stop. The reception in Great Falls, Montana, on September 29 is a good example of the excitement a caravan visit generated. On hand to greet them were the governor of Montana, Sam Ford, the mayor of Great Falls, J.C. Johnson, Miss Montana Carol Chaffin, (then Colonel) Claire Chennault of "Flying Tigers" fame, the chief of police, and numerous other local dignitaries.

A welcoming parade featuring local bands with fancy floats mustered at the Civic Center on Central Avenue and then proceeded to the Paris Department Store. The hype even included a planned flyover of P-51 Mustang fighters from the local National Guard 186th squadron.[54] This spectacle accounted for only the first few hours of the caravan's three-day stay in Great Falls, during which the tour members were treated like royalty. By the time they left Montana, they had introduced television to an estimated 23,000 people. Great Falls' population at the time was around 35,000.[55]

The caravan was such a major media event that even established celebrities came out to share the spotlight. In Jamaica, New York, Dennis James reunited with his former partner Irene Murphy for a remote version of *Cash and Carry* at Gertz Department Store. In Minneapolis, James Melton, the popular tenor for the Metropolitan Opera, was a featured guest. Eddie Anderson, known to radio and television audiences as "Rochester" on the Jack Benny show, also stopped by. In Boston, conductor Arthur Fiedler appeared. Jess Stacy, the famed jazz musician and frequent winner of *Down Beat*'s poll for best big band pianist, made an appearance. In Columbus, a young Cuban bandleader named Desi Arnaz stopped in to chat with the caravan members. Scores of politicians, both national and local, also participated. Corporate presidents stopped by. In Boise, four Nez Perce tribesmen appeared on camera, marking the first television appearance for their tribe and making them possibly the first Native Americans anywhere in the United States to be part of a live telecast.

Shows were designed to attract as much public attention as possible, and some of the segments proved highly effective at drawing crowds. Practically every store staged a contest of one sort or another. Many fielded a small-scale beauty pageant, inviting local women to compete for the title of "Miss Television." In Spokane, a "television twins" contest promised a $100 prize for the most telegenic siblings. *Charm Magazine* sponsored fashion shows featuring local models. The most effective segments, however, were the scores of interviews Jarantow and Murphy conducted with young children who chatted for the cameras while their doting parents looked on in admiration. The invitation to "See Yourself" in advance newspaper publicity attracted thousands of adults who waited in long lines just for a chance to get on camera.

Perhaps the most spectacular of the publicity stunts was the "egg drop." Although an odd and at times messy spectacle, it proved to be the most effective promotional gimmick of the entire caravan tour. U.S. Rubber's claim that its gas-filled foam rubber pads would prevent a raw egg from breaking seemed too audacious to go untested, and so the caravan fielded a special event casting Jim Hoskinson, associate editor of *PIC Magazine*, as emcee. In each of the 22 cities, a caravan member or a local notable dropped raw eggs from a tall building (often the local bank) toward the rubber pads unrolled on the sidewalk below in an attempt to see if the eggs really would bounce. In most instances, the eggs rebounded as promised (unless they missed the mat, which happened frequently), sometimes achieving a rebound height estimated between twenty-five to thirty feet. Unfortunately, their trajectories after bouncing were not always predictable. Occasionally, eggs splattered on sidewalks or on the sides of buildings.

Despite the inherent danger posed by the flying ova, large crowds of bemused spectators gathered to witness the spectacle, prompting police to rope off entire streets in order to provide enough room. In many places, radio broadcasts described each toss in lurid detail. In Waterloo, Iowa, a local newspaper was so intrigued that a photograph of an egg in flight got page two coverage.[56] In Seattle, Betty MacDonald, author of the book *The Egg and I*, dropped eggs from the twelfth floor of the Northwestern Mutual Fire Insurance Building to two Seattle Rainiers minor league baseball catchers clothed in full team uniforms waiting below to snag them.[57]

In locales where sports personalities were not available, store models or local celebrities attempted to catch the rebounding eggs. As the participants discovered, that was more easily said than done. In Great Falls, Montana, the Paris Department Store model who was selected to catch the eggs and place them in a basket repeatedly failed to do so.[58] A more catastrophic outcome occurred during a demonstration in Boise, Idaho. One dozen raw eggs were dropped from the First National Bank Building toward a team of three models from C.C. Anderson's Department Store waiting below. Apparently, one model grasped at a rebounding egg a little too forcefully, resulting in a torrent of yolk and albumen that splattered on her face and freshly coifed hair. Embarrassed, the poor woman quickly fled into the store to clean up, undoubtedly to a chorus of chuckles from the crowd. The fact that she was just one of many to suffer such a fate undoubtedly offered her little solace. Despite (or perhaps because of) the unfortunate spectacle, the store's promotion manager invited the crowd to return the next day for a repeat performance.[59]

By the end of October, the caravan had logged upwards of 15,000 highway miles—truly a monumental journey considering it was accomplished before the completion of the Interstate Highway System, not to mention the invention of cell phones or GPS navigation. Unfortunately, there is no way of knowing exactly how many people experienced television for the first time thanks to its efforts.[60] Lou Sposa was asked that question frequently, and he only replied "millions." That number seems high, but it would not be an exaggeration to put the figure in the hundreds of thousands.

Department store administrators were more than happy with the results. George Deegan, President of Morehouse-Martins Department Store in Columbus, Ohio, observed that "the public demonstrated by both attendance and interest an undiminished enthusiasm that far exceeded our expectations." Philip Troy, president of The Golden Rule in St. Paul, noted that "traffic on opening day was terrific. It looked more like Christmas than the day after Labor Day." Arthur Jerome, the sales promotion manager at Pomeroy's in Reading and Harrisburg, Pennsylvania, said that "the business and professional men contacted ... were enthusiastic in their acclaim of the Caravan itself and television in general."[61] In Grand Rapids, David Laird, the television coordinator at Herpolsheimer's, reported that "crowd reactions were most favorable" for all performances. Most everyone agreed with Donna Ames of Seattle's Bon Marché, that "the RCA Victor-Allied Stores Television Caravan has made entertainment history in the retail field in western Washington." That was certainly true at most of the other stops as well.

Public reaction to the new medium, as revealed by the survey responses, was almost universally positive. Interviewees used words like "wonderful" and "amazing" in their descriptions of the experience. One of the first questions asked by onlookers was, "How long will it be before it reaches us?"[62] One Pennsylvanian opined that "seeing makes programs more entertaining" and "I must tell my neighbors about it." Not all of the reviews were glowing, however. A tinge of skepticism remained among some newspaper opinion columnists who had attended caravan events. One writer, commenting in an otherwise favorable review, described television as a "Buck Rogers-esque gadget."[63] A San Antonio correspondent wrote that "the youngsters think that television is here to stay, although some oldsters have been heard to remark that they are as afraid of it as they were of the old Stanley Steamer of early automobile days."[64]

For the retailers who promoted the caravan tour and whose products were on display, however, the public's opinion as shoppers was far more important than their opinions of television as entertainment. Hilda Jonas's thesis, published the next year, concluded that television had a bright future as an intra-store selling device. Using the mountain of statistical information contained in the reaction surveys, Jonas found that store traffic increased on average by between 30 to 50 percent over the visit of the caravan, and participating stores reported an overall increase in sales the week of the caravan visit.

Those are impressive statistics, but they are tempered by the fact that two-thirds of the survey respondents also reported that they had never seen televisions before. Therefore, it is likely that crowd size was driven by the novelty of the visual experience and not any innate ability of television to sell products. Nevertheless, one out of every four respondents purchased something they had not originally come to buy. In many locations, however, there was little or no change in sales of the products demonstrated on the television monitors, possibly due to the fact that Allied Stores had failed to deliver enough stock to many of their stores.[65]

Ms. Jonas drew several specific conclusions from the data she collected. First, she agreed that intra-store television might best be used as a way of showcasing products, the same way stores used window displays. Second, she noted that not every item translated well visually. The best sellers were Presto pressure cookers and Hickok leather goods, and the worst sellers were dresses, fabrics, and Kem-Tone paint, leading to the logical conclusion that goods that depend on color to attract buyers fared poorly in the monochromatic medium of the time. Similarly, electric blanket sales were lackluster since temperature, heat, and the feel of the blankets could not be portrayed visually.[66]

Nevertheless, Jonas envisioned a longer-term use for intra-store television, but only under certain conditions. She reasoned (and as it turned out, accurately) that once the novelty of it wore off and without the added entertainment the caravan had staged to generate interest, intra-store television would become little more than an ancillary service to customers. A serious reading of Ms. Jonas's report might have caused department store managers to take pause, but most took away from it what they wanted to see; namely, that television was the wave of the future for retail sales. As B. Earl Puckett, president of Allied Purchasing, wrote, "television will soon be one of the most powerful factors in the movement of merchandise in retailing."[67] His sweeping statement proved several decades premature.

The study did reach one marketing conclusion that had a more immediate impact: 84 percent of all the customers polled said they would like to have a television set in their home, and about half of them expressed a willingness to pay close to the going price to obtain one. Because most of the cities visited were still without television service, department stores had few if any in stock, but one store that was well supplied reported that 18 televisions were sold during the caravan week as opposed to an average of five to ten sets in a normal week. Clearly, the caravan did succeed in driving consumer demand, but not for the sponsor's products as originally intended; television itself was the big attraction.[68]

* * *

The RCA–Allied Stores Television Caravan did for demand what the FCC color decision did for production. Thanks to both, the television industry finally blossomed. By the end of 1947 there was an explosion of new requests for station construction permits, with as many as 56 filed during the last three months alone. At one point, the stream of applications coming in to the FCC became a flood of approximately two per day. In addition, applicants who had withdrawn back in 1945 or 1946 suddenly refiled their paperwork. Smaller cities like Wilmington, Akron, Dallas, Miami, Harrisburg, and New Haven rushed to get transmission permits. In part, the boom was a response to the more bullish attitude toward licensing in Washington, D.C., and the belief among potential owners in smaller markets, many of which with only one station allotment, that they needed to move quickly before someone else got the permit.

The explosion of station applications that began late in 1947 continued well into the next year. As the January 1948 issue of *Television Magazine* put it, "1948 is being widely heralded as the year in which television will prove itself as the radio medium of the future. But, judging by the swell of new television applications ... tv's sales job, as far as the broadcasters themselves were concerned, was a 'fait accompli' in the closing months of '47."[69] Indeed, the next year did see an expansion of television service building upon the foundation created in 1947. By the summer of 1948, there were 37 on the air and 86 new stations had permission to open. A total of 302 applications for licenses had been filed, and the continuing onslaught of requests proved so demanding that the FCC imposed a freeze on granting new licenses on September 30. The FCC hoped to use the time to solve problems of station and market distribution and to resolve questions about how to best utilize the UHF band. The hiatus, which was originally supposed to last only six months, remained in place for four years.[70]

Clearly, broadcast television was here to stay, but what happened to intra-store television as a sales technique? As far as some stores were concerned, the caravan's results were proof of concept. Allied Stores envisioned a future where retailers and television broadcasters engaged in a mutually beneficial arrangement. Stores could offer space for a station's use in return for free plugs or cheap commercial time on the station's regular programming. Member department stores jumped in quickly by installing televisions to broadcast not only point-of-sale advertising but also non-commercial broadcasts originating from outside. Corporate managers recommended that 500 square feet of retail floor space be devoted to a television studio, even if the store was not prepared to do anything with it at that time. As those corporate guidelines put it, the goal was "to be ready, because, someday, all fairly large to very large department stores are going to need such space and the time is coming quickly."[71]

Despite that lofty prediction, the novelty of intra-store television soon wore off. Within a decade the sets, the coaxial cables, and the studios were no longer department store fixtures. What brought this noble experiment to an end? After all, the merchandisers of 1947 had it right: television was the wave of the future as a tool of sales and marketing. But television's forte is its ability to send messages and images over long distances and to wide audiences. That strength is neutralized if it is used simply to stimulate point-of-sale purchases to a limited audience in a specific building at a specific moment in time. In addition, the studios, technicians, actors, and sets necessary to field productions were all extremely expensive and hard to maintain; consequently, intra-store television could never replace newsprint advertising for cost effectiveness.

In the final analysis, Hilda Jonas's original observation was spot on. Despite the entertainment value and the novelty of it, intra-store television was little more than a two-dimensional store display. Over time, retailers focused more on driving demand through commercials and letting others do broadcasting.[72] Eventually, direct-to-consumer marketing succeeded where intra-store television failed. Considering the success of the cable stations Quality, Value, and Convenience (QVC) and the Home Shopping Network (HSN) today, television has once again become "the wave of the future" for product sales. Such outlets have even played a role (along with Amazon and other online retail giants) in the decline of brick-and-mortar shopping. Ironically, the device that was originally thought would bring untold prosperity to department stores became an instrument of their demise.

* * *

For the men and women who traveled the country that summer, intra-store merchandising was never really the main point of the RCA-Allied Stores Caravan. They considered themselves modern-day pioneers, introducing the new television technology to the people. Irene Murphy recalled, "We felt like we were showing people this new thing ... this wonderful thing where you could not only hear but you could see!" For most of them, the experience proved both career- and life-changing. Sam Cuff, the organizer who conceived and executed the idea, ultimately signed on with Allied Stores

Corporation as a "teleconsultant," advising stores how best to utilize their radio and television advertising budgets. He was instrumental in putting together the RCA-DuPont Color Television Caravan in 1956 and 1957, which toured the country much as its predecessor had in 1947.

Lou Sposa returned from the caravan tour to work as a freelance producer and director. After 10 more years in broadcasting, he relocated to Florida to take managerial jobs in the hospitality industry. Bernard Brink happily returned to his engineering work and served as the chief engineer on the 1956 Color Caravan tour. Lygia Jarantow left the entertainment industry, married, and moved to Portland, Oregon. Irine "Petey" Petroff left DuMont in 1948 but built upon her experiences in television as a public speaker and college lecturer. She also eventually married and left the television industry.[73]

Irene Murphy, the star and emcee of the caravan shows, still remembers 1947 as "a very exciting year." After the caravan, she returned to New York and went on to host and write a show called *The Women's Club*, which may have been America's first daytime talk show aimed at women. Debuting on WABD in 1948, the show targeted the demographic of women whose "home duties made it impossible to attend their local clubs." But *The Women's Club* was not just about homemaking; it was a show designed to expand traditional gender roles by addressing the needs of modern women.

One day a week, Murphy interviewed a woman who juggled an occupation with being a wife and mother, seeking advice on how she managed both roles. On a different day, she tackled civics and national politics featuring, for example, interviews with officers from League of Women Voters, demonstrations on how to use voting machines, or in-depth discussions with prominent politicians. International affairs occupied yet another day of the week, featuring topics such as the idea of creating a "world calendar," forging international relationships, and "building that better world everybody keeps dreaming about."[74] Among her favorite guests were the environmentalist Pearl Buck, author and journalist Robert St. John, poet Louis Untermeyer, and U.S. Senator Estes Kefauver. Her show was an impressive undertaking, made even more impressive because the production staff consisted of exactly two people; Irene Murphy and one assistant essentially put on the show all by themselves.

Despite the fact that the show aired only fifteen minutes per installment, the critics took notice. As one male reviewer put it,

> This writer's prejudiced opinion and definition of a Woman's Club has always been "an exchange where the stock in trade is gossip." Since WABD's "Woman's Club," we've changed our mind and definition somewhat. We owe the little ladies an apology, men, and the next time "the boss of the budget" announces

that she's off to a meeting, let her go. Some good can come of it. Especially if she's headed in the direction of WABD and Irene Murphy.[75]

In support of the broadcast, Murphy tapped into her education as an English major to write, publish, and distribute a newsletter to her viewers. That too was a success as she averaged 250 fan letters each week that she always answered personally. Put simply, *The Women's Club* was one of postwar television's first attempts to treat female audiences not just as housewives but as consumers of intellectual, political, and social information. Irene Murphy, the writer, producer, and star of the show, emerged as one of television's first female stars and one of WABD's most accomplished employees, both on-air and off.

Unfortunately, DuMont eventually cut back on its daytime production schedule and cancelled the show after one year on the air, so Murphy transitioned into producing and starring in commercials for the Allied Stores Corporation. She took a leap of faith with intra-store television and joined Allied Stores as the television advertising director for Joske's Department Store in San Antonio. There, she directed and starred in a half-hour show on local television called *The Peggy Wilson Show,* taking audiences through the store and displaying its wares. That job lasted for a little over a year after which she returned to New York, married, and left the industry in 1953. Combining her time on *Cash and Carry* and *Women's Club* with her work in San Antonio and on the caravan, Irene Murphy logged as many as three hundred hours in front of the camera, making her one of the most televised women of her time.

* * *

As 1947 ended, television had finally become a commercial reality. Looking back on the year and assessing its impact, a columnist recounted that "this time last year.... I never knew anybody who had seen a televised show. This year, I haven't met anyone who hasn't."[76] Television's impact went far beyond the entertainment industry. It was becoming a force for change, opening new avenues of employment and capturing the imaginations of young people across the country. For younger women especially, it was a source of empowerment that held out the promise that there were more opportunities for employment than just nursing, teaching, and secretarial work.

Irene Murphy and Irine "Petey" Petroff, two perfect examples of this promise coming to fruition, remained lifelong friends who vowed to tell the story of their caravan adventure someday in print. The two started to author a book or screenplay and even put several chapters on paper, but family obligations, distance, and time halted the effort.[77] It is interesting to note that they said very little about their experience to their families. Petroff's daughters do not recall that she ever mentioned the caravan, other than to say that she got a lot of negative attention from men who questioned whether it was "proper" for a woman to work as a camera operator. Murphy's children admit that they knew nothing of their mother's fame until much later in life. One can only wonder how many other women have similar stories of success and accomplishment that are now lost to time.

The year 1947 was one of many television "firsts." The opening sessions of Congress were televised for the first time and Harry Truman became the first president to address the nation over television. The World Series was first televised that year. More importantly, it was the year that production log jams were finally broken, making possible the explosion of television production in 1948 and the years to follow. It was also the year that television broke through to the American heartland. Thanks to the RCA Caravan and its appeal to "See Yourself" in department stores that summer, average citizens finally got an intimate look at the new medium. Although intra-store television never took off, television's impact on consumer thinking and demand was transformative in the long run.

Ironically, the year that witnessed television finally "coming of age" also produced a technological innovation that would revolutionize electronics. On December 15, 1947, Bell Laboratories physicists John Bardeen and William Brattain first demonstrated a device that could boost energy output well beyond that of the normal diode tubes then in use in radio and television receivers. That device, eventually dubbed the "transistor," would completely transform the broadcasting industry.[78] Transistorized circuitry was still years off, but thanks to Bardeen, Brattain, and others, televisions eventually became smaller, cheaper, and more dependable than ever. As a result they became a fixture in every home in America, eventually overtaking and supplanting radio and newsprint as the preferred source of news and entertainment; a position it held until only recently when electronic devices took over as America's preferred source of news.[79]

Epilogue

As 1947 drew to a close, people across the globe again found themselves wishing for a better new year. Although the previous 12 months had brought great progress, many problems persisted. In Germany, another cold winter loomed, and although the occupation authorities scored successes in restoring economic and political life on the local level, Cold War disputes continued to hamper efforts to unify the four zones into a single state. Any such prospects were dashed completely in 1948, as arguments over currency reform drove the U.S.S.R. and the West to the brink of war and all but ensured that Germany would be partitioned into two states.

The situation was equally dire in Asia, where the new nation of Pakistan was struggling to survive. From its first days, the fledgling country had to contend with a non-existent industrial base, an on-going refugee crisis, regional sectarianism, and a territorial dispute with India over Kashmir. Its problems demanded a bold and energetic leadership that the sickly Jinnah, who had only nine more months to live, could no longer provide. There was still more rebuilding to do in Britain, and food rationing continued as a way of combatting shortages. Even in the United States, citizens still had to contend with inflation and restrictions on food consumption. For those who struggled to deal with these issues, 1947 bore little significance as a critical moment in history.

It is only with the passing of time that historians can reflect on and appreciate all that had been accomplished in 1947. One fact is indisputable: the world became "smaller" that year. The Truman Doctrine and the flood of humanitarian support the United States gave to Europe laid the foundation of trust and friendship that culminated in a trans–Atlantic economic, defensive, social, and intellectual partnership that has endured for decades. Then, as if to give metaphoric expression to those ties, 1947 ended for the northeastern seaboard of the United States much as it had begun for London and Hamburg.

Over Christmas week, a snowstorm of epic proportions paralyzed New England and the mid–Atlantic states. The storm was particularly brutal in New York City, where snow started to fall during the morning hours of December 26 and persisted all day, dumping over 25 inches in a 24-hour period.[1] Intercity transportation ground to a halt as drifting snow blocked streets, curtailing the delivery of coal and oil and threatening to bring about a potential heating crisis for millions. The city devolved into what some called a "ghost town." One account put the death toll at 31.

Some notables were caught up in the storm. Stan Kenton and his band were staying in New York and were booked to play the Meadowbrook Ballroom in New Jersey beginning on December 24. After two successful nights, the massive snowfall put an end to any hopes of traveling out of the city. Kenton and the Meadowbrook ownership agreed to void the remainder of the contract and, in a gesture typical of the band leader's largesse, Kenton refused payment for the first two nights, calling it his "Christmas present" to the owners. Fortunately, the band could still generate income by performing during the day at the Paramount Theater on Broadway and 43rd street during Christmas week.

Kenton's crew stayed in the city and worked the Paramount shows before ending their schedule of public appearances and going on hiatus for much of January 1948. Television stations also felt the impact of the storm. Many had to curtail broadcasting, but the major stations in New York City continued with evening programming. Again, the snow proved fortuitous because it ensured that those people who owned sets would be "glued" to them; either to watch for news or weather updates or simply for entertainment to while away the hours.

For those contemporaries residing outside the U.S. northeast, 1947 passed unremarkably. Wendell Smith settled into his dual role as reporter for the *Chicago Herald American* and *The Pittsburgh Courier*. He continued to sing Robinson's praises in his newspaper articles, but in truth there were signs of tensions in their personal relationship. The two men had decided to "cash in" on the Robinson's celebrity by collaborating on an autobiography. The volume, entitled *My Own Story*, was in fact mostly written by Smith over several months following the end of Jackie's inaugural season and hurriedly published in May of 1948. Unfortunately, several egregious errors in the text cast a pall over the entire work.[2]

In addition, Smith's articles had attacked Jackie for reporting to spring training in January 1948 slightly overweight. As the new year went on, Smith continued to criticize Robinson. "We are sure," editorialized Smith in June 1948, "that he won't let himself overstuff again this winter. He's learned his lesson."[3] Although Smith was only trying to goad Robinson into staying in shape, his criticisms strained their relationship to the point where it became a factor in the ultimate dissolution of their partnership.

Senator Vandenberg ushered in the New Year by doing what he did best, making headlines. Ever since his reelection in 1946, he had hinted that his present term would be his last, but many took that to mean that he might consider a run for president in 1948. Although Governor Thomas Dewey and Senator Robert Taft were the favorites to be the Republican nominee, many saw Vandenberg as a possible dark horse candidate or deal broker at a stalemated convention. On December 31, he put any such contentions to rest. In a letter to his home delegation, Vandenberg announced that he did not wish to have his name brought forward as a presidential candidate. He explained, "I am confident that I can best serve my country by completing my present term in the Senate."[4] He went back to work as Senate President pro tempore and Chairman of the Foreign Relations Committee. Several months later, he was diagnosed with lung cancer, the illness that eventually claimed his life in 1951.

It is impossible to probe all the events of 1947 that point to the emergence of a modern, interdependent world in just one volume. Many other topics deserving of our attention must go unexplored here because of space limitations. For example, in late summer, diplomats from 16 European nations gathered in Paris to discuss how best to distribute Marshall Plan money coming from the United States. Their discussions ultimately led to the creation of the Organization for European Economic Cooperation (OEEC), the first major step in bringing former adversaries together in an environment of mutual cooperation and joint decision making. Out of that same spirit emerged the movement to integrate Europe, eventually leading to the creation of the Common Market, the European Community, and culminating in the European Union.[5]

In the arts, Tennessee Williams' *A Streetcar Named Desire* opened on Broadway in New York City on December 3. The play, which explores the darker sides of human sexuality including exploitation, spousal abuse, and rape, was a bold departure from the drama of the past that tended to overly romanticize the human experience.[6] On June 24, Kenneth Arnold, a civilian aviator from Boise, Idaho, was flying from Washington State to Oregon and saw nine objects in the sky he could not identify. The initial accounts of his encounter described the objects as "saucerlike"[7] and thus began a year the National Air and Space Museum calls "the year of the Flying Saucer."[8] Less than a month later, the Roswell, New Mexico *Daily Record* reported the capture of a "flying saucer" on its front page.[9] In more tangible aviation news, Chuck Yeager broke the sound barrier in the X-1 aircraft in October.[10] On television, both the *Howdy Doody Show* and *Meet the Press* debuted.

These are but a few examples (some more profound than others) of events that influenced generations to come—all from a year chock full of transitional moments. The events chronicled here can only provide a brief glimpse into the transformations the world experienced during 1947—a most remarkable year.

Chapter Notes

Introduction

1. The United Kingdom had to contend with bread rationing (which had not been necessary during the war), thanks to the torrential rains and poor wheat crop of 1946. Ireland suffered from the same bad harvests, and had it not been for a *levée en masse* of agricultural labor that summer, the citizens of the Emerald Isle would have faced starvation conditions by the end of the year. Similar shortfalls occurred across most of the continent.

2. Proclamation 2714, Truman Library, https://www.trumanlibrary.gov/library/proclamations/2714/cessation-hostilities-world-war-ii. Accessed August 2023.

3. "Truman Declares Hostilities Ended, Terminating Many Wartime Laws: Republican Chiefs Commend Action," *New York Times*, January 1, 1947.

4. "New Era for the Mines," *Times* (London), January 1, 1947.

Chapter 1

1. Alexander Häusser and Gordian Maugg, *Hungerwinter: Deutschlands humanitäre Katastrophe 1946/47* (Berlin: Propyläen, 2009), 13–14.

2. Over the night of December 12, the region surrounding Hannover-Braunschweig recorded a bone-chilling overnight low of 0°F (-18°C). Häusser and Maugg, *Hungerwinter*, 14.

3. Thomas Berger and Karl-Heinz Mueller, *Lebenssituationen 1945–1948* (Hannover: Niedersächsische Landeszentrale für politische Bildung, 1983), 74.

4. Hans Schlange-Schöningen, *Im Schatten des Hungers* (Hamburg: Verlag Paul Parey, 1955), 114–5.

5. Similar to American Quonset huts, Nissen huts were semi-permanent storage structures made of corrugated steel that could be used for human habitation. Cold and drafty even in the best of circumstances, the Nissen huts at least provided some shelter from the elements.

6. "Der Tod mit dem Aktenzeichen 07," *Die Zeit* (1947:03), January 16, 1947. Accessed online at http://www.zeit.de/1947/03/der-tod-mit-dem-aktenzeichen-07.

7. "17 Deaths from Cold at Hamburg," *Times* (London), January 9, 1947.

8. "Der Tod mit dem Aktenzeichen 07," *Die Zeit*.

9. Roughly, "hamstering."

10. Häusser and Maugg, *Hungerwinter*, 160–1.

11. The actual text of the sermon goes on to say that the goods should be returned or paid for as soon as possible, but most people conveniently forgot that part of the sermon. The word is still in use today. http://institutionen.erzbistum-koeln.de/historischesarchiv/archivschaetze/fringsen.html. Accessed November 2014. The original manuscript of the sermon can be found at the Historical Archive of the Archbishopric of Cologne.

12. Häusser and Maugg, *Hungerwinter*, 168.

13. Berger and Mueller, *Lebenssituationen*, 78.

14. Häusser and Maugg, *Hungerwinter*, 152.

15. Häusser and Maugg, *Hungerwinter*, 170–1. See also Karl-Heinz Rothenberger, *Die Hungerjahre nach dem Zweiten*

Weltkrieg (Boppard am Rhein: Harald Boldt Verlag, 1980), 153.

16. Häusser and Maugg, *Hungerwinter*, 179.

17. "Snow and Gales: Disorganization of Traffic," *Times* (London), January 7, 1947, and "Another Fall of Snow," January 8, 1947.

18. Alex J. Robertson, *The Bleak Midwinter: 1947* (Manchester: Manchester University Press, 1987), 8.

19. "Monthly Weather Report of the Meteorological Office," HMSO, vol. 64, no. 1 (January 1947).

20. "Heavy Falls of Snow: Villages Isolated by Drifts," *Times* (London), January 27, 1947.

21. "50 M.P.H. Gale," *Times* (London), January 27, 1947.

22. "Further Falls of Snow," *Times* (London), January 28, 1947.

23. Monthly Meteorological Report, January 1947.

24. Kevin C. Kearns, *Ireland's Arctic Siege: The Big Freeze of 1947* (Dublin: Gill and Macmillan, 2012), 3–4.

25. Observatories at Kew recorded no sunshine whatsoever from February 2 to 22, setting a record. Monthly Weather Report of the Meteorological Office, HMSO, February 1947. See also Robertson, *Bleak Midwinter*, 10.

26. "More Snow in the South," *Times* (London), January 29, 1947.

27. *Times* (London), January 30, 1947.

28. David Kynaston, *A World to Build* (London: Bloomsbury, 2007), 194.

29. "Snowstorm in the North: Buses trapped in Drifts," *Times* (London), February 5, 1947.

30. "Snowstorm." *Times* (London).

31. Kearns, *Arctic Siege*, 8.

32. "Gale After the Snow," *The Western Times* (Exeter), February 14, 1947.

33. Monthly Weather Report, HMSO, March 1947.

34. This comparison to the Blitz was repeated time and again in the decades following the catastrophe. See C.A. Jones, et al., "Examining the Social Consequences of Extreme Weather: The Outcomes of the 1946/47 Winter in Upland Wales, U.K.," *Climatic Change* 113:35–53 (2012).

35. "Serious Dislocation of Traffic: Main Routes Still Blocked by Drifts," *Times* (London), March 8, 1947.

36. "Serious Dislocation," *Times* (London).

37. Robertson, *Bleak Midwinter*, 17.

38. "Cadbury's to Close: More Firms Short of Coal," *Times* (London), February 5, 1947.

39. "Power Cuts and Industry," *Times* (London), February 8, 1947.

40. Kynaston, *World to Build*, 194.

41. "Cabinet and Coal: Hope of Avoiding Domestic Cut," *Times* (London), January 1, 1947.

42. "Further Falls of Snow," *Times* (London), January 28, 1947.

43. "All Britain Freezes," *Times* (London), January 30, 1947.

44. The cut did not apply to the north and northeast of Britain, or to southern Wales and the southwest. "Electricity Supplies Cut Off Today," *Times* (London), February 10, 1947.

45. Peter Tanner, "British Fuel Crisis Hits Entertainment Hard," *Downbeat*, March 12, 1947, 16.

46. "Special Coal Effort this Weekend" and "Slight Rise in Temperature," *Times* (London), February 15, 1947. The BBC resumed regular evening broadcasting on March 11, but daytime broadcasts were still curtailed. See "Main Routes Cleared," *Times* (London), March 10, 1947.

47. Ironically, Parliament was debating the food situation—and discussing possible further cuts in the bread and bacon rations—just one day before the initial storms hit the southeast.

48. "Snowbound Village asks for Food by Plane," *Yorkshire Post*, February 8, 1947.

49. "Many at Huggate Had No Food Left," *Yorkshire Post*, February 10, 1947. See also "Heavy Snow in the South," *Times* (London), February 10, 1947.

50. "Dale Hamlet's Plight," *Yorkshire Post*, March 5, 1947.

51. Kearns, *Arctic Siege*, 10.

52. "A Winter's Dale: Weather Memories from Upper Teesdale," North Pennines AONB Partnership, Oral History Project, 7. Downloadable at https://silo.tips/queue/a-winter-s-dale-weather-memories-from-upper-teesdale?&queue_id=-1&v=1697033918&u=MjYwMDo2YzYwOjUzMDA6NWE2OjFkMjE6ODI4ODo0NGVkOjkyODg=.

53. "New Threat to Coal," *Western Morning News*, February 22, 1947.

54. C.A. Jones, et al., "Examining the Social Consequences of Extreme Weather," *Climatic Change* 113:1 (July 2012), 45.
55. Jones, et al., "Extreme Weather," 46.
56. Cedric Roberts, MBE, "The 1947 Winter in Halesowen, West Midlands," https://www.swanstonweather.co.uk/Pages/Index.html. Accessed August 2023.
57. "Traffic Chaos after Heavy Snowstorms," *Times* (London), March 6, 1947.
58. "Transport Stopped in Many Areas," *Times* (London), March 7, 1947.
59. "North Isolated by Snow: Rising Floods," *Times* (London)," March 14, 1947.
60. "Rising Floods in Thames Valley: Worst for 53 Years," *Times* (London), March 17, 1947.
61. The volume of onrushing waters was so great that it caused measuring devices fail. D. Barker, *Harvest Home: The Official Story of the Great Floods of 1947 and Their Sequel* (London: HMSO, 1948), 18.
62. Barker, *Harvest Home*, 82.
63. "1947 U.K. River Floods: 60-Year Retrospective," *Risk Management Solutions*, 2007, 2–4.
64. "1947 Floods," *Risk Management Solutions*, 7. A complete accounting of the flooding can also be found in B. Howorth, "The Spring Floods of 1947," *Journal of the Institution of Water Engineers*, vol. 2, issue 1 (1948) and in Barker, *Harvest Home*.
65. Michael Sissons and Philip French, eds., *Age of Austerity: 1945–1951* (Oxford: Oxford University Press, 1986), 37.
66. Kearns, *Ireland's Arctic Siege*, 309–310.
67. "England Swept by a Destructive Gale," *Times* (London), March 17, 1947.
68. "Relief of Distress in Flooded Areas," *Times* (London), March 25, 1947.
69. Kynaston, *World to Build*, 201. See also Sissons and French, 37.
70. Robertson, *Bleak Midwinter*, 128. In 2007, an insurance report concluded that if a flood similar to the 1947 event struck again, it would cause between $8.8 and $11.8 billion in damage. See "1947 Floods," *Risk Management Solutions*, 11.
71. Fritz Bela Groissmayr, *Berichte des Deutschen Wetterdienstes in der U.S.-Zone*, Nr. 10 (Bad Kissingen: Deutscher Wetterdienst in der U.S.-Zone, 1949), 18.
72. "The Winter's Weather," *Times* (London), March 1, 1947.

73. "Saskatchewan Blizzards," *Times* (London), February 10, 1947.
74. It was the coldest February in fifty-two years. L.H. Seamon, "The Weather of 1947 in the United States," *Monthly Weather Review*, vol. 75, no. 12. (December 1947). Later that year, Floridians experienced what has since been called "The Great Flood of 1947," a period of four months of soaking rain punctuated by a 155-mph hurricane that hit in early September.
75. Groissmayr, *Berichte*, 18.
76. "Kalt, Kälter, am Kältesten," *Der Spiegel*, February 8, 1947, 14.

Chapter 2

1. "Ruhr Hunger March," *Times* (London), March 29, 1947.
2. Christoph Klessman and Peter Friedemann, *Streiks und Hungermärsche im Ruhrgebiet 1946–48* (Frankfurt: Campus-Verlag, 1977), 47.
3. Large demonstrations had started in Essen a month earlier but remained relatively localized. Klessman, *Streiks*, 45.
4. The workers also wanted land reform and the socialization of mines.
5. Black market profiteers commonly adulterated food to increase the profitability of the merchandise. Milk and butter were frequent targets. See Hans-Ulrich Sons, *Gesundheitspolitik während der Besatzungszeit* (Wuppertal: Peter Hammer Verlag, 1983), 113–114.
6. "Ruhr Hunger March," *Times* (London), March 29, 1947.
7. "Steine statt Brot," *Der Spiegel*, vol. 1, nr. 14, April 3, 1947.
8. Paragraph 32. The full text of JCS 1067 is readily available online. One site is https://history.state.gov/historicaldocuments/frus1945v03/d351. Accessed September 2023.
9. JCS 1067.
10. Henry Morgenthau was FDR's Secretary of the Treasury. His plan proved to be a propaganda gold mine for the Nazis, who used it to convince their citizens of the horrors that awaited them should they lose the war.
11. At the Quebec Conference in September 1944, the United Kingdom accepted JCS 1067 "in principle" in return for U.S. concessions in the territorial

division of Germany. See Lucius D. Clay, *Decision in Germany* (New York: Doubleday, 1950), 11.

12. Beate Ruhm von Oppen, *Documents on Germany* (London: Oxford University Press, 1955), 113–118.

13. Clay, *Decision in Germany*, 73.

14. Clay, *Decision in Germany*, 77.

15. Byrnes' Stuttgart speech can be found online at http://usa.usembassy.de/etexts/ga4-460906.htm. Accessed September 2023.

16. Much of JCS 1067 had been changed, watered-down, or ignored anyway over the previous eighteen months. Still, Bizonia began with no official restatement of policy.

17. Professor Alan Milward investigated the nature of the "crisis of 1947" thoroughly in *The Reconstruction of Western Europe: 1945-1951* (Berkeley: University of California Press, 1984). He reinforces the claim that the food crisis was most acute in Germany, stating "it could not be shown that any population outside of Germany was in danger of starving and even their diet was slightly improved over the previous year" (3).

18. Louis P. Lochner, *Herbert Hoover and Germany* (New York: Macmillan, 1960), 177.

19. War Dept. Memorandum, January 16, 1947. National Archives and Records Administration (NARA), Harry S. Truman Presidential Library and Museum (HSTLM), White House Central Files, Official File 950-B (Economic Mission as to Food and Its Collateral Problems). Voorhees later claimed credit for the idea of asking Herbert Hoover to lead the mission.

20. There are many good biographies of Herbert Hoover. Perhaps the best is George H. Nash's, *The Life of Herbert Hoover* (New York: W.W. Norton, 1988). Equally valuable is William Leuchtenberg's contribution on Hoover in the American Presidents Series published by Macmillan (2009). Unfortunately, most scholars have chosen to concentrate on his life up to and including his presidency, particularly focusing on his administration's handling of the Great Depression. Only a few have written on his post-presidential years. The most notable scholarship here is Gary Dean Best's work, *The Life of Herbert Hoover: Keeper of the Torch* (New York: Palgrave Macmillan, 2013).

21. Truman issued a number of invitations to other prominent Republicans too.

22. Timothy Walch and Dwight M. Miller, *Herbert Hoover and Harry S. Truman: A Documentary History* (Worland WY: High Plains Publishing Co., 1992).

23. Walch and Miller, *Hoover*, 43.

24. Walch and Miller, *Hoover*, 98–9. Truman's letter can be found at https://www.trumanlibrary.gov/node/317994. Accessed September 2023.

25. Walch and Miller, *Hoover*, 99. Hoover's response can be found at https://www.trumanlibrary.gov/node/317995. Accessed September 2023.

26. Secretary Patterson to President Truman, January 20, 1947, NARA, HSTLM, President's Secretary Files, General File Box 106.

27. Edgar Rickard Diaries, entry for Thursday, January 16, 1947, NARA, Herbert Hoover Presidential Library and Museum (HHLM), West Branch, Iowa.

28. Walch and Miller, *Hoover*, 100.

29. Eugene Lyons, *Herbert Hoover: A Biography* (Garden City, NY: Doubleday, 1964), 390.

30. Rickard Diaries, Tuesday, January 28, 1947, NARA, HHLM.

31. NARA, HHLM, President's Secretary Files, Box 950-B (miscellaneous file).

32. Hugh Gibson, who chronicled the trip in a diary, remarked that the railroad car they were given was luxurious, complete with a bathtub "big enough for Himmler and Goering." Entry for Wednesday, February 5. http://www.hoover.org/library-archives/collections/food-mission-diaries-hugh-gibson-1946-and-1947. Accessed September 2023.

33. Gibson Diary, entry for Saturday, February 8.

34. Calorie delivery levels dropped steadily in the first months of 1947, and according to Clay, by April the average consumer was getting only 1040 calories per day. Clay, *Decision in Germany*, 268.

35. Nitrogen production had been strictly controlled as a war material and limited to 40 percent of 1936 production by the Level of Industry Plan.

36. Illegal pig feedings were not the only problem. German farmers were feeding grains to livestock rather than surrendering them to occupation authorities.

Notes—Chapter 2

37. Notes of meeting on February 7, NARA, HHLM, Box 318 (Trips: 1947 Germany and Austria).

38. Gibson Diary, entry for Monday, February 10, 1947.

39. Gibson Diary, entry for Monday, February 10, 1947.

40. The rest of the group had taken a train to Berlin because their pilots refused to fly in the icy conditions.

41. Memo of meeting made by Hugh Gibson, NARA, HHLM, Box 318, Trips file: memos of conversations.

42. The briefing with Attlee apparently did not go well. Hugh Gibson recorded that Attlee gave "laconic approval" to the idea of reducing the burdens on taxpayers but said little else and offered nothing of substance to the conversation other than to say, "This has been very interesting." Memo of meeting, NARA, HHLM, General File Box 318 (Trips 1947: Germany and Austria).

43. Not so for the 72-year-old Hoover, who was nursing a bad head cold the entire time. The changes in cabin pressure burst an eardrum, deafening him for months thereafter.

44. Report No. 1 can be found archived online in its entirety at https://hoover.archives.gov/sites/default/files/research/ebooks/b3v5_full.pdf, 269–285.

45. A 10-in-1 ration was a package of canned foods designed to feed ten soldiers one meal.

46. Report No. 2 concerned Austria and is out of the scope of our discussion here.

47. Herbert Hoover, *Addresses Upon the American Road: 1945-1948* (New York: Van Nostrand and Co., 1949), 83–97. Available online at https://hoover.archives.gov/sites/default/files/research/ebooks/b3v5_full.pdf.

48. Lochner, *Hoover and Germany*, 186.

49. Joan Wilson, *Herbert Hoover: Forgotten Progressive* (Prospect Heights, IL: Waveland Press, 1992), 259–260.

50. Hoover, *Addresses Upon the American Road*, 137.

51. Hoover, *Addresses Upon the American Road*, 310.

52. The French were furious that they had not been consulted. See Bidault to Marshall, July 17, 1947, *Foreign Relations of the United States (FRUS) 1947, Council of Foreign Ministers; Germany and Austria*, 991–2.

53. Ruhm von Oppen, *Documents*, 239–245.

54. The text of JCS 1779 can be found in Department of State, *Germany 1947-1949: The Story in Documents* (Washington, D.C.: Government Printing Office, 1950), 33–41. It was also printed in the *New York Times*, July 16, 1947.

55. U.S. War Department to Military Governor for Germany (Clay), *FRUS 1947, Council of Foreign Ministers; Germany and Austria*, Vol II, 1010.

56. Clay to Hoover, June 8, 1947, NARA, HHLM, Post-Presidential Individual Correspondence File, Box 37 (Clay).

57. Stolper to Hoover, July 19, 1947, NARA, HHLM, Post-Presidential Individual Correspondence File, Box 223 (Stolper).

58. Press release, U.S. War Department, March 17, 1947. NARA, HHLM, Post-Presidential Individual Correspondence File, Box 244 (Voorhees).

59. Theodore A. Wilson and Richard D. McKinzie, "Save Wheat, Save Meat, Save the Peace,'" in *Prologue, The Journal of the National Archives*, vol. 3, no. 3, Winter 1971.

60. Report from Dept. of Army, Food Adminstrator for Occupied Areas signed N.H. Vissering to Maurice Pate, March 12, 1948. NARA, HHLM, Food Emergency Committee, Box 144.

61. Most of the time, the meals were not prepared at the schools per se but in private kitchens that were monitored for proper sanitation. "Child Feeding Program," *Weekly Information Bulletin*, Military Government (No. 103, July 28, 1947), 3.

62. Report from the Hessian Minister for Culture and Education, *Die Schulkinderspeisung in Hessen*, NARA, HHLM, Post-Presidential Subject File, Box 169 (Germany).

63. Report from the Hessian Ministry of the Interior, Medical Division. *Die Ernährungs- und Gesundheitszustand der Kinder und Jügendlichen in Hessen im Hinblick auf die Hoover-Speisung*, January 31, 1948, NARA, HHLM, Post-Presidential Subject File, Box 169 (Germany).

64. NARA, HSTLM, Official File 198 Germany (Box 829). Last name withheld.

65. NARA, HHLM, Post-Presidential Subject File, Box 169 (Germany). Name withheld.

66. More letters can be found in Lochner, *Hoover and Germany.*
67. If there is such a thing as an "official" ending to the idea of quadripartite control, it is most likely when General Sokolovsky stormed out of the ACC meeting in July of 1948 in disagreement over the currency reform issue. Thereafter, no serious attempts were made to draw the Russians into any policy agreements.
68. Lochner, *Hoover and Germany*, 180.
69. Rickard Diary, *Review of the Year*, NARA, HSTLM.
70. Rickard Diary, Sunday, February 23, NARA, HSTLM.
71. John W. Snyder interviews, Oral History at Truman. http://www.trumanlibrary.org/oralhist/snyder30.htm#1161.
72. Clay, *Decision in Germany*, 268.
73. Steve Neal, ed., *HST Memories of the Truman Year* (Carbondale: Southern Illinois University Press, 2003), 71–7. Transcriptions of the Truman Library Oral History Project.
74. Clipping from the *Daily Mirror*, May 2, 1947, NARA, HHLM, Edgar Rickard files.
75. Sokolsky clipping, May 3, 1947, NARA, HHLM, Edgar Rickard files.

Chapter 3

1. "Truman Acts to Save Nations from Red Rule: Asks 400 Million to Aid Greece and Turkey," *New York Times*, March 13, 1947.
2. The text of this speech is available online in a variety of locations. See, for example, National Archives website at https://www.archives.gov/milestone-documents/truman-doctrine. An audio recording can be found at https://www.trumanlibraryinstitute.org/truman/historic-speeches/. Accessed September 2023.
3. Edgar O'Ballance, *The Greek Civil War* (New York: Praeger, 1966), 124.
4. O'Ballance, *Greek Civil War*, 128.
5. David Close, *Origins of the Greek Civil War* (London: Longman, 1995), 190–1.
6. Arnold A. Offner, *Another Such Victory* (Stanford: Stanford University Press, 2002), 197.
7. Or Archibald Clark-Kerr, as he was known before his elevation to the peerage.
8. Quoted in Stephen George Xydis, *Greece and the Great Powers 1944–1947: Prelude to the Truman Doctrine* (Thessaloniki: Institute for Balkan Studies, 1963), 475.
9. Xydis, *Greece and the Great Powers*, 400–1.
10. Xydis, *Greece and the Great Powers*, 478.
11. For a Washington insider's account of the events, see Dean Acheson, *Present at the Creation* (New York: W.W. Norton, 1969), 220–3.
12. Gerald G. Bogert, entry on Arthur Hendrick Vandenberg in *Dictionary of American Biography*, 181.
13. Dean Acheson, *Sketches from Life of Men I Have Known* (New York: Harper and Bros., 1961), 125.
14. *Memorial Services for Arthur Hendrick Vandenberg, 82nd Congress, first session* (Washington, D.C.: Government Printing Office, 1951), 50.
15. C. David Tompkins, *Senator Arthur H. Vandenberg: The Evolution of a Modern Republican* (Lansing: Michigan State University Press, 1970), 1–2.
16. Tompkins, *Senator Arthur H. Vandenberg*, 6.
17. Tompkins, *Senator Arthur H. Vandenberg*, 13.
18. The Zimmerman Telegram was a secret German state department message to their legation in Mexico, promising the Mexican government territorial rewards at the expense of the United States if it should side with Germany in any potential war with the U.S. The British had intercepted the telegram, decoded it, and forwarded it on to Washington, hoping to spike anti-German sentiment in the U.S.
19. Many shared his criticism, and the Senate eventually rejected both treaties.
20. Tompkins, *Senator Arthur H. Vandenberg*, 20–5.
21. Quoted from the *Herald*, in Tompkins, *Vandenberg*, 33.
22. Tompkins, *Senator Arthur H. Vandenberg*, 45.
23. Arthur H. Vandenberg and Arthur H. Vandenberg, Jr., *The Private Papers of Senator Vandenberg*, edited by Joe Alex Morris (Cambridge, MA: Riverside Press, 1952), 16.

24. So named because the Republican Party retreat was held at Mackinac Island on the Upper Peninsula of his home state of Michigan.

25. Vandenberg, *Private Papers*, 74.

26. Vandenberg, *Private Papers*, 135.

27. Vandenberg, *Private Papers*, 139. Writing three years later during the height of the tensions with the Soviet Union, Vandenberg recounted that at the time he had anticipated the "Moscow menace" and had been motivated to advocate some means of confronting communist expansion after the war's end.

28. Vandenberg, *Private Papers*, 140.

29. Harry S. Truman, *Memoirs. Volume 1: Year of Decisions* (Garden City, NY: Doubleday, 1955), 21. The definitive study of the relationship between Truman and Vandenberg is by Lawrence J. Haas, *Harry and Arthur: Truman Vandenberg, and the Partnership that Created the Free World* (Lincoln: Potomac Books, 2016).

30. Truman, *Memoirs*, 145.

31. Senator Thomas "Tom" Connally of Texas (Democrat) also accompanied them.

32. According to Byrnes, Vandenberg and Connally spent a total of 213 days away from their offices in 1946 to attend meetings and conferences. See James F. Byrnes, *Speaking Frankly* (New York: Harper and Brothers, 1947), 235.

33. Joseph Hernon, *Profiles in Character: Hubris and Heroism in the U.S. Senate* (Armonk, NY: M.E. Sharpe, 1997), 170.

34. "Vandenberg Denies '48 Aim but Avoids a Ban on 'Draft,'" *New York Times*, December 18, 1946 (University of Michigan, Bentley Historical Library, Vandenberg archive, microfilm, reel 9).

35. Byrnes apparently was a difficult man to work for; State Department employees often found his style abrasive and he was not one to delegate authority to subordinates. See John Lewis Gaddis, *The United States and the Cold War, 1941-1947* (New York: Columbia University Press, 1972), 347.

36. Robert Taft of Ohio, the powerful Republican chairman of the Senate Policy Committee and noted isolationist, was "accidently" omitted from the invitation list. Vandenberg pointed out the "omission" at the start of the meeting.

37. In his memoirs Acheson compared the meeting to "Armageddon." Acheson, *Present at the Creation*, 219.

38. The phrase has since common parlance in the lexicon of governmental and foreign affairs.

39. George F. Kennan, *Memoirs* (Boston: Little, Brown, 1967), 319–320.

40. Kennan, *Memoirs*, 321.

41. Truman's State Department had already recommended this approach in a memorandum written for the State, War, and Navy Conference Committee (SWNCC) known as FPI 30. See Howard Jones, *A New Kind of War* (Oxford: Oxford University Press, 1989), 41.

42. Vandenberg, *Private Papers*, 344.

43. Vandenberg, *Private Papers*, 340.

44. Vandenberg, *Private Papers*, 351.

45. Acheson, *Present at the Creation*, 223-4. Acheson described Vandenberg's approach to legislation as "a kind of political transubstantiation." First, he would feign ignorance and skepticism while he studied the proposal (the "gestation" period), then he would find some minor fault with it. Once that fault was rectified, he would announce his "conversion" to it. Acheson called this procedure "applying the trademark." Dean Acheson, *Sketches from Life* (New York: Harper and Brothers, 1961), 127.

46. Vandenberg, *Private Papers*, 347.

47. Vandenberg, *Private Papers*. The entire speech can be found under the title "The Whole Greek Loan Story" in the Congressional Record, proceedings and debates of the 80th Congress, First Session.

48. Jones, *New Kind of War*, 61.

49. Offner, *Another Such Victory*, 207–8. See also O'Ballance, *Greek Civil War*, 131.

50. When Tito refused to comply, it added to the already sizeable list of disagreements between the two men, which led ultimately to the rift between the Soviet Union and Yugoslavia.

51. Letter to the Rev. Richard V. Grace, March 7, 1947 (Bentley Historical Library, Vandenberg archive, microfilm, reel 4). Underlining and punctuation as in original.

52. "Vandenberg is 67," *New York Times*, March 23, 1951 (Bentley Historical Library, Vandenberg archive, microfilm, reel 9).

53. *Memorial Services, 82nd Congress*, 34.

54. Acheson, *Sketches from Life*, 130.

55. "World Capitals Mourn Death of Sen. Vandenberg," *Grand Rapids Press*, April 20, 1951 (Bentley Historical Library, Vandenberg archive, microfilm, reel 9).

56. Just about everything in Vandenberg's career, from his rhetoric to his impact on foreign policy, has been studied by academics. Among the many dissertations are Newell S. Moore, *The Role of Senator Arthur H. Vandenberg in American Foreign Affairs* (Ph.D. dissertation, George Peabody College for Teachers of Vanderbilt University, 1954), Ryh-hsiuh Yang, *The Role of Chairman Arthur H. Vandenberg of the Senate Foreign Relations Committee in the 80th Congress, 1947-1948.* (Ph.D. dissertation, New School for Social Research, 1966); and Ronald Frank Lehman, II, *Vandenberg, Taft, and Truman: Principle and Politics in the Announcement of the Truman Doctrine* (Ph.D. dissertation, Claremont Graduate School, 1975).

Chapter 4

1. Clement Attlee, address to Parliament February 20, 1947. Text of parliamentary announcement and debate is at *Hansard's Parliamentary Debates* [House of Commons], 5th Series, Vol. 433, cols. 1395-1398. Hansard's inaccurately records the date as February 10 instead of February 20. Accessed September 2023.

2. Population statistics cited here are based on the 1941 census and published in the world press. See O.H.K. Spate, *India and Pakistan: A General and Regional Geography* (London: Methuen, 1954), 128-132.

3. Four out of every ten Muslims lived in the Hindu-dominated Indian heartland. Spate, *India and Pakistan*, 128.

4. There is a long-standing debate about the effects of British rule in India. Western historians have tended to focus on what they consider the "positive" aspects of the Raj. Asian historians focus on the exploitative nature of colonial rule. For the Asian perspective, see Shashi Tharoor, *Inglorious Empire* (London: Hurst, 2017).

5. Hector Bolitho, *Jinnah: Creator of Pakistan* (London: John Murray, 1954), 45.

6. Bolitho, *Jinnah*, 40.

7. It is possible that his birthday was in October, not December, as birth certificates were not routine in this part of India until years later. Stanley Wolpert, *Jinnah of Pakistan* (New York: Oxford University Press, 1984), 5. See also Yasser Hamdani, *Jinnah: A Life* (London: Pan Macmillan, 2020).

8. Bolitho, *Jinnah*, 5.

9. Quoted in Wolpert, *Jinnah*, 19.

10. Quoted in Wolpert, *Jinnah*, 34.

11. The origins of "Pakistan" lie in an acronym based on the regions comprising the country (P for Punjab, A for Afghani regions, K for Kashmir, S for Sindh, etc.)

12. Ayesha Jalal, *The Sole Spokesman* (Cambridge: Cambridge University Press, 1985), 12-13.

13. Penderel Moon, *Divide and Quit*, edition contained in *The Partition Omnibus* (Oxford: Oxford University Press, 2002), 21.

14. Jalal, *Sole Spokesman*, 60.

15. Although this was a breakthrough for the Indian independence movement, neither the Congress nor the League accepted the proposals. Hindus thought it did not safeguard unity enough and Muslims thought it did not assure self-determination enough.

16. Yasmin Khan, *The Great Partition* (New Haven: Yale University Press, 2007), 36.

17. Jalal, *Sole Spokesman*, 150.

18. Interview with Masood Ghaznavi, November 16, 2010.

19. Ghaznavi interview.

20. Quoted in Riaz Ahmad, "Muslim Punjab's Fight for Pakistan: League's Agitation Against the Coalition Ministry of Sir Khizr Hayat Khan Tiwana, January-March 1947," *Pakistan Journal of History and Culture*, vol. XXVIII, no. 1, 2007. Accessed at http://www.nihcr.edu.pk/Downloads/Punjab_Muslim.pdf.

21. Khalid Bin Sayed, *Pakistan: The Formative Phase 1857-1948* (Oxford: Oxford University Press, 1968), 137.

22. For a while, it seemed as if the Cabinet Mission might have looked favorably on the idea of a Pakistan, had Jinnah been willing to relinquish some of his territorial demands. But Jinnah proved unwilling to compromise.

23. This again raises the questions of Jinnah's true motivations. Moon, *Divide and Quit*, 50-51.

24. Moon, *Divide and Quit*, 53.
25. Bin Sayed, *Pakistan*, 146–7.
26. Stanley Wolpert, *Shameful Flight* (Oxford: Oxford University Press, 2006), 108.
27. Khan, *Great Partition*, 63.
28. Khan, *Great Partition*, 63. Wolpert puts the figure of wounded at 16,000. *Shameful Flight*, 120.
29. Quoted in Pakistan Historical Society, *History of the Freedom Movement: Vol. 4* (Karachi: Pakistan Historical Society, 1970), 154.
30. Nehru and most of the Congress were not happy with the decision, and eventually Gandhi himself regretted making the concession. Bin Sayeed, *Pakistan*, 158.
31. Jalal, *Sole Spokesman*, 226.
32. Khizar's government also outlawed a militant Hindu group. Moon, *Divide and Quit*, 75.
33. Some of those who were arrested with Ghaznavi eventually became high judges and ministers in the Pakistani government. Ghaznavi Interview.
34. Quoted in Wolpert, *Shameful Flight*, 160.
35. V.P. Menon, *The Transfer of Power in India* (Princeton: Princeton University Press, 1957), 361.
36. Up until this point, the viceroy's staff had been very scrupulous about sharing information with both sides equally. See H.V. Hodson, *The Great Divide* (London: Hutchinson, 1969), 296.
37. Menon, *Transfer of Power*, 361.
38. Alan Campbell-Johnson, *Mission with Mountbatten* (New York: E.P. Dutton, 1953), 93.
39. Bin Sayed, *Pakistan*, 175.
40. Historians have ever since debated whether Nehru's decision was a naïve attempt to seize independence while he could, or a calculated attempt to hamstring the creation of Pakistan.
41. This led to some confusion over who received what. For example, the volumes of the *Encyclopedia Britannica* were distributed alternately between the two countries. Khan, *Great Partition*, 118.
42. Mountbatten had hoped to be accepted as Governor-General of both India and Pakistan. When Jinnah demanded to be named governor-general of Pakistan instead, he earned Mountbatten's eternal enmity.
43. Gandhi did not attend the inaugural ceremonies, deciding instead to fast in Calcutta. Wolpert, *Shameful Flight*, 171.
44. Ghaznavi interview.
45. Khan, *Great Partition*, 134–5.
46. Khan, *Great Partition*, 136.
47. Khan, *Great Partition*, 155. Some estimates put the figure as high as seventeen million.
48. Ghaznavi interview.
49. Ghaznavi interview.
50. S. Gopal, ed., *Selected works of Jawaharlal Nehru*, Series 2, Vol. 3 (New Delhi: Jawaharlal Nehru Memorial Fund distributed by Oxford University Press, 1984), 99.
51. See the report reproduced in its entirety in Hodson, *Great Divide*, 548–552.
52. Wolpert, *Shameful Flight*, 2.
53. Masood Ghaznavi eventually took a position as a professor at Rosemont College in Pennsylvania, where he taught History until his death in 2013. The author dedicates this chapter to his memory.

Chapter 5

1. "Lady Astor Backs Palestine Policy," *New York Times*, Saturday May 24, 1947.
2. Obit clipping dated January 21, 1976. "Death at 85 of Mr. Rex Stranger," Hampshire County Library, Biography files.
3. "Soton says big 'Thank You,'" *Southern Evening Echo*, October 28, 1970, Southampton Public Libraries, Biography files.
4. "Councillor R.J. Stranger, M.C. Mayor of Southampton," *Southern Daily Echo*, November 9, 1943, Southampton Public Libraries, Biography files.
5. "Soton says big 'Thank You,'" Southampton Public Libraries, Biography files.
6. *Southampton and D-Day*, Oral History, City Heritage, Southampton City Council, 1994, 4.
7. Martin Doughty and Ken Ford, eds., *Hampshire and D-Day*, Hampshire County Council, 1994, 122–123.
8. Molly Trimble, "Former Lord Mayor Keeps Promise with American GI," *Bergen Record*, USA (date unknown), Stranger files, Folder D/Z 472, Southampton, U.K.
9. Account of Stranger's speech in text of sermon by the Rev. W. Wilson Carvell,

June 8, 1947, Southampton Archives, folder D/Z 428, Acc. 3925.
10. Interview with Kathryn (Shimer) Ruggiero, 2003.
11. Interview with John Robert Shimer, 2003.
12. "Sgt. P.S. Shimer Killed in Action," *Chambersburg Public Opinion* (hereinafter *CPO*), April 30, 1945.
13. NARA, RG 338 (Records of U.S. Army Commands 1942–) 14th Port history file, October 1944.
14. Text of broadcast, "We the People" program, Empire Broadcasting Corporation, June 1, 1947, Southampton Archives, folder D/Z 428, Acc. 3925.
15. "Southampton Port of Embarkation," NARA, RG 336, Historical Program files, ETO—Ports General, Box 509, 16.
16. U.S. Population Statistics for 1950, http://www.infoplease.com/ipa/A0004986.html. Accessed September 2023.
17. "Sgt. P.S. Shimer Killed in Action," *CPO*, Apr. 30, 1945.
18. "We the People" program text.
19. Clipping from the *News Chronicle*, June 9, 1947. Southampton Public Libraries, Stranger biography files.
20. "Town to Greet Wartime Head of British City," *CPO*, May 22, 1947.
21. Harry S. Truman papers, Official file #200, Box 839, NARA, Harry S. Truman Library.
22. "May 30 Fixed for Greeting Noted Briton," *CPO*, May 24, 1947.
23. Opinion/editorial, *CPO*, May 26, 1947.
24. "British Youth to Get County Fruit at Xmas," *CPO*, May 27, 1947.
25. A 'carload' was approximately equivalent to six hundred bushels.
26. "Ulster United Soccer Team Tops German-American All-stars, 3-2," *New York Times*, May 26, 1947.
27. "Noon Luncheon at Wilson Completes Community Welcome to Strangers," *CPO*, May 31, 1947.
28. President Truman was visiting his ailing mother; Marshall, Martin, and Myers all sent regrets; Kiser was not in the country.
29. "Ex-Mayor Presents $4,000 Trust Fund to Child's Mother," *CPO*, May 31, 1947.
30. "Ex-Mayor Presents $4,000 Trust Fund to Child's Mother," *CPO*, May 31, 1947.
31. "Local Rotarians Recognize Visit of Former Mayor," *CPO*, May 31, 1947.
32. Hassett to Etter, May 26, 1947. Truman papers, Official file #200, Box 839. NARA, Harry S. Truman Library.
33. "Noon Luncheon at Wilson Completes Community Welcome to Strangers," *CPO*, May 31, 1947.
34. "We the People" text of broadcast.
35. "'Tokens of Affection' from Franklin County," *Southern Daily Echo*, Southampton, December 20, 1947.
36. "Councillor R J. Stranger Decorated," *Southern Daily Echo*, November 4, 1947.
37. "Soton says Big 'Thank You,'" *Southern Evening Echo*, Southampton Public Libraries, Biography files.
38. "Rex Stranger to be Feted at Dinner Monday," *CPO*, May 25, 1960.
39. "Visiting Briton Places Wreath for War Dead," *CPO*, May 31, 1960.
40. Extract from minutes 30th Meeting Principal Personnel Officers Committee, 24 June 1946. National Archives (U.K.) Reference CAB 80/54/82. FUSBC brochure. Francis Pickens Miller papers collection, General File, Box 13. George C. Marshall Foundation, Lexington, VA.

Chapter 6

1. He did reach base on an error and eventually scored. The box score for that day can be found at http://www.baseball-almanac.com/boxscore/04151947.shtml. Accessed October 2023.
2. The first biography of Jackie Robinson came off the presses in 1948, one year after he broke in with the Dodgers. Countless others have been published ever since. See the bibliography for a short list of best books on Robinson.
3. Professor Chris Lamb's work has brought many of these unsung heroes to light. See *Blackout: The Untold Story of Jackie Robinson's First Spring Training* (Lincoln: University of Nebraska Press, 2004).
4. Wendell Smith's life and career have been brought vividly to life by Jonathan Eig in his book, *Opening Day: The Story of Jackie Robinson's First Season* (New York: Simon and Schuster, 2007).
5. Transcript of Smith recollections,

Wendell Smith papers, National Baseball Hall of Fame, 9.

6. One of the players was Mike Tresh, who went on to have a successful major league career with the Chicago White Sox. There was evidently no personal animosity between the two men, as they remained "the closest of buddies" long after they went their separate ways. *Pittsburgh Courier*, January 27, 1940.

7. Smith papers, Hall of Fame.

8. Smith papers, Hall of Fame. See also Eig, *Opening Day*, 132.

9. Smith papers, Hall of Fame. Available also at Jerome Holtzman, *No Cheering in the Press Box* (New York: Henry Holt and Co., 1995), 312–324.

10. Jerome Holtzman, "Wendell Smith—A Pioneer for Black Athletes," *The Sporting News*, June 22, 1974.

11. David K. Wiggins, "Wendell Smith, the Pittsburgh Courier-Journal and the Campaign to Include Blacks in Organized Baseball, 1933-1945," *Journal of Sport History*, vol. 10, no. 2 (Summer 1983), 10.

12. Holtzman, "Wendell Smith."

13. Wendell Smith, "Smitty's Sports Spurts," *Pittsburgh Courier*, December 10, 1938.

14. Chris Lamb, *Blackout: The Untold Story of Jackie Robinson's First Spring Training* (Lincoln: University of Nebraska Press, 2004), 30.

15. Wendell Smith, "Says Organized Baseball Willing to Accept Colored Players," *Pittsburgh Courier*, February 25, 1939.

16. Smith, "Smitty's Sports Spurts," *Pittsburgh Courier*, March 11, 1939.

17. Smith, "Cincinnati Reds' Manager, Players Laud Negro Stars," *Pittsburgh Courier*, July 15, 1939. Whether or not Frick meant that is a matter of conjecture. Nowhere in the article does Frick actually say what Smith purports him to say. Smith may have based his inference on Frick's comment that "the only way a manager can develop team spirit is to keep his men together…. Ballplayers who were not broadminded enough would take advantage of the situation and use it to further their own cause."

18. Smith Papers, Hall of Fame, 2.

19. Dean replied, "No I wouldn't care, all I want is my money." *Pittsburgh Courier*, August 19, 1939.

20. The series ran from July 15 to September 2, 1939. A more complete accounting of the interviews can be found in Chris Lamb, "Baseball's Whitewash: Sportswriter Wendell Smith Exposes Major League Baseball's Big Lie," *Nine—A Journal of Baseball History and Culture*, vol. 18, no. 1 (Fall 2009).

21. David Falkner, *Great Time Coming: The Life of Jackie Robinson from Baseball to Birmingham* (New York: Simon & Schuster, 1996), 95–6. Kelly Rusinack has explored the scope of the relationship of the Communist party and baseball integration in Joseph Dorinson and Joram Warmund, *Jackie Robinson: Race Sports and the American Dream* (Armonk, NY: M.E. Sharpe, 1998), 80.

22. Smith papers, 3. See also Arnold Rampersad, *Jackie Robinson: A Biography* (New York: Alfred Knopf, 1997), 121.

23. Smith papers, Hall of Fame, 3.

24. Brian Carroll, *When to Stop the Cheering?* (New York: Routledge, 2007), 97.

25. See also Wiggins, "Wendell Smith."

26. "Smitty's Sports Spurts," May 25, 1940.

27. "Smitty's Sports Spurts," March 16 and May 25, 1940.

28. Smith papers, 3. See also Jules Tygiel, *Baseball's Great Experiment* (New York: Oxford University Press, 1997), 40 and Carroll, *Cheering*, 106. Smith never quite forgave Benswanger for this slight. He made sure to relate the entire incident in Robinson's biography published the next year. See Jackie Robinson and Wendell Smith, *Jackie Robinson: My Own Story* (New York: Greenberg, 1948), 32.

29. Carroll, *Cheering*, 129.

30. "Smitty's Sports Spurts," December 11, 1943.

31. Howard Bryant, *Shut Out: A Story of Race and Baseball in Boston* (Boston: Beacon Press, 2002), 29.

32. In his later recollections, Wendell Smith claimed to have introduced Muchnick to the idea for this subterfuge in a long-distance telephone call. "[The idea] hit home with him," Smith recalled. "He said he would. And he did." Smith papers, Hall of Fame, 5. See also Bryant, *Shut Out*, 29.

33. Roger Birtwell, "Javery Gives 5 Blows as Braves Win, 3–1," *Boston Daily*

Globe, April 12, 1945. The Braves, according to Bryant, "flatly refused" to give the men a tryout. Bryant, *Shut Out*, 29.

34. Some authors claim that FDR's death that same day was the reason for the cancellation, but Roosevelt died in the late afternoon. Additionally, Game 2 of the City Series was played that evening as scheduled. Harold Kaese, "Culler's Hit in 9th Deciding Blow," *Boston Daily Globe*, April 13, 1945. See also Bob Lemoyne, "Jackie Robinson: From Boston 'Tryout' to a Negro Leagues Star, https://sabr.org/journal/article/jackie-robinson-in-1945-from-boston-tryout-to-a-negro-leagues-star/#calibre_link-2221. Accessed October 2023.

35. Newspaper accounts say that General Manager Ed Collins met the players and gave them Red Sox uniforms for the tryouts. "Three Negroes Given Workout by Red Sox," *Boston Globe*, April 16, 1945. Sources disagree about manager Joe Cronin's participation. Contemporary accounts, including Robinson and Smith (1948), the *Baltimore Afro-American* (April 21, 1945), and the Associated Press put Cronin at the scene. Isadore Muchnick recalled that he spoke to Cronin personally after the tryout ended (Clif Keane, "Muchnick Says Cronin Impressed with Robby," *Boston Globe*, April 29, 1959). But some authors, including Tygiel, have him absent. Tygiel, *Great Experiment*, 44. Smith's reminiscences in later years also have him absent due to a broken leg, but in fact Cronin broke it four days *after* the Robinson tryout. (See Smith papers, Hall of Fame, 6.) Cronin himself said many years later that he "remembered" the tryout well, and that he told the players that as manager he could not hire them.

36. Robert Peterson, *Only the Ball Was White* (New York: McGraw Hill, 1970), 185.

37. Milt Gross, "Jackie's Red Sox Tryout," *The Miami News*, April 21, 1959.

38. Smith to Collins, April 27, 1945. Smith papers, Hall of Fame.

39. Collins to Smith, May 11, 1945. Smith papers, Hall of Fame.

40. John C. Chalberg, *Rickey and Robinson: The Preacher, the Player, and America's Game* (Wheeling: Harlan Davidson, 2000), 17.

41. Chalberg, *Rickey and Robinson*, 27.

42. Whether Rickey ever intended to field such a team is an open question. Many authors feel that the idea was simply a front to hide his true intentions to add a black ballplayer to the Dodger organization. See Scott Simon, *Jackie Robinson and the Integration of Baseball* (Hoboken: John Wiley and Sons, 2002), 57.

43. Wendell Smith, "Jackie Robinson: Rickey Made His Epochal Decision on Wild May 8, 1945," *Chicago Herald American*, August 23, 1947.

44. Smith, "Rickey Made His Epochal Decision."

45. Accounts of Robinson's meeting with Rickey are by now legendary. See Harvey Frommer, *Robinson and Rickey: The Men Who Broke Baseball's Color Barrier* (New York: Macmillan, 1982).

46. Smith to Rickey, January 14, 1946. Smith papers.

47. Tygiel, *Great Experiment*, 107.

48. Some accounts claim that it was a demand, not a request.

49. Wendell Smith, "Jackie Robinson's Story the Saga of a New America," *Chicago Herald American*, August 21, 1947.

50. Baseball reference.com, http://www.baseball-reference.com/minors/team.cgi?id=7d25f8c5. Accessed July 2019.

51. Robinson and Smith, *My Own Story*, 111.

52. Smith to Rickey, November 27, 1946. Smith papers, Hall of Fame. The two men conducted their conversations frequently in writing without mentioning Robinson by name in order to preserve secrecy. Rickey tried to prevent word of a possible promotion to the majors from leaking out prematurely.

53. In his April 5 column, Smith informed his readers that he had information from an "unimpeachable source" that Robinson would be with the Dodgers before opening day.

54. Wendell Smith, "Sports Beat," *Pittsburgh Courier*, April 12, 1947.

55. In this case, Smith let the words of Dave Egan, sports reporter for *Boston Daily Record*, to speak for him. Quoting from Egan's column, Smith wrote "The war against bigotry in baseball will not be won until every team in every league judges every man on the basis of his ability to play ball. That will not happen tomorrow, nor the day after tomorrow, but happen it must

if the American dream of equal opportunity for all its citizens is to be realized." Smith, "Sports Beat," May 3, 1947.

56. Smith, "Sports Beat," May 31, 1947.

57. Smith, "Sports Beat," May 3, 1947.

58. Smith, "Sports Beat," August 9, 1947.

59. Wendell Smith, "Negro National Loop Folds: AL Takes Over," *Chicago Herald American*, December 1, 1948. The remaining teams were merged into the Negro American League, which would continue on in the 1950s, but as the quality of the baseball suffered, so too did the League. It collapsed in the early 1960s.

60. The initial contacts between the *Herald American* and Smith may have been due to Roger Treat, a sportswriter for the *Herald* who was a prominent critic of racism in sports throughout his career.

61. Smith, "Sports Beat," August 23, 1947. Mounting pressures from the HUAC most likely also influenced Smith's first article for the *Chicago Herald American*, a very pro-America piece titled "Jackie Robinson's Story the Saga of a New America," which he was writing at about the same time.

62. For more information, see Brian Carroll, "Wendell Smith's Last Crusade: The Desegregation of Spring Training 1961" in *The Cooperstown Symposium on Baseball and American Culture: 2001* (Jefferson, NC: McFarland, 2002).

63. Smith, "The Sports Beat," February 23, 1946.

64. Rich Westcott, *The Mogul: Eddie Gottlieb, Philadelphia Sports Legend and Pro Basketball Pioneer* (Philadelphia: Temple University Press, 2008), 111.

65. Smith, "Sports Beat," November 23, 1946.

66. Smith, "Sports Beat," November 23, 1946.

67. Smith, "Sports Beat," January 11, 1947.

68. Smith, "Sports Beat," January 25, 1947.

69. Oddly enough, when the Baseball Hall of Fame decided in 1971 to honor great ballplayers from the Negro leagues, both Smith and Gottlieb were picked to serve on the selection committee.

70. Smith papers, Hall of Fame, 1.

71. Smith to Rickey, November 27, 1946. Smith papers, Hall of Fame.

72. Robinson and Smith, *My Own Story*, 111.

73. Smith to Robinson, February 4, 1947. Smith papers, Hall of Fame.

74. Lamb, *Blackout*, 111.

Chapter 7

1. This story has been retold many times and is famous in the folklore surrounding Stan Kenton's career. Like many such stories, the details vary from version to version. The version presented here is a composite assembled from two different accounts that span several decades. Most of it relies on information Kenton gave to Ted Hallock during an interview for *Down Beat* magazine six months after the incident took place. See "'World Needs Strong Music,' Cries Kenton, 'So Let 'em Have It,'" *Down Beat* (November 19, 1947). Some ancillary details come from Kenton's recollections given to biographer Carol Easton 25 years later. See Carol Easton, *Straight Ahead: The Story of Stan Kenton* (New York: Morrow, 1973), 112–3.

2. Quoted in Joachim E. Berendt, *The Jazz Book: From Ragtime to Fusion and Beyond* (Brooklyn: Lawrence Hill Books, 2009), 237.

3. Although big bands differ in size and personnel, typical big band instrumentation includes four trumpets, three or four trombones, four or five saxophones, and three or four rhythm (drums, bass, piano, guitar). In contrast, a "combo" is a group featuring six or fewer performers.

4. "Dance band" is also a valid name for groups of this type.

5. It was also this emphasis on individuality, combined with its African roots, that prompted the Nazis to ban jazz music and swing dancing as "degenerate."

6. For a good synopsis, see Frank Tirro, *Jazz: A History* (New York: W.W. Norton, 1977).

7. Edward F. Gabel, *Stan Kenton: The Early Years 1941–1947* (Lake Geneva, WI: Balboa Books, 1993), 41.

8. Gabel, *Stan Kenton*, 23.

9. United Service Organizations (USO) provides entertainment for American troops stationed abroad.

10. Tires were particularly difficult to come by.

11. For the story of these all-girl bands see Sherrie Tucker, *Swing Shift* (Durham: Duke University Press, 2000). The use of the term all-girl, without quotation marks, conforms with Prof. Tucker's preferences.

12. A great deal has been published about Stan Kenton and his music. Perhaps the most authoritative is by Michael Sparke, *Stan Kenton: This Is an Orchestra* (Denton: University of North Texas Press, 2010). Others include Steven Harris and Pete Rugolo, *The Kenton Kronicles* (Pasadena, CA: Dynaflow Publications, 2000).

13. His date of birth has been inaccurately reported as February 12, 1912.

14. Details of Kenton's early life come from a narrative written by Bud Freeman in 1955 for a promotional insert for a Capitol records album release, entitled "The Kenton Era" (Creative World-ST 1030), 1955.

15. Harris, *Kenton Kronicles*, 9–10.

16. William F. Lee and Audree Coke Kenton, *Stan Kenton: Artistry in Rhythm* (Los Angeles: Creative Press of Los Angeles, 1980), 45.

17. Sparke, *Stan Kenton: This Is an Orchestra*, 17. See also Harris, *Kenton Kronicles*, 10.

18. "Facing the Music," *Radio Mirror*, vol. 26, no. 2 (July 1946), 4.

19. George Simon, *The Big Bands* (New York: Macmillan, 1967), 294.

20. Harris, *Kenton Kronicles*, 15.

21. Sources differ on the length of stay. One claims the band lasted ten days, another three weeks. See Harris, *Kenton Kronicles*, 16, and Lee, *Stan Kenton: Artistry in Rhythm*, 47–8.

22. Lee, *Stan Kenton: Artistry in Rhythm*, 48. Simon, co-editor at *The Metronome*, admitted twenty years later that he never quite reconciled himself with Kenton's brand of music. See Simon, *Big Bands*, 293.

23. Freeman, "Kenton Era."

24. According to Gabel, he admitted his vision as early as 1942. Gable, *Kenton*, 38.

25. "I'll Go Back to a Saloon If I Fail!" *Down Beat*, February 1, 1943, 15.

26. "Kenton Style Altered Drastically," *Down Beat*, July 1, 1943, 21.

27. Readers old enough to remember *The Tonight Show* with Johnny Carson will be familiar with the concept of a background band. In this case, Doc Severinson and the Tonight Show Orchestra carried on the tradition.

28. Sparke, *Kenton*, 25. Harris, *Kronicles*, 21.

29. Gabel, *Kenton*, 66. Les Brown replaced Kenton.

30. Although these songs had been a staple of Kenton's live performances, a union recording ban kept Capitol from recording them until 1943.

31. Lee, *Stan Kenton: Artistry in Rhythm*, 78–81.

32. Bill Gottlieb, "Posin," *Down Beat*, December 16, 1946, 5.

33. Lillian Arganian, *Stan Kenton: The Man and His Music* (East Lansing, MI: Artistry Press, 1989), 43.

34. Sparke, *This Is an Orchestra*, 46.

35. "Band of the Year: Stan Kenton," *The Metronome* (January 1947), 45.

36. Gabel, *Kenton*, 95–6.

37. Art Pepper, *Straight Life: The Story of Art Pepper* (New York: Schirmer Books, 1979), 103.

38. Harris, *Kronicles*, 40.

39. Pepper, *Life*, 104.

40. Pepper, *Life*, 104.

41. Pepper, *Life*, 102.

42. Pepper, *Life*, 109.

43. Michael Levin, "Leaders, Men and Buyers All Hit Sour Notes," *Down Beat*, November 18, 1946, 1.

44. There has been a tendency in some political circles to attribute the eclipse of big bands to the enforcement of this tax, but that is an oversimplification ignoring the other social and economic factors contributing to the decline.

45. Ticket prices varied but could range from $1.75 to $4.00 or more.

46. "Leaders," *Down Beat*, November 18, 1946, 4.

47. Lee, *Stan Kenton: Artistry in Rhythm*, 90.

48. Gabel, *Stan Kenton*, 106.

49. Charlie Spivak, Skinnay Ennis, and several other bands adopted the same tactic. "Bands Cut One-Night Bite on Coast," *Variety*, February 12, 1947, 38.

50. "Kenton's Popularity No Accident, His P.A. Proves," *Down Beat*, January 1, 1947, 15.

51. "Kenton Krew Hops to Hollywood," *Capitol News* (February 1947), 7. See also "Kenton Goes 50 percent Commercial on Wax," *The Billboard*, January 11, 1947, 36.

52. The negotiated price of $6,500 was $600 under what Kenton was charging at the time. *Variety*, March 5, 1947, 44. See also "Kenton Krew Hops to Hollywood," *Capitol News*, February 1947, 7. The amount of cash it took to field the Kenton band was, for its time, staggering. By now, the orchestra had burgeoned to twenty-five musicians with the addition of a five-man vocal group called The Pastels. But that number does not include the publicity man, the photographer, the band secretary, an arranger, and others with the band, now totaling thirty-two persons.

53. "Kenton Forced West to Play Avodon Date," *Down Beat*, January 29, 1947, 6.

54. "Stan Kenton Tells Avodon to Kill Airtime," *Down Beat*, February 12, 1947, 1.

55. In response to the lackluster attendance during weekdays, the Avodon went to weekends-only after the Kenton gig, following a trend that other ballrooms had inaugurated. "Avodon Biz Bad, Cut to Three Nights Weekly," *Down Beat*, March 12, 1947, 14.

56. "Coast Ops Cheered by Kenton," *Variety*, April 9, 1947, 41.

57. Bob Kennedy, "Swing Session," *Swing*, vol. 3, no. 5 (May 1947), 58.

58. "Kenton Crew On Back-Breaking Trek," *Down Beat*, March 12, 1947, 6.

59. "Kenton Calls Off Decision to Disband Until Pacted Dates Are Played Out," *Variety*, April 9, 1947, 39.

60. "Kenton Ignores Health Warning," *Capitol News*, May 1947, 5.

61. "Stan Nixes Out Vacation Keeps Band in Prospect of Nervous Breakdown," *Down Beat*, April 23, 1947, 1.

62. Some writers have said he "collapsed" but both the recollections of band member Milt Bernhard and a review of the concert published six days later in the University of Alabama's newspaper, *Crimson-White*, makes no mention of any physical crisis occurring at any time that day. See Sparke, 61–2.

63. "Kenton Too Ill to Go On, Plans Up in Air," *Down Beat*, May 7, 1947, 2.

64. "I'll Be Back Soon: Stan Kenton Improves," *Capitol News*, June 1947, 5.

65. "Kenton to Rebuild Band On Coast: Rehearsals Begin Sept 15, Several Stars Won't Return," *Down Beat*, August 13, 1947, 1.

66. "Kenton Rolls Again This Month," *Capitol News*, September 1947), 2.

67. "Musso to Lead Sidemen while Kenton Recups," *Variety*, May 14, 1947, 45.

68. Despite Kenton's overtures and offers of higher pay, Vido Musso, Kai Winding, and Boots Mussili did not return. Easton, *Straight Ahead*, 118.

69. "Stan Kenton Resumes Record-Cracking Ways," *Variety*, October 8, 1947, 42.

70. "Kenton to Rebuild Band on Coast: Rehearsals Begin September 15, Several Stars Won't Return," *Down Beat*, August 13, 1947, 1.

71. "'You Won't Lose with Me,' Kenton Tells Ops and Really Means It," *Variety* (October 29, 1947), 51.

72. "World Needs Strong Music," *Down Beat*, November 19, 1947, 1.

73. "World Needs Strong Music," *Down Beat*, 7.

74. "World Needs Strong Music," *Down Beat*, 7.

75. "World Needs Strong Music," *Down Beat*, 7.

76. "Kenton Breaks It Up On Chi Jazz Date," *Variety*, November 26, 1947, 46.

77. "Kenton Crew Pours New Life Into Town at the Commodore," *Down Beat*, December 17, 1947.

78. Bernie Woods, "Band Review," *Variety*, December 3, 1947, 42.

79. Woods, "Band Review," 42.

80. "Artistry in Kenton," *Radio Mirror*, March 1948, 6.

81. "Band Review," *Variety*, December 3, 1947, 42.

82. "Artistry in Kenton," *Radio Mirror*, March 1948, 6.

83. " Kenton Wants to Drop Dance Beat for Jazz," *Variety*, November 12, 1947, 48.

84. The Petrillo ban was an attempt by the leader of the American Federation of Musicians, James Petrillo, to keep unionized musicians from making recordings unless broadcasters paid royalties into a fund for out of work musicians. A similar ban had been done during the war (1942–1944) and this one was to start on January 1, 1948. It lasted eleven months before a settlement was reached.

85. Michael Levin, "Poll Winner Says Jazz Orks Can't Play Dance Jive," *Down Beat*, January 14, 1948, 1.

86. Levin, "Poll Winner," 18.

87. "Music: He Calls It Progress," *Time*, March 1, 1948. https://content.time.com/time/subscriber/article/0,33009,794298,00.html

88. Harris, *Kenton Kronicles*, 47.

89. Nat Shapiro and Nat Hentoff, *Hear Me Talkin' to Ya: The Story of Jazz as Told by the Men who made it* (New York: Dover Publications, 1955), 387.

90. Sparke, *This Is an Orchestra*, 73.

91. In one case, a brawl erupted between patrons wanting progressive concert music and those wanting dance. Freeman, Capitol promo material.

92. Sparke, *This Is an Orchestra*, 89.

93. A notable example is his composition, *4'33,"* which is composed entirely of silence punctuated by incidental noises made by the audience and orchestra.

94. Levin, "Poll Winner," 1.

95. Easton, *Straight Ahead*, 177–8.

Chapter 8

1. Herpolsheimer's was a favorite Christmastime destination because of Santa's Rocket Express, a monorail train for children installed inside the store in 1949. The train has been restored and can be seen in the Grand Rapids Public Museum. The store no longer exists, but its memory lives on as the department store depicted in the 2004 movie *The Polar Express*.

2. *Television: The Business Magazine of the Industry*, vol. IV, no. 3 (March 1947), 1.

3. Norm Goldstein, *The History of Television* (New York: Portland House, 1991), 56–7. See also Stephen Herbert, *A History of Early Television* (New York: Routledge, 2004), 152.

4. Herbert, *Early Television*, 155.

5. James Von Schilling, *The Magic Window: American Television 1939–1953* (New York: Haworth Press, 2003), 8. Bloomingdale's also placed television monitors in their store windows so passersby could see the opening of the Fair and other newsworthy events from the sidewalk. I.A. Hirschmann, "Television—A New Dimension in Department Store Advertising," *Television Magazine* (Spring 1944), 10.

6. Herbert, *Early Television*, 155–6, *New York Times*, April 30, 1939.

7. Von Schilling, *Magic Window*, 43–46.

8. That price, according to inflation calculators, equates to $4,800 (with an additional $680 installation) in 2023 dollars. DuMont, which specialized in the high-end market, was selling consoles for a whopping $2,495 ($34,350). There was a cheaper model available, the Motorola Model VT-71 with a seven-inch screen that sold for $180.

9. "How to Buy a Television Set," *Television Magazine*, vol. III, no. 10 (December 1946), 15–17.

10. Ed Reitan, *CBS Color Television System Chronology*, http://earlytelevision.org/Reitan/CBS_Chronology_rev_h_edit.html. Accessed September 2023.

11. *Television Magazine*, vol. IV, no. 3 (March 1947), 4.

12. *Television Magazine* (March 1947), 9.

13. C.B. Jolliffe, et al., "Status of Color Television," *RCA Radio Age Magazine*, vol. 6, no. 1 (January 1947), 9–11.

14. "Color Decision," *Television Magazine*, vol III, no. 4 (April 1947), 7.

15. "Color Decision," *Television Magazine*. The debate over standardizing a common color broadcast system continued well into the 1950s.

16. Albert Abramson, *The History of Television, 1942–2000* (Jefferson, NC: McFarland, 2003), 22.

17. These figures are based on estimates collected by the Radio Manufacturer's Association (RMA) and published in *Television Magazine*, which purported to be an observer of the entire television industry.

18. The February 1947 issue contradicts this number, quoting a figure of only 10,000. This number is most likely erroneous and may have been a typographic error.

19. Production continued to accelerate exponentially in 1948.

20. The remaining station was WRBG in Schenectady, New York, located at the General Electric plant there.

21. One interesting byproduct of the 1947 expansion was the introduction of newspapers as players in the television market. Five of the nine new stations were owned by newspapers, and at least forty-eight new applications were filed by newspapers.

22. "Television Outlook in St. Louis," *Television Magazine*, vol. IV no. 5 (May 1947), 9.

23. "Television for St. Louis," *Radio Age*, vol. VI, no. 3 (April 1947), 15.

24. "The DuMont-Wanamaker Bombshell," *Televiser*, vol II, no. 1 (September–October 1945), 43.

25. I.A. Hirschmann, "Television in the Retail Field," *Journal of Marketing*, vol. 8, Nno. 4 (April 1944), 396.

26. For an excellent account of the history of postwar intra-store television, see Anna McCarthy, *Ambient Television* (Durham: Duke University Press, 2001), 63–88.

27. The sample included 250 stores. "Department Store Survey Weighs Television," *Television Magazine* (January 1945), 13.

28. The list includes Macy's, Gimbel's, Bambergers, Abraham & Strauss, and Bloomingdales.

29. "Gimbel's (Phila) Launches Tele Series on WPTZ-Philadelphia," *Televiser*, vol. 3, no. 4 (July–August 1946), 33. See also Broadcast Pioneers of Philadelphia webpage at http://www.broadcastpioneers.com/bp/1945tv.html. Accessed April 2024.

30. "250,000 See Store Video," *Radio Age*, vol. V, no 2 (January 1946), 28.

31. "Intra-store Television," *Film World and AV News Magazine*, vol. II, no. 3 (March 1946), 127.

32. "Kaufmann's (Pitts) Stages RCA Intra-Store Video," *Televiser*, vol. 3, no. 4 (July–August 1946), 33.

33. "Television Develops New Presentation of War News as Events Occur Swiftly," *Broadcasting Magazine*, vol. 21, no. 24 (December 15, 1941), 16.

34. Samuel H. Cuff, "Open Letter to B. Louis Posen," *Televiser*, vol. 1, no. 2 (winter, 1945), 49.

35. Cuff's idea may have arisen out of that same issue of *Televiser*, which contained an article by Bud Gamble describing his 1939 cross-country tour demonstrating Farnsworth television in eighty-eight cities. Gamble's article happened to be published on the page 48, right before Cuff's article on page 49.

36. Other sponsors included United States Rubber Company, Koroseal, National Pressure Cooker Company, and Hickok Manufacturing.

37. The cameras sent were first put in service in 1939 and were not equipped with the viewfinders or turret lenses more modern ones had.

38. All of the great stores that once comprised this chain are now gone. What is left of this corporation has been absorbed into Macy's Group, Inc.

39. Louis Sposa, *Television Primer of Production and Direction* (New York: McGraw Hill, 1947). The book is available online at https://archive.org/details/televisionprimer00sposrich. Accessed October 2023.

40. "Louis Sposa 'Holds the Hand of the Agency' for DuMont," *Television Showman*, April 29, 1946. Clipping courtesy of Ms. Terry Rosa. I am indebted to Ms. Rosa and her family for giving me access to a scrapbook containing a wealth of information and reminiscences about Lou's career.

41. *Daily Northwestern*, February 22, 1944, 2. See also article byline on February 2, 1945, 3. The author is indebted to Jill Tunkavige and Diane Conklin, Irine Petroff Davidson's daughters, for granting access to Petey's scrapbook.

42. Stephen Michael Shearer, *Patricia Neal: An Unquiet Life* (Lexington: University Press of Kentucky, 2006), 26.

43. Lady Behind Camera Tells of Work in Television," *Minneapolis Star Ledger*, October 11, 1947, 7.

44. "'Television Girl' Told her Job for Men," *The Cincinnati Post* (date uncertain, possibly July 23, 1947), 8.

45. Lou Sposa said that she was THE first in an interview with *Syracuse Post-Standard* newspaper (June 19, 1947), but other sources, including contemporary radio interviews, claim she was "one of three."

46. "Lady Behind Camera," 7. Reflecting on Petey's attire, Irene Murphy commented, "In those days, none of us wore pants!" (interview with the author).

47. "Television Here for Demonstration," *Tampa Times*, July 30, 1947, 16.

48. I am indebted to Irene Murphy McInerney, whose personal reminiscences, photos, and documents make up much of this chapter.

49. Dennis James had a long career on television as a game show host. See Adam Nedeff, *Okay? Okay! Dennis James' Lifetime of Firsts* (Albany, GA: BearManor Media, 2017). Dennis James was Lou Sposa's brother.

50. At the time, there were no earpiece monitors connecting a performer to the control room. Last minute directions came via the telephone, and on-air directions were all relayed by hand signals. Interview with Irene Murphy McInerney.

51. Interview with Irene Murphy McInerney.

52. At first, the crew tried doing four but soon found that too demanding.

53. Bernie Brink took much of the equipment ahead on an airplane in order to set the equipment up early.

54. Advertisement, *Great Falls Tribune*, September 29, 1947, 7.

55. Estimate based on census figures, http://population.us/mt/great-falls/. Accessed September 2023.

56. "This Egg Dropped 8 Stories; Bounces," *The Daily Courier* (Waterloo, Iowa), August 18, 1947, 2.

57. Advertisement in *Seattle Times*, September 16, 1947, 18.

58. "Television Company to Minneapolis," *Great Falls Tribune*, October 2, 1947, 9.

59. "3000 Witness Boise's First Telecast Show," *The Idaho Statesman*, September 12, 1947, 17.

60. No official attendance figures were compiled.

61. Manuscript notes in possession of Irene Murphy McInerney. Used with permission.

62. McInerney manuscript notes.

63. Fred Posey, "Television Appears Simple in Demonstration," *The Columbus Dispatch*, July 16, 1947, 2-A.

64. "Television Debut in S.A." *San Antonio Light*, August 13, 1947, 4-A.

65. Hilda Jonas, *The Value of Intra-Store Television as a Sales Promotion Medium* (New York: New York University School of Retailing, 1948), 2–9.

66. Jonas, *Intra-Store Television*, 8–9.

67. "Gertz Store Drops Curtain on 5-Day Television Show," *Long Island Star Journal*, June 7, 1947, 2.

68. Jonas, *Intra-Store Television*, 7.

69. "Washington," *Television Magazine*, vol. V, no. 1 (January 1948), 8.

70. Von Schilling, *Magic Window*, 109. See also "Radio & TV: TV Thaw," *Time*, April 21, 1952. https://content.time.com/time/subscriber/article/0,33009,889476,00.html Accessed September 2023.

71. Allied Stores Corporation, *Television: A General Guide for Your Information*, April 1950, 1 (provided courtesy of Irene McInerney).

72. Some had predicted already in 1944 that television was too expensive for effective use in department stores. See Ben E. Posen, "Can Television Pay Its Way?" *Televiser*, vol. 1, no. 1, Fall 1944, 41.

73. Petey's husband, Marshall Davidson, served as director and eventually Vice President for CBS News.

74. "It's No Joke, Son," article written by Irene Murphy, date unknown (1949?), clipping courtesy Irene Murphy McInerney.

75. "Murphy's Meetings," article by Ross, *Television World*, clipping courtesy Irene Murphy McInerney.

76. "Television," *Life Magazine*, December 1, 1947, 117.

77. Many of the details described in this chapter come from the manuscripts they wrote, and I am indebted to both the Davidson family and the McInerney family for allowing me access to those documents.

78. For a scientific but readable account of the early history of the transistor, see Lillian Hoddeson, et al., *Out of the Crystal Maze* (New York: Oxford University Press, 1992), 466–476.

79. A Pew research study done in 2016 revealed that television was the preferred source of news for most Americans. By 2020, a new survey revealed that over half of the respondents preferred a digital device. The numbers of respondents preferring television declined every year from 2020 to 2022. http://www.journalism.org/2016/07/07/pathways-to-news/ and https://www.pewresearch.org/journalism/fact-sheet/news-platform-fact-sheet/ both accessed September 2023.

Epilogue

1. The snow accumulation broke a record that had stood since 1888. "Record Snow Buries New York City," *Life Magazine*, January 8, 1948.

2. For example, Jackie's birth name is incorrectly given as John and his mother's name is also incorrect. See Rampersad, *Jackie Robinson*, 207.

3. Smith, "Sports Beat," *Pittsburgh Courier*, June 5, 1948.

4. Paul Healy, "Include Me Out of Race: Vandenberg," *New York Daily News*, January 1, 1948, 2.

5. A good introduction to the history of European integration is Desmond Dinan, *Ever Closer Union: An Introduction to European Integration* (Boulder: L. Rienner, 4th Edition, 2010). More specific histories include Richard T. Griffiths, *Explorations in OEEC History* (Paris: Organization for Economic Cooperation and Development, 1994) and Richard T. Griffiths, *Thank You M. Monnet, Essays on the history of European Integration* (Leiden, Netherlands: Leiden University Press, 2014).

6. Williams' *Streetcar* has been the subject of countless dissertations, theses, and journal articles, making it one of the most analyzed dramas in the recent history.

7. "Sights 'Saucers' Flitting in Air," *The Spokesman-Review* (Spokane, WA), June 26, 1947.

8. https://airandspace.si.edu/stories/editorial/1947-year-flying-saucer. Accessed August 2023.

9. "RAAF Captures Flying Saucer on Ranch in Roswell Region," *Roswell Daily Record*, July 8, 1947.

10. See Tom Wolfe, *The Right Stuff* (New York: Farrar, Straus and Giroux, 1979), among other sources.

Bibliography

Archival Sources

Bentley Historical Library, University of Michigan. Arthur H. Vandenberg papers.
George C. Marshall Foundation, Lexington, Virginia. Francis Pickens Miller papers.
Gloucestershire Archives (U.K.).
Hampshire County (U.K.) Library, Biography files.
National Archives and Records Administration, Harry S. Truman Presidential Library and Museum, Independence, Missouri.
National Archives and Records Administration, Herbert Hoover Presidential Library and Museum, West Branch, Iowa.
National Archives and Records Administration, Still Pictures Branch, College Park, Maryland.
National Baseball Hall of Fame, Cooperstown, NY. Wendell Smith files.
Southampton Archives (U.K.).
Southampton City Libraries (U.K.).

Articles and Books

Abramson, Albert. *The History of Television, 1942–2000*. Jefferson, NC: McFarland, 2003.
Acheson, Dean. *Present at the Creation: My Years in the State Department*. New York: W.W. Norton, 1969.
_____. *Sketches from Life of Men I Have Known*. New York: Harper and Brothers, 1961.
Ahmad, Riaz. "Muslim Punjab's Fight for Pakistan: League's Agitation Against the Coalition Ministry of Sir Khizr Hyat Khan Tiwana, January-March 1947." *Pakistan Journal of History and Culture*, Vol. XXVIII, no. 1, 2007.
Ali, Chaudhri Muhammad. *The Emergence of Pakistan*. New York: Columbia University Press, 1967.
All-India Muslim League, and Syed Sharifuddin Pirzada, ed. *Foundations of Pakistan: All-India Muslim League Documents, 1906–1947*. Vol. 2: 1924–1947. Karachi: National Publishing House, 1970.
Ambrose, Stephen E., and Douglas Brinkley. *Rise to Globalism: American Foreign Policy Since 1938*. 8th rev. ed. New York: Penguin, 1997.
Arganian, Lillian. *Stan Kenton: The Man and His Music*. East Lansing, MI: Artistry Press, 1989.
Bandopadhaya, Sailesh KuMarch. *Quaid-I-Azam: Mohammad Ali Jinnah and the Creation of Pakistan*. New Delhi: Sterling Publishers, 1991.
Barker, D. *Harvest Home: The Official Story of the Great Floods of 1947 and Their Sequel*. London: HMSO, 1948. Later edition by Providence Press, 1985.
Barnouw, Erik. *The Golden Web: 1933–1953* of *A History of Broadcasting in the United States*. V. 2. New York: Oxford University Press, 1968.

_____. *Tube of Plenty: The Evolution of American Television.* 2nd rev. ed. New York: Oxford University Press, 1990.
Beisner, Robert L. *Dean Acheson: A Life in the Cold War.* New York: Oxford University Press, 2006.
Best, Gary Dean. *The Life of Herbert Hoover: Keeper of the Torch, 1933–1964.* New York: Palgrave Macmillan, 2013.
Bolitho, Hector. *Jinnah: Creator of Pakistan.* London: J. Murray, 1954.
Bryant, Howard. *Shut Out: A Story of Race and Baseball in Boston.* Boston: Beacon Press, 2002.
Byrnes, James F. *Speaking Frankly.* New York: Harper and Brothers, 1947.
Campbell-Johnson, Alan. *Mission with Mountbatten.* London: Hale, 1972; reprinted, New York: Atheneum, 1985.
Carroll, Brian. *When to Stop the Cheering? The Black Press, the Black Community, and the Integration of Professional Baseball.* New York: Routledge, 2009.
Challener, Richard D. *From Isolation to Containment, 1921–1952: Three Decades of American Foreign Policy from Harding to Truman.* New York: St. Martin's Press, 1970.
Close, David Henry. *The Origins of the Greek Civil War.* London: Longman, 1995.
Collins, Larry, and Dominique Lapierre. *Freedom at Midnight.* New York: Simon & Schuster, 1975.
Dorinson, Joseph, and Joram Warmund, eds. *Jackie Robinson: Race, Sports, and the American Dream.* Armonk, NY: M.E. Sharpe, 1998.
Doughty, Martin, and Ken Ford, eds. *Hampshire and D-Day.* Devon: Hampshire Books, 1994.
Easton, Carol. *Straight Ahead: The Story of Stan Kenton.* New York: Morrow, 1973.
Eig, Jonathan. *Opening Day: The Story of Jackie Robinson's First Season.* New York: Simon & Schuster, 2007.
Falkner, David. *Great Time Coming: The Life of Jackie Robinson, from Baseball to Birmingham.* New York: Simon & Schuster, 1995.
Feather, Leonard, and Ira Gitler. *The Biographical Encyclopedia of Jazz.* Oxford: Oxford University Press, 1999.
Frommer, Harvey. *Rickey and Robinson: The Men Who Broke Baseball's Color Barrier.* New York: Macmillan, 1982.
Gabel, Edward F. *Stan Kenton: The Early Years, 1941–1947.* Lake Geneva, WI: Balboa Books, 1993.
Gaddis, John Lewis. *The United States and the Origins of the Cold War, 1941–1947.* New York: Columbia University Press, 1972.
George, T.J.S. *Krishna Menon: A Biography.* New York: Taplinger, 1965.
Gilmartin, David. *Empire and Islam: Punjab and the Making of Pakistan.* Berkeley: University of California Press, 1988.
Gitler, Ira. *Swing to Bop: An Oral History of the transition in jazz in the 1940s.* New York: Oxford University Press, 1985.
Haas, Lawrence J. *Harry and Arthur: Truman, Vandenberg, and the Partnership that Created the Free World.* Lincoln: Potomac Books, 2016.
Hamdani, Yasser Latif. *Jinnah: A Life.* London: Macmillan, an imprint of Pan Macmillian, 2020.
Harris, Steven D., and Pete Rugolo. *The Kenton Kronicles: A Biography of Modern America's Man of Music, Stan Kenton.* Pasadena: Dynaflow Publications, 2000.
Hasan, Mushirul. *India's Partition: Process, Strategy and Mobilization.* New Delhi: Oxford University Press, 2001.
Häusser, Alexander, and Gordian Maugg. *Hungerwinter: Deutschlands humanitäre Katastrophe 1946/47.* Berlin: Propyläen, 2009.
Herbert, Stephen. *A History of Early Television* of Routledge Library of Media and Cultural Studies. London: Routledge, 2004.
Hernon, Joseph M. *Profiles in Character: Hubris and Heroism in the U.S. Senate, 1789–1990.* Armonk, NY: M.E. Sharpe, 1997.
Hess, Gary Newton. *An Historical Study of the DuMont Television Network.* New York: Arno Press, 1979 (reprint of 1960 Ph.D. dissertation).

Hirschmann, I.A. "Television in the Retail Field." *Journal of Marketing*, Vol. 8, No. 4 (April 1944).
Howard, Herbert H. "Television Station Ownership in the United States: Comprehensive Study 1940-2005." *Journalism and Communication Monographs*. Association for Education in Journalism and Mass Communication, vol. 8 issue 1 (Spring 2006).
Howorth, B., B.E. Mowbray, W.H. Haile, and G. Cubley Crowther. "The Spring Floods of 1947." *Journal of the Institution of Water Engineers*, vol. 2, issue 1 (1948).
Ikram, S.M. *Indian Muslims and Partition of India*. New Delhi: Atlantic Publishers and Distributors, 1995.
Isaacson, Walter, and Evan Thomas. *The Wise Men: Six Friends and the World They Made: Acheson, Bohlen, Harriman, Kennan, Lovett, McCloy*. New York: Simon & Schuster, 1986.
Jalal, Ayesha. *The Sole Spokesman: Jinnah, the Muslim League and the Demand for Pakistan*. Cambridge: Cambridge University Press, 1985.
Jinnah, Mahomed Ali. *Jinnah. Speeches and Statements 1947-1948*. 5th ed. Karachi: Oxford University Press, 2009.
Jonas, Hilda, and New York University School of Retailing. *The Value of Inter-Store Television As a Sales Promotion Medium: Based on Field Survey of Allied Stores-R.C.A. "Television Caravan." A Study of the Bureau of Retail Research*. New York: New York University School of Retailing, 1948.
Jones, C.A., S.J. Davies, and N. Macdonald. "Examining the Social Consequences of Extreme Weather: The Outcomes of the 1946/47 Winter in Upland Wales, U.K. *Climatic Change* 113, 2012.
Jones, Howard. *A New Kind of War: America's Global Strategy and the Truman Doctrine in Greece*. Oxford: Oxford University Press, 1989.
Jones, Joseph M. *The Fifteen Weeks (February 21-June 5, 1947)*. New York: Viking Press, 1955.
Kearns, Kevin C. *Ireland's Arctic Siege: The Big Freeze of 1947*. Dublin: Gill and Macmillan, 2012.
Kemp, Anthony. *Southampton at War 1939-1945*. Southampton: Ensign, 1989.
_____. *Springboard for Overlord: Hampshire and the D-Day Landings*. Horndean: Milestone Publications, 1984.
Kennan, George F. *Memoirs: George F. Kennan. Vol. 1, 1925-1950*. Boston: Little, Brown, 1967.
Khan, Yasmin. *The Great Partition: The Making of India and Pakistan*. New Haven: Yale University Press, 2007.
Kleindienst, Jürgen. *Morgen Wird Alles Besser: West-Deutschland 1947-1953*. Berlin: Zeitgut Verlag, 2008.
Kynaston, David. *A World to Build*. London: Bloomsbury, 2007.
Lamb, Alistair. *Birth of a Tragedy Kashmir 1947.* Hertingfordbury: Roxford Books, 1994.
_____. *Kashmir: A Disputed Legacy, 1846-1990*. Hertingfordbury: Roxford Books, 1991.
Lamb, Chris. "Baseball's Whitewash: Sportswriter Wendell Smith Exposes Major League Baseball's Big Lie." *Nine—A Journal of Baseball History and Culture*, Vol. 18, No. 1 (Fall 2009).
_____. *Blackout: The Untold Story of Jackie Robinson's First Spring Training*. Lincoln: University of Nebraska Press, 2004.
Lee, William F., and Audree Coke Kenton. *Stan Kenton: Artistry in Rhythm*. Los Angeles: Creative Press of Los Angeles, 1980.
Lochner, Louis P. *Herbert Hoover and Germany*. New York: Macmillan, 1960.
Lyons, Eugene. *Herbert Hoover: A Biography*. Garden City, NY: Doubleday, 1964.
Mansergh, N., E.W.R. Lumby, and Penderel Moon, eds. *India: The Transfer of Power 1942-1947.* 12 vols. London: HMSO, 1970-1983.
Marschall, Rick. *The History of Television*. London: Bison Books, 1986.
McCarthy, Anna. *Ambient Television: Visual Culture and Public Space*. Durham: Duke University Press, 2001.
McClellan, Lawrence. *The Later Swing Era: 1942-1955*. Westport, CT: Greenwood Press, 2004.

McCullough, David. *Truman.* New York: Simon & Schuster, 1992.
Meijer, Hendrik. *Arthur Vandenberg, The Man in The Middle of the American Century.* Chicago: University of Chicago Press, 2017.
Memorial Services for Arthur Hendrick Vandenberg, 82nd Congress, first session. Washington, D.C.: USGPO, 1951.
Murray, Michael D., and Donald G. Godfrey, eds. *Television in American: Local Station History from Across the Nation.* Ames: Iowa State University Press, 1997.
Naim, C.M., ed. *Iqbal, Jinnah and Pakistan: The Vision and the Reality.* Syracuse: Maxwell School of Citizenship and Public Affairs, Syracuse University, 1979.
Nash, Lee, and George Fox College. *Understanding Herbert Hoover: Ten Perspectives.* Stanford, Calif: Hoover Institution Press, Stanford University, 1987.
National Documental Centre (Pakistan), and Rukhsana Zafar. *Disturbances in the Punjab 1947: A Compilation of Official Documents.* Islamabad: Government of Pakistan, Cabinet Division, National Documentation Centre, 1995.
Neal, Steve, ed. *HST: Memories of the Truman Years.* Carbondale: Southern Illinois University, 2003.
O'Ballance, Edgar, and C.M. Woodhouse. *The Greek Civil War, 1944–1949.* New York: Praeger, 1966.
Offner, Arnold A. *Another Such Victory: President Truman and the Cold War, 1945–1953.* Stanford: Stanford University Press, 2002.
Page, David, Anita Inder Singh, Penderel Moon, G.D. Khosla, and Mushirul Hasan. *The Partition Omnibus: Prelude to Partition/the Origins of the Partition of India 1936–1947/ Divide and Quit/Stern Reckoning.* New York: Oxford University Press, 2002.
Pakistan Historical Society. *A History of the Freedom Movement. Volume 4: 1936–1947.* Karachi: Pakistan Historical Society, 1970.
Pandey, B.N. *The Break-up of British India.* New York: St. Martin's Press, 1969.
The Partition of Punjab: A Compilation of Official Documents. Lahore: Sang-e-Meel, 1993.
Pepper, Art, and Laurie Pepper. *Straight Life: The story of Art Pepper.* New York: Schirmer Books, 1979.
Peterson, Robert. *Only the Ball Was White: A History of Legendary Black Players and All-Black Professional Teams.* New York: McGraw-Hill, 1970.
Philips, C.H., and M.D. Wainwright, eds. *The Partition of India: Policies and Perspectives 1935-47.* London: Allen and Unwin, 1970.
Prasad, Bimal, and Rajendra Prasad Academy. *Pathway to India's Partition: Vol III. The March to Pakistan, 1937–1947.* New Delhi: Manohar Publishers, 2009.
Qureshi, Ishtiaq Husain. *The Struggle for Pakistan.* Karachi: University of Karachi, 1965.
Rampersad, Arnold. *Jackie Robinson: A Biography.* New York: Alfred A. Knopf, 1997.
Robertson, Alex J. *The Bleak Midwinter: 1947.* Manchester: Manchester University Press, 1987.
Robinson, Jackie, Wendell Smith and Branch Rickey. *Jackie Robinson: My Own Story, as Told to Wendell Smith.* New York: Greenberg, 1948.
Robinson, Jackie. *Baseball Has Done It.* Edited by Charles Dexter. Philadelphia: Lippincott, 1964.
Sayeed, Khalid B., and George Cunningham. *Pakistan: The Formative Phase 1857–1948.* 2nd ed. London: Oxford University Press, 1968.
Schofield, Victoria. *Kashmir in Conflict: India, Pakistan and the Unending War.* London: I.B. Tauris, 2003.
Sfikas, Thanasis. "Attlee, Bevin and a 'Very Lame Horse': The Dispute over Greece and the Near East, December 1946–January 1947." *Journal of Hellenic Diaspora,* Vol. 18 (September 1992).
Shapiro, Nat, and Nat Hentoff. *Hear Me Talkin' to Ya: The Story of Jazz as Told by the Men who Made It.* New York: Dover Publications, 1955.
Shearer, Stephen. *Patricia Neal An Unquiet Life.* Lexington: University Press of Kentucky, 2006.
Simon, George T., and Frank Sinatra. *The Big Bands.* New York: Macmillan, 1967.
Sissons, Michael, and Philip French, eds. *Age of Austerity 1945–1951.* Oxford: Oxford University Press, 1986.

Smith, Richard Norton. *An Uncommon Man: The Triumph of Herbert Hoover.* New York: Simon & Schuster, 1984.
Sons, Hans-Ulrich. *Gesundheitspolitik während der Besatzungszeit: das öffentliche Gesundheitswesen in Nordrhein-Westfalen 1945-1949.* Wuppertal: Peter Hammer Verlag, 1983.
Southampton City Council. *Southampton and D-Day.* Southampton (U.K.), 1994.
Sparke, Michael. *Stan Kenton: This Is an Orchestra!* Denton: University of North Texas Press, 2010.
Tharoor, Shashi. *Inglorious Empire: What the British Did to India.* London: Hurst, 2017.
Tirro, Frank. *Jazz: A History.* New York: W.W. Norton, 1977.
Tompkins, C. David. *Senator Arthur H. Vandenberg: The Evolution of a Modern Republican, 1184-1945.* East Lansing: Michigan State University Press, 1970.
Truman, Harry S. *Memoirs. Volume 1 Year of Decisions.* Garden City, NY: Doubleday and Co., 1955.
_____. *Off the Record: The Private Papers of Harry S. Truman.* Robert H. Ferrell, ed. New York: Harper and Row, 1980.
Tucker, Sherrie. *Swing Shift: "All-Girl" Bands of the 1940s.* Durham: Duke University Press, 2000.
Tygiel, Jules. *Baseball's Great Experiment: Jackie Robinson and His Legacy.* New York: Oxford University Press, 1997.
Ulanov, Barry. *A History of Jazz in America.* New York: DaCapo Press, 1972.
Vandenberg, Arthur, and Arthur Vandenberg, Jr. *The Private Papers of Senator Vandenberg.* Edited by Joe Alex Morris. Cambridge, MA: Riverside Press, 1952.
Von Schilling, James A. *The Magic Window: American Television 1939-1953.* New York: Haworth Press, 2003.
Walch, Timothy, and Dwight M. Miller. *Herbert Hoover and FDR, a Documentary History.* Worland, WY: High Plains Publishing Company, 1992.
Weinstein, David. *The Forgotten Network: DuMont and the Birth of American Television.* Philadelphia: Temple University Press, 2004.
Westcott, Rich. *The Mogul: Eddie Gottlieb, Philadelphia Sports Legend and Pro Basketball Pioneer.* Philadelphia: Temple University Press, 2008.
White-Spunner, Barney. *Partition: The Story of Indian Independence and the Creation of Pakistan in 1947.* Noida: Simon & Schuster India, 2018.
Wiggins, David K. "Wendell Smith, the Pittsburgh Courier-Journal and the Campaign to Include Blacks in Organized Baseball, 1933-1945." *Journal of Sport History,* Vol. 10, No. 2 (Summer 1983).
Wilson, Joan Hoff. *Herbert Hoover: Forgotten Progressive.* Prospect Heights, IL: Waveland Press, 1992.
Wilson, Theodore A., and Richard D. McKinzie. "Save Wheat, Save Meat, Save the Peace: The Food Crusade of 1947." *Prologue,* vol. 3 (Winter 1971).
Wolpert, Stanley. *Jinnah of Pakistan.* Oxford: Oxford University Press, 1984.
_____. *Shameful Flight.* Oxford: Oxford University Press, 2009.
Woods, Bernie. *When the Music Stopped: The Big Band Era Remembered.* New York: Barricade Books, 1994.
Xydis, Stephen George. *Greece and the Great Powers 1944-1947; Prelude to the "Truman Doctrine."* Thessaloniki: Institute for Balkan Studies, 1963.

Newspapers

Akron Beacon Journal
Boston Daily Globe
Boston Herald
Boston Traveler
Chambersburg (PA) *Public Opinion*
Chicago Herald American
Cincinnati Enquirer
Columbus Dispatch
Dallas Morning News
Derby (U.K.) *Telegraph*
Dover (U.K.) *Express*
Dundee (U.K.) *Courier*
Easton (PA) *Express*
Gloucestershire Echo
Grand Rapids (MI) *Herald*
Great Falls (MT) *Tribune*

The Guardian
Harrisburg (PA) *Evening News*
Harrisburg Telegraph
Hull (U.K.) *Daily Mail*
Idaho Daily Statesman
Lake Charles (LA) *American-Press*
Long Island (NY) *Star-Journal*
Minneapolis Star Tribune
Nashua (IA) *Reporter*
New York Times
Paterson (NJ) *Evening News*
Paterson Morning Call
Pittsburgh Courier
Pottstown (PA) *Mercury*
Reading (PA) *Eagle*
San Antonio Evening News
San Antonio Express
San Antonio The Light
Seattle Times
Southern Daily Echo, Southampton (U.K.)
Southern Evening Echo, Southampton
Spokane Daily Chronicle
Syracuse (NY) *Post-Standard*
Tampa Morning Tribune
Tampa Times

Times (London)
Waterloo (IA) *Daily Courier*
Western Times, Exeter, Devonshire (U.K.)
Yorkshire Post and Leeds Intelligencer (U.K.)

Periodicals

Billboard
Broadcasting Telecasting
Capitol News
Downbeat
Film World and AV News
Life
Look
Metronome
Radio Mirror
RCA Radio Age
Sporting News
Swing
Televiser
Television
Time
Variety

Online Resources

Fauvell, D. "Famous British Winters." *Netweather.tv*, n.d. https://www.netweather.tv/weather-forecasts/uk/winter/famous-winters.

Gibson, Hugh. Diary of Trip February 2–February 22. https://www.hoover.org/library-archives/collections/food-mission-diaries-hugh-gibson-1946-and-1947.

Hoover, Herbert. *Addresses upon the American Road Volume 5: 1945–1948*. https://hoover.archives.gov/sites/default/files/research/ebooks/b3v1_full.pdf.

Isobar maps of European Weather. http://www.wetterzentrale.de/topkarten/fsreaeur.html.

Kynaston, David. "Cheer Up—At Least it Isn't 1947." *Mail Online*, January 11, 2010. http://www.dailymail.co.uk/news/article-1242189/Cheer-At-1947--winter-power-cuts-TV-baths-children-sent-bed-dinner-wasnt-food.html.

MET Office. "Monthly Weather Reports—1940's." https://digital.nmla.metoffice.gov.uk/SO_34786917-b714-4a96-8766-b6b71b7cea8f/.

MET Office. "Severe Winters." https://www.metoffice.gov.uk/weather/learn-about/weather/case-studies/severe-winters.

The President's Economic Mission to Germany and Austria. *Report No. 1 German Agriculture and Food Requirements*. https://web.archive.org/web/20160303172202/http://www.trumanlibrary.org/whistlestop/study_collections/marshall/large/documents/index.php?pagenumber=1&documentdate=1947-02-26&documentid=5166.

The President's Economic Mission to Germany and Austria. *Report No. 3 German Agriculture and Food Requirements*. http://www.trumanlibrary.org/hoover/internaltemplate.php?tldate=1947-03-18&groupid=5170&collectionid=hoover.

Rennell, Tony. "Britain 1947: Poverty, queues, rationing—and resilience." *Mail Online*, 20 November 2007. https://www.dailymail.co.uk/news/article-495096/Britain-1947-Poverty-queues-rationing--resilience.html.

United States Population Statistics for 1950. http://www.infoplease.com/ipa/A0004986.html.

Vosbein, Terry. *All Things Kenton*. https://allthingskenton.com/table_of_contents/articles/.

Wainright, Martin. "The Great Floods of 1947." *The Guardian*, July 25, 2007. http://www.theguardian.com/world/2007/jul/25/weather.flooding1.
Wedder, Noel. http://stankenton.org.
"Winter 1947 in the British Isles." https://www.swanstonweather.co.uk/Pages/Index.html.

Index

Acheson, Dean 59, 65–68, 70, 73–74
Adams, Paul 178
Adelphi College 177
Afghanistan 81
Akron, Ohio 188
Alabama 140, 156
Albania 56
Alderson, Bill 22
Alexander, Lord A.V. (Albert Victor) 83
All-India Muslim League 76–82, 84–87, 90–93
Allied Control Council 31–33, 38, 47
Allied Purchasing 187
Allied Stores Corporation 177, 187, 189–191
Almeida, Laurindo 154, *162*
Amazon 189
Ames, Donna 186
Amritsar, India 81, 88
"And Her Tears Flowed Like Wine" 148
Anderson, Eddie 184
Apartheid 77
Appropriations Committee, U.S. Senate 44
Arkansas 140, 157, 178
Armenian massacres 97
Armstrong, Louis 141
Arnaz, Desi 184
Arnold, Kenneth 195
"Artistry in Bolero" 150
"Artistry in Rhythm" 145, 148; album 150; concert 159
Assam, India 76
Associated Press 98
Astor, Lady Nancy 100–101
Athens, Greece 55–56
Attlee, Clement 7, 41, 75, 89, 201n42; Labour government 8, 27, 41, 57, 75, 80, 83
Austin, Texas 156
Austin Motor Works 19

Austria 25, 30, 34–35
Avodon Ballroom 155
Avon (river) 23
Azores 38

Bahawalapur, Pakistan 81
Balboa peninsula, California 144, 158
Balochistan 76, 81, 86, 92–94
Baltimore, Maryland 146, 155, 161, 171–173
Baltimore Afro-American 122
Bamberg, Germany 105
Bangladesh 97
Bankhead, Dan *130*, 134
Banks, Ernie 134, 136
Bardeen, John 192
Basie, Count 142; orchestra 155
Bassett Green School 112
Bath, England 23, 25
Bavaria 29, 105
BBC *see* British Broadcasting Corporation
bebop 153, 161, 164
Beck, William 106, 112
Belgium relief efforts 38, 40
Bell Telephone Laboratories 167, 192
Bengal 76, 87, 90–92, 94, 97–98
Bennett, Rep. John 67
Benswanger, Bill 123, 207n28
Benton, Illinois 179
Berlin, city of 16, 38, 40–41, 167
Bermuda 38
Bessie, Alvin 133
Bevin, Ernest 41, 46
Bielefeld, Germany 28
big band 140–143, 147, 152–153, 164, 209n3; *see also* swing
Bihar 86

225

Index

Birmingham, Alabama 19, 25
Bizonia 6, 34, 42–43, 46–48, 50
Blackburn, England 19
Blitz *see* bombings
Bloomingdale's Dept. Store 167, 212*n*5
Boise, Idaho 183–185, 195
Bolitho, Hector 77
Bombay 78
bombings 2, 5, 11, 98, 101, 115
Bon Marché Dept. Store 177, 186
Boston, Massachusetts 124–126, 135, 146, 150, 177, 183–184; Symphony Hall 161
Boston Braves 117, 124–125
Boston Red Sox 124–125
Bournville, England 19
Brattain, William 192
Braunschweig, Germany 28, 197*ch*1*n*2
Bridges, Sen. Styles 33
Brink, Bernard A. 177–178, 190
British Automobile Association 23
British Broadcasting Corporation (BBC) 21, 198*n*46
British Information Service 106–107
Broadway 145, 194–195
Bronx 180
Brooklyn 126, 136
Brooklyn Dodgers 117–118, 121, 125–133, 137–138
Brown, Les 154
Brown Dodgers 126
Broz, Josip *see* Tito
Brussels, city of 25
Bublé, Michael 164
Buck, Pearl 190
Buddhists 76
Bulgaria 55–56
Bureau of Retail Research (NYU) 177
Bury St. Edmunds, England 23
B.V.D. clothing 176
Byrnes, James 33, **64**–65, 73–74, 203*n*35

cabaret tax 152–153, 210*n*44
Cabinet Mission to India 83–85, 204*n*22; plan 83–85, 87
Cadbury 19
Café Rouge (New York City) 148
Cage, John 164, 212*n*93
Calcutta, city of 86
California 137, 140, 144, 147, 157–158
Camden, New Jersey 112, 181–182
Campanella, Roy 130, 134, 136
Camus, Albert 164
Canada 108
capitalism 27, 67, 126
Capitol Records 154–155, 157–158
Carnegie Hall 161

Cash and Carry 180, 184, 191
C.C. Anderson's Dept. Store 185
Cedar Grove, New Jersey 146; *see also* Meadowbrook Ballroom
Cedar Grove Cemetery 111, 115
Cedar Lane Club 156
Central Electricity Board (CEB) 20–21
Chaffin, Carol 184
Chambersburg, Pennsylvania 104, 107–113, **114**, 115; Rotary Club 110–111; town council 106–107
Chandler, Happy 134
Charles, Ray 163
Charm magazine 176, 184
Chase Hotel (St. Louis) 132
Chechnya 98
Chennault, Col. Claire 184
"Chiapas" 163
Chicago, Illinois 133, 136, 142, 147, 157, 172; Civic Auditorium 158; Opera House 161
Chicago Cubs 134
Chicago (Herald) American 133–134, 139, 194
Chicago Press Club 136
Chicago Sun-Times 136
Children of Southampton Fund 107
Christians 76
Christy, June 148, **149**–151, 156–157, 160
Churchill, Prime Minister Winston 55, 75, 80, 86; government 101
Cincinnati, Ohio 172–173
Cincinnati Reds 121, 126
"City of Glass" 161; album 163
Civil Affairs Units, U.S. military 30
Clay, Lt. Gen. Lucius D. 33–34, 37–**39**, 40, 47, 52, **64**
Cleveland, Pres. Grover 59
Cleveland, Ohio 172–173
Cleveland Buckeyes 124
Cleveland Indians 134
coal 1, 12–14, 18, 23, 194; looting 14; shortages 5, 7, 19–20; U.K. nationalization 7–8
Cold War 50, 69–70, 113, 193
College of New Rochelle 180
Collins, Eddie 124–125, 208*n*35
Cologne, city of 14
colonialism 95
Color Television 168–170, 172, 188, 190
Colorado 144
Columbia Broadcasting System (CBS) 168–170, 172–173
Columbia College 113
Columbus, Ohio 184, 186
Commodore Hotel (New York City) 158

Index

Common Market 195
Commonwealth of Nations, British 80, 85, 87, 89, 90, 92, 109
Communism 7, 27, 30, 33, 50, 54, 66–68, 70–73, 134
Concert in Progressive Jazz: album 158
"Concerto to End All Concertos" 155, 161
Congress, U.S. 6, 34, 36, 54, 58, 61–62, 66–68, 70, 73, 123, 192; House of Representatives 44, 65, 69; Senate 59–63, 65, 66, 68–69, 73, 74, 195
Connally, Sen. Thomas **64,** 65
Connick, Harry, Jr. 164
Cooper, Bob 151–152
Cooperstown *see* National Baseball Hall of Fame
Copland, Aaron 148
Cornwall 18, 23
Costanzo, Jack 154
Council for Relief Agencies Licensed to Operate in Germany (CRALOG) 40
Cripps, Sir Stafford 80, 83; mission 83
Croix de Guerre 101
Cronin, Joe 125, 208*n*35
Cuba 129, 130, 138
Cuff, Sam 175–**178**, 182, 189, 213*n*35
Czechoslovakia 98, 119

D-Day 30, 101, 102, 104; H-Hour of 102
Daily Worker 120, 122, 123, 133–134
Dallas, Texas 156, 188
Darnton, Robert 2
Dawes, V.P. Charles 61
Daytona Beach, Florida 127–129
Dean, Dizzy 121
Dean, Paul ("Daffy") 121
decolonization 8
Deegan, George 186
DeLand, Florida 129
Delhi, city of 81
Deluxe Hotel (St. Louis) 132
democracy 7, 30, 33, 41, 55, 57, 66, 67, 70–73, 97, 115, 117, 133
Democratic National Committee 68
Democratic Party 7, 59, 60
denazification 28, 31, 38–39, 41, 43, 46
Denmark 25
Department of Agriculture, U.S. 38
Department of State, U.S. 33–34, 37, 45, 46, 57–58, 70
Detroit, Michigan 118, 131, 172
Detroit Tigers 118
Devon 17, 18, 23
Dewey, Gov. Thomas 195
Dibben, Mayor Frank 112

Dies Committee *see* House Un-American Activities Committee
direct action 85–87, 96
disease 34
displaced persons 1–2, 13, 38, 42, 92, 94
Dixieland 141, 153
Doby, Larry 134
Dolgoch, Wales 22
domiciles 13, 14, 197*ch*1*n*5
Doolittle, Lt. Gen. Jimmy 115
Dorsey, Tommy 154, 158
Dover, England 17
Down Beat 147, 152, 153, 158–161, 184
Draper, Brig. Gen. William H. 38, **39**
Dresden, city of 25
Dublin 18, 26
Duff, Gov. John H. 107
Duffy, Hugh 125
Duke of Gloucester 24
Dumbarton Oaks Conference 62
DuMont: laboratory 177; network 169, 170, 172–174, 177, 190, 191
Dunkirk 101
Durocher, Leo 121
Düsseldorf, city of 28

"Eager Beaver" 148, 162
EAM (*Ethnikó Apeleftherotikó Métopo*) 55–56
East Timor 98
East-West All-Star Game 132
Easton, Pennsylvania 182
Ebbets Field 117, 126
Eckstein, Billy 154
EDES (*Ethnikós Dimokratikós Ellinikós Syndesmos*) 55–56
Edgewater Beach Ballroom 158
Egan, Dave 208*n*55
Egan, Wish 118
The Egg and I 185
egg drop 185–186
Eisenhower, Gen. Dwight D. 107, 114, 115
ELAS (*Ellinikós Laïkos Apeleftherotikós Stratós*) 55–56
electricity 5, 7, 12–13, 20–21, 198*n*44; *see also* Central Electricity Board
Elks Club 107
Ellington, Duke 142, 147, 160
Ely, England 24
Empire State Building 167
English Channel 101
Etter, William 107, 109, 111
European Community 195
European Recovery Program *see* Marshal Plan
European Union 195

Index

The Face of the War 175
Fair Lawn, New Jersey 178
Falklands War 116
famine 7, 29–30, 32, 50; *see also* food
farms 18, 22, 24, 29, 40, 42, 57, 80, 200*n*36; U.K. sheep production 22
Farnsworth televisions 168; tour 174, 213*n*35
Federal Communications Commission (FCC) 169–170, 172–173, 175, 188
Federation of Old Age Pensioners' Clubs 113
Fellowship of US-British Comrades 114–116
Fenway Park 125
Ferguson, Sen. Homer 73
Ferris, Sen. Woodbridge 61
Fiedler, Arthur 184
First World War *see* World War I
FitzGerald, Dennis A. 38, **39**
flooding: of Mississippi River 35; in U.K. 18, 23–24, 199*n*61
Florida 26, 67, 129, 130, 190
flying saucers 2, 195
Folkestone, England 17
food 1, 5, 7, 11–14, 18, 21–22, 25–27, 29–30, 32, 34–36, 40, 58, 80, 193, 197*Intro*. *n*1, 200*n*17; milk procurement 37, 47; production 22; school feeding program 42, 47–**49**, 50, 52, 201*n*61; *see also* farms
Food Administration, U.S. 34
Food Emergency Committee 35, 38
Ford, Pres. Gerald 74
Ford, Henry 118
Foreign Policy, U.S. 6, 51, 54, 59, 61–65, 67–69, 72–74
Foreign Relations Committee, U.S. Senate 61, 65, 66, 68, 195
Fort Worth, Texas 156
France 30, 66, 101, 104, 105, 119
Frankfurt, city of 26, 27, 38
Franklin County, Pennsylvania 108, 111, 112; Horticultural Society of 110, 112
Frecon, Robert 108
Freemantle, England 101
Frick, Ford 120, 124, 207*n*17
Frings, Cardinal Josef 14

Gabel, Ed 150
Gandhi, Mohandas Karamchand (Mahatma) 2, 77–80, 82, 87, 89–91, 96, 98
Ganges river 76
Gastel, Carlos 155, 162
General Electric Corporation 169
George (King of Greece) 56
George Washington Bridge 181
Georgetown (Washington D.C.) 62
Germany 1, 6–7, 30, 33–35, 37, 42–44, 58, 101, 105, 119; bifurcation 50, 193; occupation 6, 26, 28–32, 42; weather 11–13, 16, 26–27, 193, 197*ch*1*n*2; *see also* zones of occupation
Gertz Dept. Store 175, 176, 184
Gestapo 56
Gettysburg (battle of) 104
Ghaznavi, Masood 75, 81–**82**, 86, 88, 89, 92–95, 98, **99**
Gibson, Hugh 38, 41
Gibson, Josh 121, 124
Gillespie, Dizzy 153; combo 160
Gimbels Dept. Store 175, 176
GIs 101, 102, 104, 105, 111
Glendale, California 144
Gohkale, Gopal Krishna 78
The Golden Rule Dept. Store 186
Goodman, Benny 141, 142, 145, 154
Göttingen, city of 15
Gottlieb, Ed 135–136
Graettinger, Bob 161, 163
Grand Rapids, Michigan 59, 73, 74, 166, 186
Grand Rapids Herald 60, 61
Grantham, England 18
Great Britain 6–9, 33, 75, 80, 96, 100, 101, 167, 193; German zonal occupation authorities 31, 49, 50; India and 75, 77, 80; occupation of Greece by 56–57, 65–66; trans-Atlantic friendships with 110–116; weather in 16–27
Great Depression 61, 96, 122, 141, 143, 144; of 1893 59
Great Falls, Montana 184, 185
Great Ouse (river) 24
Great Partition 95–96, 98
Great War *see* World War I
Greece 7, 8, 54; civil war in 55–58, 70–72; debate over aid to 66–69; World War II and 55–56
Gross, Chester 107, 109
Gulf Oil Corporation 176
Gulf War 116

Hagen, Germany 28
Hague Peace Convention (1899) 60
Hamble, England 101
Hamburg 12–13, 40–41, 193
Hamilton, Alexander 59
Hamstering (*hamstern*) 13–14; *hamsterfahrt* **15**, 29
Harridge, William 124
Harrisburg, Pennsylvania 186, 188

Index

Harvard University 124
Hassett, William 111
Havana, city of 129
Havens, Paul Swain 110, 111
Hawaii 175
Hawkins, Coleman 141, 153
Henderson, Fletcher 141
Herman, Woody 147, 153, 154
Herpolsheimer's Dept. Store 166, 186, 212*n*1
Hester, Col. Hugh 38, 40
"Hey Jude" 163
Hickok leather goods 187
Hill, Benjamin T., Jr. 178
Hindus 76, 79–81, 84–87, 89, 95–96, 98
Hitler, Adolf 8, 55, 96, 97, 119–120
Hoagland, Everett 144
Holland 25
Hollywood 144, 155, 157
Hollywood Bowl 161
Hollywood Canteen 147
Home Shopping Network (HSN) 189
Homestead Grays 124, 132
Hoover, Herbert 7, 34–*39*, 51–53, 58, 167; reports findings 40–49, 58
Hoover Dam (Grand Coulee Dam) 52
Hoover vacuums 176
Hooverspeisung see food: school feeding program
Hope, Bob 147
Hoskinson, Jim 178, 182, 185
Hotel Washington (Chambersburg) 109, 111
House Beautiful magazine 176
House of Commons 25, 86; *see also* Parliament
House of Representatives, U.S. *see* Congress, U.S., House of Representatives
House Un-American Activities Committee 123, 133
Howdy Doody Show 195
Hubble, Carl 121
Huggate, England 21–22

Idaho 183
Imperial Chemical Industries (ICI) 19
imperialism *see* colonialism
India 8, 75–80, 82–93, 95–98, 193
India Independence Bill 92
Indian National Congress 76–80, 83–87, 90–91
Indus river 76
inflation 80, 152, 168, 193
"Innovations in Modern Music" 162
Internal Revenue Service (IRS) 163

Interstate Highway System 186
Iqbal, Muhammad 79
Ireland 16–18, 22, 24, 25
Irish Republican Army (IRA) 98
Islam 79, 81, 96
Isle of Sheppey 17
Isles of Scilly 17
Ives-Quinn Act 124

Jains 76
Jamaica, New York 175, 184
James, Barbara 112
James, Dennis 180, 184, 213*n*49
James, Harry 154
Japan 5, 54, 61, 62, 80, 127
Jarantow, Lygia 178, *181*, 182, 184, 190
jazz 141–143, 147, 152, 153, 163; progressive 150, 154–155, 158, 160–164; *see also* big band; swing music
J.C. Penney 104
JCS 1067 31–34, 44; revocation 46, 50, 199*n*11, 200*n*16
JCS 1779 46
Jeeps (Willys-Overland) 166, 180–181, 183, 184
Jerome, Arthur 186
Jethroe, Sam 124
Jews 8, 76, 97, 119–120
J.G. Taylor-Spink Award 136
Jim Crow 8, 119, 129
Jinnah, Muhammad Ali 2, 8, 75, *82*–92, 96; early life and career 77–80; post-independence 98, 193
Johnson, J.C. 184
Johnston, Ralph "Red" 178
Joint Chiefs of Staff 65
Jonas, Hilda 177, 187, 189
Jones, Jo 141
Jordan Marsh Dept. Store 177
Joske Brothers Dept. Store 177, 191

Kalamazoo, Michigan 72
Kalat, Pakistan 98
Kammeyer, Günther 14–15
Kansas City, Missouri 142
Kansas City Monarchs 125, 135
Karachi, city of 77, 92
Kashmir 76, 79, 193; war in and partition of 97
Kaufmann's Dept. Store 175
Keating, Maj. Gen. Frank 38
Kefauver, Sen. Estes 190
Kem-Tone paint 187
Kennan, George F. 66
Kenton, Stanley Newcomb 9, 140, 152–160, *162*–163, 194, 209*n*1, 211*n*52; legacy

164–165; new progressive jazz orchestra 158–161, 163; orchestra 144–146, 148, *149*; touring 150, *151*, 154–157
Kenton, Violet 154, 163
Khan, Liaquat Ali 79
Khan, Syed Ahmad 77, 79
Khan, Yasmin 86
Khizar, Hyat *see* Tiwana, Khizar Hayat
KHJ radio (Los Angeles) 144
Kiser, Col. Sherman L. 107
Kohlenklau see coal
Königstein, Germany 38
Korean War 116
Kottkamp, Horace A. 107–108, 113
KSD-TV (St. Louis) 172–173
Kurdistan 98

Labour Party 113
Lacy, Sam 118, 122, *130*
Lahore, Pakistan 82
Lahore resolution 79–80
Laird, David 186
Lake Charles, Louisiana 183
Lake District 17
Lake Worth Casino 156
Lamb, Chris 129, 138
Landis, Kenesaw Mountain 119, 122, 124
Landon, Alfred 61
Lardner, Ring, Jr. 133
Large, David Clay 2
Larson, Erik 2
Laubach's Dept. Store 182
Lavagetto, Cookie 121
League of Nations 60
Leeds, England 18
Legion of Honor (France) 113
Leicester, England 25
Lend-Lease 101
Leningrad, city of 25
Level of Industry Plan 32, 34, 44, 50; revised 46–47
Levin, Michael 159
Levy, Hank 163
Lewis, Ira 122
Ley, Sgt. Murray 103
Lizard Point, England 17
Lochner, Louis P. 38, 51
Lockton, England 18
London 7, 16–18, 23, 25, 41, 78–79, 87, 193; underground 17
Long Island 183
Look magazine 150
Lord Inverchapel 41, 57, 109, 111
Los Angeles, California 140, 142, 144, 148, 155, 159, 172, 173
Louis, Joe 120, 136

Louisiana 156, 183
Luftwaffe 19
Lyric Theater (Baltimore) 155

Maas Brothers Dept. Store 177
MacArthur, Gen. Douglas 73
"Macarthur Park" 163
MacDonald, Betty 185
Mackinac Charter 62
Macy's Dept. Store 167, 174
Major League Baseball 8, 117, 118, 120–123, 127, 129, 131–132, 134, 137
malnutrition 7, 16, 34
Manne, Shelly 148, 152, 160, *162*
Market Weighton, England 18
Marshall, George C. 46, 65, 67, 73–74, 107
Marshall Plan 2, 44–45, 51, 72, 73, 195
Martin, State Sen. Edward 107
Martin, Rep. Joseph 45
Martin, Pepper 121
Martin, Sen. Topher 65
Mason, Col. Frank E. 38
Massachusetts 65, 124
McClelland, Hugh 109, 111
McConnellsburg, Pennsylvania 103, 111
McDonald, R.C. 110
McKechnie, Bill 121
McNarney, Gen. Joseph T. 38
McNeill, Hector 41
Meadowbrook Ballroom 146, 156, 194
Medal of Freedom (U.S.) 113
Medway (river) 23
Meet the Press 195
Mehaffey, Marian *see* Shimer, Marian
Meier, Hugo 38
Melton, James 184
Memorial Day 108–109, 113, 115, 144
Menon, V.P. 90; plan 90–91
The Metronome 145, 146
Metropolitan Opera 184
Meyer, Col. Leo 102, 107–109
Miami, Florida 188
Milhaud, Darius 147, 148, 159
Military Cross 101
Miller, Glenn 145
"Millionth Yank" *see* Shimer, Sgt. Paul James
Mills College 148
Ministry of Fuel and Power (U.K.) 21, 23
Minneapolis, Minnesota 178, 183, 184
Mississippi 140
Missouri 55, 64, 105
Mr. X *see* Kennan, George F.
Montana 184
Montreal Royals 127, 129, 134, 138
Morehouse-Martins Dept. Store 186

Index

Morgan, Sir Frederick E. 115
Morgenthau Plan 31–33, 37, 43, 199n10
Moscow 25; foreign ministers conference in 46
Most Valuable Player Award 129
Mountbatten, Viscount 89–92, 98
Muchnick, Isadore 124–125
Mughals 75
Munich 12
Murphy, Irene 9, 166, 180, *181*, 182, *183*, 184, 189–192
Murrow, Edward R. 165
Muslim League *see* All-India Muslim League
Muslims 76, 77, 79, 80, 82–89, 91, 96, 98
Musso, Vido 157
Mustang, P-51 184
My Own Story 194
Myers, State Sen. Francis J. 107

National Baseball Hall of Fame 118, 137
National Basketball Association 135
National Broadcasting Company (NBC) 168, 172, 173; radio 148
National League 120; Negro 132, 135
Nazism 7, 38–39, 100, 119, 209n5; *see also* denazification
Neal, Patricia 179
Negro leagues 123, 125, 126, 209n59; *see also* National League, Negro
Nehru, Jawaharlal 82, 84, 85, 89, 90, 92, 95
New Deal 61
New Haven, Connecticut 188
New Jersey 112, 194
New York City 38, 42, 45, 100–101, 108, 112, 117, 122, 131, 141, 142, 144–146, 148, 154, 156–160, 167, 171–175, 178–182, 190, 191, 194–195
New York Giants 121
New York Herald Tribune 63
New York Sportswriters' Club 134
New York State 26, 118, 124, 191
New York University 177
New York Yankees 131
Newark, New Jersey 161, 181
Newbald, England 18
Newcombe, Don 130
Nez Perce tribe 184
Nicklas, Charles 107
North Atlantic Treaty Organization (NATO) 71–73
Northumberland, England 17
Northwest Frontier Provinces (India) 76
Northwestern University 179
Nottingham, England 24

Oakland, California 144
O'Day, Anita 148
Office of Military Government for the United States (OMGUS) 33, 40
Ohlsdorf, Germany 14
one-night stand 143, 144, 146, 148, 150, 154, 158, 160
O'Neil, Buck 134
Opelousas, Louisiana 156
Operation Iraqi Freedom 116
Operation Undertone 105
"Opus in Pastels" 150
Oregon 155, 190, 195
Organization for European Economic Cooperation (OEEC) 72, 195
Ott, Mel 121
Oughtershaw, England 22

Paige, Satchell 121, 124
Pakistan 8, 75, 79, 80, 82–85, 89, 91–98, 193, 204n11
Palatinate 105
Palestine 100, 101
Palladium Theater 144–145, 147–*149*
Panama 130, 138
Paramount Theater 194
Paris, city of 25, 195
Paris Dept. Store 184, 185
Parker, Charlie 153, 160
Parliament (U.K.) 75, 80, 92, 98, 100, 113
Parses 76
Partlow, Roy 130
Pasadena, California 159
Passaic, New Jersey 181
Patterson, Robert 35, 36, 47, 107
"Peanut Vendor" 148, 162
Pearl Harbor 61, 123, 145, 168, 175
The Peggy Wilson Show 191
Pembrokeshire, Wales 24
Pennsylvania 26, 103, 108, 115, 156, 182, 186
Pethick-Lawrence, Lord Frederick 83
Petrillo Recording Ban 160, 211n84
Petroff, Irine "Petey" 179–*180*, *183*, 190–192
Philadelphia, Pennsylvania 135, 136, 146, 168, 171–173
Philadelphia Athletics 135
Philadelphia Phillies 135
Philadelphia Stars 124, 135
Philadelphia Warriors 135
Philco 169
Pic magazine 176, 178, 185
Pittsburgh, Pennsylvania 120, 132, 133, 175
Pittsburgh Courier 8, 119, 122–123, 127–128, 133–134, 137, 194

Index

Pittsburgh Pirates 123
Plantation Club 156
Pleasure Pier Ballroom 156
Poland 55, 122
Pomeroy's Dept. Store 182, 186
Poole, England 101
Port Arthur, Texas 156
Porter, Paul 58
Portland, Oregon 190
Potsdam Accords 32, 33, 43, 46, 50
Prague, city of 26
Presto pressure cookers 187
Proclamation 2714 5–6
"Prologue Suite" 161
Public Health Service, U.S. 38
Public Opinion (Chambersburg, Pennsylvania) 106, 107
Puckett, B. Earl 187
Punjab 76, 80–82, 87–94, 97–98

Quaid-e-Azam 77, 82, 92
Quality, Value, and Convenience (QVC) 189
Queen Elizabeth (ship) 100, 106
Quetta, Pakistan 81, 93, 98

racism 8, 119, 134
Radcliffe, Sir Cyril 92
Radcliffe line 93, 97
Radio Corporation of America (RCA) 168–170, 176; DuPont Color Television Caravan tours 190; 1939 television tour 174
Raeburn, Boyd 153
ragtime 141, 153
Raj 76–77, 204n4
rationing *see* food
Ravel, Maurice 148
Rayburn, Sen. Samuel 65
RCA-Allied Stores Television Caravan 166, 178, 180–190, 192
Reading, Pennsylvania 182, 186
Reece, B. Carroll 68
refugees 1, 38, 92–94, 97; *see also* displaced persons
Regina, Saskatchewan 26
Rendezvous Ballroom 144, 158, 164
reparations 32, 42, 46, 50
Republican Party 6, 58–61, 63, 66–67; national convention 168; presidential administrations 34
Republicans 6, 36, 45, 51, 55, 61, 62, 64, 68, 69, 74, 195
Rich, Buddy 153
Rickard, Edgar 35–37, 52
Rickey, Orla 126

Rickey, Wesley Branch 122, 125–135, 137–138
Robeson, Paul 122
Robinson, Jack Roosevelt 8, 117, 118, 124, 126–131, 135–139, 194
Rockefeller Plaza 180–181
Rodino, Capt. Peter W. 115
Rodney, Lester 122, 133
Romania 55, 56
Rome, city of 41
Roosevelt, Pres. Franklin Delano 35, 63, 167; administration 62
Roosevelt Hotel 122
Roseland Ballroom 145–146
Roswell, New Mexico 195; *Daily Record* 195
Rotary Club (Chambersburg) 110, 113
Rowe, Billy 128
Royal Air Force (RAF) 21–22
Royal Irish Fusiliers 101
rubber production 19, 143
Rugolo, Pete 148–149, 160
Ruhr valley 12, 28–30, 39–40, 43

Saarland 105
Safranski, Eddie 148, 160, **162**
Sain, Johnny 117
"St. James Infirmary" 148
St. John, Robert 190
St. Louis, Missouri 131–132, 172–173
St. Louis Browns 173
St. Louis Cardinals 121, 122, 132, 173
St. Louis Post-Dispatch 173
St. Paul, Minnesota 183, 186
Salisbury, Maryland 104
San Antonio, Texas 177, 186, 191
San Francisco Conference 63
Sanford, Florida 127–129
Sartre, Jean-Paul 164
Scandinavia 11
Schlange-Schöningen, Dr. Hans 28
Scotland 23
Seattle, Washington 177, 185, 186; Rainiers (baseball team) 185
Sebrell, Dr. William H. 38
Second World War *see* World War II
Selby, England 24
Senate, U.S. *see* Congress; Senate
Setzer, Brian 164
Shaw, Artie 142, 145
Sherman Hotel (Chicago) 157
Sherwin-Williams Paints 176
Shibe Park 135
Shimer, John R. 103, 105
Shimer, Marian 104, 106, 110–112
Shimer, Patricia Ann 104, 106, 109, 110, 113

Index

Shimer, Sgt. Paul S., Jr. *103*–106
Shimer, Paul, Sr. 103
Sikhs 76, 81, 86, 89, 91, 93, 95–98
Simla, India 84, 90
Simon, George 146
Sinatra, Frank 163
Sindh 76, 77
Sinti-Roma 8
Sixteenth Amendment 60
Slapton Ley (lake) 18
Smith, Bessie 141
Smith, Wendell 8, 118–129, *130*–135, *136*–139, 194
Smith, Wyonella 119
Smith-Connally Act 6
Sokolosky, George 52
South Africa 77
Southampton, England 101–102, 104–108, 110, 112–115
Southeastern High School (Detroit) 118
Soviet Union 7, 25, 31, 46, 50, 56, 66, 71, 98, 113, 123, 193
Der Spiegel 29
Spokane, Washington 184
Sporting News 122
Sportsman's Park 132
Sposa, Louis A. 177–*178*, 186, 190
Stacy, Jess 184
Stalin, Josef 7, 71, 97
Stamford, England 18
Stanford University 34
Stanley Steamer 186
Stark, Charles 180
Stolper, Gustav 38, 47, 51
Stranger, Reginald (Rex) James 101–102, *103*–106, 107–*114*, 115, 116
Stravinsky, Igor 147, 148, 159
"A Streetcar Named Desire" 164, 195
Stuttgart, Germany 33, 40–41
Stuttgart speech 33
Sudetenland 119
Sukeforth, Clyde 127
swing dancing 9, 141, 142, 209*n*4
Swing magazine 155
swing music 141–143, 148, 161

Taft, Sen. Robert 195
"Talk About a Lady" 148
Tampa, Florida 177, 179
"Tampico" 148
Tedder, Air Marshal Arthur 115
Teegarden, Jack 154
Telefun 182
Televiser 175
television 9, 164, 166–169, 173–174, 188–189, 191; marketplace application 174–176, 188–189, 192; production of receivers 170–172; *see also* RCA-Allied Stores Television Caravan
Television Magazine 168, 170, 174, 188
Terry, Bill 121
Tery, Joseph 178
Texas 140, 156, 157
Texas A&M 156
textile industry 19–20
Thames river 23, 24
Third Division, U.S. Seventh Army 105
Third Reich 30, 105
"This I Believe" (radio series) 165
"Time for a Change" 163
Times (London) 17, 18, 23, 24
Tito (Josip Broz) 55, 56, 71, 203*n*50
Tiwana, Khizar Hayat 81, 87; government 89
Trade Union Athletics Association, New York 123
Transistor 192
transportation 1, 17–19, 21, 23, 28, 29, 34, 143, 163, 194; railroads 12, 19, *20*, 23, 94, 143, 200*n*32
Transportation Corps, U.S. Army 101–103
Trent (river) 23
Troy, Philip 186
Truman, Pres. Harry S. 2, 5–7, 35–37, 41–45, 48, 51–52, 54–55, 58, 63–67, 72, 74, 107, 192; Democratic administration 6, 7, 44–47, 51, 58, 64, 70, 71
Truman Doctrine 7, 54, 66–70, 72–73, 193
Trumbo, Dalton 133
Tsaldaris, Greek Prime Minister Constantinos 56, 58, 67; government 57
Turkey 7, 8, 54, 57, 58, 66, 68, 71, 72
Tuscaloosa, Alabama 140, 156
Tygiel, Jules 128

UHF band 169, 188
Ukraine 97
Ulanov, Barry 145
Ulster United (soccer team) 108
unemployment 20, 35, 43
United Kingdom *see* Great Britain
United Nations 5, 58, 62, 68, 71
United Nations Relief and Rehabilitation Agency (UNRRA) 62
United Services Organizations (USO) 143, 209*n*9
United States 7, 8, 41, 42, 44, 47, 60, 98, 104, 106, 123, 133, 140, 142, 145, 148, 161, 167–169, 173, 174, 176, 184; foreign policy 6, 51, 54, 59, 61–69, 72–74; intervention in Greece by 57, 58, 70–72; isolationism 63, 72, 74; postwar occupation

policies 31–34, 49–50; trans–Atlantic friendships with 101–102, 108–114; weather in 26, 192–193
University of Alabama 156
University of California Los Angeles (UCLA) 124
University of Delaware 1
University of Texas 156
Untermeyer, Louis 190
Upper Teesdale, England 22
Urdu 78
U.S.S.R. *see* Soviet Union

Vandenberg, Aaron 59
Vandenberg, Sen. Arthur 2, 7, 58–**64**, 65–**69**, 72–74, 194–195
Vann, Robert L. 119
Variety 159, 165
Vaughn, Arky 121
V-E Day 126
Venezuela 127
Versailles Treaty 60
Veterans of Foreign Wars (VFW) 107
viceroy 76, 80, 83, 86, 89, 90; *see also* Mountbatten, Viscount; Wavell, Lord Archibald P.
Vienna, city of 25, 26, 41
Vietnam conflict 116
Villa Maria Academy 180
Voorhees, Tracy S. 34, 38

WABD (New York City) 172, 174, 175, 177, 179, 190–191; *Teleshopping with Martha Manning* 174
Wagner, Honus 121
Walcott, Jersey Joe 133
Wales 22, 23
Wallace, V.P. Henry A. 65
Wanamaker's Dept. Store 174, 175
War Department, U.S. 47, 106
Warsaw Pact 71
Washington, D.C. 7, 31, 36, 57, 58, 61, 62, 67, 74, 108, 109, 161, 167, 171, 172, 188
Washington (state) 155, 183, 186, 195
Waterloo, Iowa 185
Wavell, Lord Archibald P. 80, 84–86, 89
WBKB (Washington, D.C.) 172
WCBS (New York City) 172
WCBW (New York City) 169
"We the People" (radio show) 111
weather 5, 8, 11, 25, 34, 38; in Great Britain 16–24; in Ireland 16–18, 22, 24, 25; in occupied Germany 11–16, 41; in United States 26, 108–109, 117, 193–194
W8XCT (Cincinnati) 172
West Virginia State College 119
Westinghouse Appliances 176
WEWS (Cleveland) 172
Weymouth, England 101
WGN-TV (Chicago) 136
White House 34, 35, 37, 48, 54, 63, 65
Whiteman, Paul 141
Wichita, Kansas 144
William Penn Hotel (Pittsburgh) 120
Williams, Marvin 124, 135
Williams, Tennessee 164, 195
Williams, Tom 25
Wilmington, Delaware 188
Wilson, Pres. Woodrow 60
Wilson College 110, 111
Winding, Kai 148
Wingert, Edmund 111
WMAL (Washington, D.C.) 172
WMAR (Baltimore) 172
WNBT (New York City) 172, 175
WNBW (Washington, D.C.) 172
Wolverhampton, England 19
The Women's Club 190–191
Woodall, Larry 125
Woods, Bernie 159
World War I 34, 37, 60, 77, 96
World War II 2, 5, 35, 55, 63, 77, 79, 90, 94, 96, 114–116, 123, 143, 164
Worlds' Fair, (New York City) 123, 167
WPTZ (Philadelphia) 172, 175
Wright, Johnny 128–130
W6XAO (Los Angeles) 172
W6XYZ (Los Angeles) 172
WTTG (Washington, D.C.) 172
Württemberg 29
WWJ (Detroit) 172

X-1 195

Yalta conference 31, 63, 71 accords 32, 46, 50
Yeager, Chuck 195
Yorkshire, England 17, 21, 24
Yugoslavia 55, 56, 98

Zanuck, Col. Darryl F. 115
zones of occupation 6, 28, 29, 31–33, 36–40, 42, 43, 47, 50, 193